Some Things Are Worth Fighting For

Dr. Rickey McCray, Jr.

Washington Way Publishing
Pooler, GA
www.washingtonwaypublishing.com

DEDICATION

This book is dedicated to my dad, Dr. Rickey A. McCray Sr., my grandmother Pearl Meyers, and my mother-in-law Mary Francis Akers who passed away before I could write this book. I am grateful for how they prayed, believed, supported, taught, corrected, loved, and accepted me for who I am.

I am a better man because of them.

Dr. Rickey McCray

Table of Contents

Dr. Rickey McCray

ACKNOWLEDGMENTS

My wife, Robyn McCray. You are my strength. You are my backbone!
You make me a better man. There is no way I could have done this
without you. I thank and praise God daily for you coming into my life.
Life is better because I am with you. Thank you for allowing me to dream
big and go after those big dreams even when it is scary. Thank you for
allowing me to do me. Thank you for being involved with the girls when I
was reading, writing, studying, preaching, or just plain tired! I fall in love
with you all over again every year! You never cease to amaze me with your
creativity, hard work, dedication, loyalty, intelligence, hospitality, and your
beautiful smile! I love you!

INTRODUCTION

Have you ever tried to make sense of the impossible? My father and I had a love-hate relationship due to years of disappointment and broken promises. He was notorious for getting my hopes high by telling me he would come and pick me up. I would get my bag packed and he would not show up. Time after time, I was left waiting at the door, embarrassed that I believed he would show up again.

Occasionally, he would try to make up for that lost time by offering his unsolicited advice about relationships and life. And each time he did this, I reminded him he had missed that time and opportunity. As the years went on, more things were said and done that made my dream of us having a relationship filled with trust, honesty, depth and friendship seem more like a fantasy than a reality.

I remember one incident where my mother tried to console me after my father did not show up as he promised. She asked me, "Why do you keep putting yourself through this? You know how he is. Why are you fighting so hard for this relationship with your dad?" I remember vividly that I did not have an answer. I was speechless. It was one of the few times I did not have a quick comeback.

The truth is, I could not understand it myself. Why was I fighting so hard for a relationship when it seemed like I was the only one who wanted it? However, my mother's question would continue to ring in my ears for years to come. *"Why are you fighting so hard for this relationship with your dad?"* I would spend the next 18 years trying to answer the most difficult question ever asked to me.

One of the most challenging things to do in a relationship after being hurt is to reconcile with that person. It can seem almost impossible. It is as if each time we are hurt, there is a layer of defense added on to the fortress that we are building in our hearts to protect ourselves. And if you are anything like me, I had constructed an elaborate, impenetrable fortress with a state-of-the-art security system equipped with a sophisticated firewall, infrared beams invisible to the human eye, and capped off with an isolating panic room. Nothing was getting near my heart, and unfortunately, nothing was getting out either.

This fortress of protection that I created was safe and comfortable. For years it served me well. I had been hurt many times by my father and thought my fortress would protect me from being hurt again. My heart would be protected from being disappointed, lied to, and betrayed. However, what I did not anticipate, was the very thing I constructed to protect myself from being hurt by my father, became a prison that kept me from connecting with other people.

If I was ever going to get out of my self-made prison, it would take a miracle. With the help of God, it would take me doing the impossible. If I was to ever reconcile with my father, the impossible was doing the work within me. Reconciliation is soul work. And you cannot do this kind of work without working on your soul.

For me, the soul work was taking a long hard look in the mirror and asking myself these questions:

Are you the man you claim to be?

Are you the same man on the inside that you want people to think you are on the outside?

Do your behaviors, actions, and intentions reflect what you say you believe and the God, you say you believe in?

Are you truly living like the Jesus you say you follow and encourage others to follow?

Soul work is consistently checking yourself to make sure who you are lines up with what you say you believe. Then, making the appropriate adjustments in words and deeds. Soul work not only transforms you into a better person, it also changes those who are connected to you.

Reconciliation is a journey. It is not something achieved through halfhearted attempts. You will have to sacrifice more than you agreed upon, give more than you think is fair and sometimes receive less than you know you deserve. However, if you take this journey as I did, you will find that it will all be worth it somehow.

But why should you keep reading? If you ever felt like or said, "I can never get past what they did to me!" This book is for you. In this book, you will discover that judging people based on their worst moments could ultimately shut you off from some of the best parts of them. And whether you know it or not, the best of them may be what you need to become the best you. Forgiveness and reconciliation are possible even when it seems out of reach. After reading this book, I hope you will release whatever has had you bound, break generational curses, have a clear conscience, a freed heart and a deeper, more profound relationship with God and others.

Follow me as I recall and reflect on my journey to reconciliation with my father through a collection of stories. I share the soul work I had to do, tearing down the walls around my heart and answering my mother's question, "Why are you fighting so hard for this relationship with your dad?"

Dr. Rickey McCray

ONE

"My parents' relationship was a roller-coaster ride. The highs were extremely high, fun and loving. But the lows were dark and scary."

WHEN I FIRST LEARNED HOW TO FIGHT FOR THOSE I BELIEVE IN

Where did I learn to fight for relationships? We all are products of our environments. Whether it is taught, or we learned it by watching. Some things we do consciously, others subconsciously. For example, if a person is nervous, they may consciously choose to chew gum to calm their nerves. In addition, subconsciously, when they're nervous they may pace the floor or talk to themselves and not realize they are doing the same thing their father did when he was nervous. We often do not recognize the things we are doing unconsciously until we do the work of reflecting or someone else points it out. If I want to find out why I fight so hard for people I am in relationship with, I must go back to one of my earliest memories where I have seen it done.

One Saturday morning my mom sat us down on the couch when my sister, Racheal, was eight years old, I was five years old, and my twin brothers, Reuben and Ryan, were four years old. My dad was not home at the time. We were used to him being gone because of work or church. Therefore, it was normal for my mom to communicate with us about what was going on or what we needed to do. Especially, if there was a major decision being made or we were in trouble. Which for me, trouble was my middle name. I had a knack for getting under people's skin and upsetting them with my antics. However, this talk was not about being in trouble, it was much more intense. Nothing could have prepared us for what she was getting ready to say.

"I sat y'all down to tell y'all that y'all have a little sister," my mom said, with a slight quiver in her voice. We were all shocked! "How do we have a little sister? Did you have another baby? Were you pregnant and we did not know?" I asked. She did her best to explain. While my mother and father were separated, he had been with another woman. She got pregnant and had a little girl, named Ricketa.

We had so many questions. What did Ricketa look like? Where was she? Why had we not seen her? When will we see her? But more importantly, I wanted to know, was my mom going to stay married to my dad? Would they get a divorce? I was scared because I thought I would not see my dad again. I thought this meant he was going to leave us.

There was an awkward pause, you could tell my mom was thinking this is too much for these kids to go through. But then she assured us that they would not get a divorce. "I'm going to stay, and your dad and I are going to fight for our marriage and our family." That was a relief for my brothers and me, but my sister Racheal felt a little different because her relationship with my dad was different from my brother's and my relationship.

My parents' tumultuous relationship created a strain between my father and his children. Racheal learned how damaging my dad's actions were to their relationship all too soon. My parents met at a church service in Indianapolis, Indiana. My sister was three years old. Racheal's father and my mother had dated in high school but were no longer together at this time. Unfortunately, Racheal's biological father had been killed by his wife during a domestic dispute the following year. My father would be the only father Racheal remembers.

My parents dated about four months before getting married. After the wedding, my mom moved to Marion, Indiana, my dad's hometown. Indianapolis, where my mom grew up, was considered the big city compared to Marion. It was a major adjustment for my mom and sister leaving all their family and friends to move to a small town where they knew no one. Little did my mother and sister know, relocating would be the least of their problems.

My mother told me the story of when they brought me home from the hospital, my dad told Racheal not to pick me up and try to hold me because I was too little and she might drop me. Well of course when they laid me down on the bed and left the room, Racheal picked me up. She told my parents she just wanted to hold her little brother. However, when our dad came back into the room, she got scared and threw me on the bed. My dad pushed her, yelled at her, and spanked her. She was devastated. All she saw was how nice our dad had been to her up to that point. This was the first time she saw the angry and violent side of him.

The next couple of years was rough for my parents. My dad, who worked at General Motors, was continuously being laid off. My parents constantly argued, and my father was physically abusive to my mom. If that was not enough, they had my twin brothers, Rueben and Ryan, in the middle of all that. Because my sister was older and understood what was going on, she had a front-row seat to the madness.

My parents' relationship was a roller-coaster ride. The highs were extremely high, fun and loving. But the lows were dark and scary. The mood and atmosphere in our house was always unpredictable. My dad would do something great and spectacular to surprise everyone, usually with gifts or a trip. Or the surprise would be yelling, shouting, fussing, or fighting. We all walked on eggshells because we did not know which person we would get.

Finally, the pressure of taking care of a growing family during financial uncertainty, miscommunication, and physical abuse proved too much for my parents. After four years of marriage, they decided to get a divorce. For my brothers and I, this meant leaving our home in Marion, but for Racheal it meant going back home to Indianapolis.

We moved to Indianapolis and lived with my grandparents. It was always fun there. We had a big family with lots of cousins. My sister was happy being back in Indianapolis. She was back in her element with people she knew and could depend on. She was especially close with my grandmother.

My grandma Pearl was like a second mom to my brothers and me, but she was a refuge for my sister. Whenever things got bad in my parents' marriage, my grandmother would drive to Marion and get Racheal to stay with them for a while. So, for Racheal, Indianapolis and my grandmother were symbols of a safe place.

Less than a year after we returned to Indianapolis, my parents started having coffee together. My dad would drive to Indianapolis to visit us for a few moments and then ask my mom out, just to talk. Within a couple of months of "talking," we moved back to Marion again. My parents decided to give it another try and get remarried. My mom was hopeful, my brothers and I were excited to be back with my dad. But Racheal was sad because going back to Marion meant uncertainty and the fear of not knowing when something bad would happen again.

Racheal would sit alone in her room while the rest of us would watch movies or TV as a family. I asked her why she did not join us, and she would not answer. She later shared how she had had enough of seeing Dad treat her differently based on how he and Mom were doing. If my dad was mad at my mom, he seemed to take it out on Racheal. He would either be mean to her or not talk to her at all. She sometimes felt like an outsider because she had a different biological father. For Racheal, my dad's love for her was conditional at best. Which caused her to feel isolated and sometimes alone.

Being alone was not something my brothers Reuben and Ryan knew about. They were inseparable. They were always together, running around laughing at everyone and everything. They had their own inside jokes and gestures. It was almost as if they knew what each other were thinking. They had their wonder twin powers activated.

But as much as they were together, they were still two different people. Ryan was the spirited one who always spoke up and often did so for Reuben. Ryan was adventurous and would try new things. He also had a wicked temper. One day, I remember he got mad at me for taking one of his toys and he chased after me. I darted through the front door, slamming the glass screen door behind me, thinking it would slow him down. But instead of him trying to open the screen door, he jumped headfirst through it as if he was Superman. Except he only made it halfway through the glass. Glass was everywhere, and some of it cut his stomach because he was still lodged in the screen. Thankfully, it was not as bad as it seemed. My mother was so upset with us. She helped Ryan get out of the screen, cleaned his wounds, and bandaged him up. And she gave me a good tongue lashing because she said I was the older brother, and I should have been more responsible.

Reuben was the thoughtful and sensitive twin. He was not quick to anger and wanted everyone to get along. He was the peacemaker. Reuben could see perspectives from both sides of an argument. He did not like picking sides and chose to be neutral. He played the role of a middle child perfectly. Rueben also did not like seeing other people hurt physically or emotionally.

When Reuben was five years old, he had a health scare. One day he came in from playing outside and complained about not feeling well. My mom noticed little bumps all over him that looked like measles. Within hours he had a fever, and one eye was swollen shut. My mom gave him children's Tylenol and put an ice pack on his eye, but nothing changed.

They rushed him to the emergency room. The doctors ran all the tests they knew to run but could not diagnose what was causing my brother to be sick. Things turned for the worst. His fever shot up, his hands and feet started peeling. The swelling over his eye grew larger and the skin on his eyelid begin to split open. And if that wasn't bad enough, he lost sight in his other eye. My parents were afraid my brother would not live. The doctors in Marion determined that they needed to send him to a specialist in Indianapolis.

My parents, who were strong in their faith in God, called on their friends to pray for my brother. Several pastors came to the hospital to pray for him. They surrounded him and prayed that God would heal his body. Miraculously, within hours Reuben's fever went away, and the bumps began to leave. He regained his eyesight. The doctors did not know what to make of it. After running more test, they decided that he was getting well enough that they did not need to send him to Indianapolis. The only thing they needed to do was sew his eyelid back together.

When Rueben made it home, he was lying in my mom's lap and said, "Mom, I'm glad this happened to me and not Ryan."

"Why do you say that, Reuben?" my mom asked.

Reuben looked at her and said, "Because I don't think Ryan could have handled this happening to him." Despite the scary, life-threatening situation Reuben had just gone through, he was still thinking about how he would rather go through the hurt than see his brother be hurt.

Reuben got his heart from our mother. My mother was the most energetic, charismatic, beautiful woman you could ever meet. She loved people and was always trying to help anyone she could. People who met her were always amazed about her ability to talk almost anyone into anything. She had a particular way of encouraging you to believe you could do anything. Whether she was speaking in the pulpit as an evangelist or just with you one on one, you felt like you had the loudest cheerleader cheering you on to greatness. It was almost as if her energy was contagious, and if you were anywhere in earshot, you might catch it too.

She was also a dreamer. Most dreamers are limited to only seeing the possibilities of their own dreams. However, my mom was not just a dreamer, but what I call a dream bearer—meaning, she could see the possibilities in other people's dreams and help support their dreams to bring them to fruition. I believe this, along with her charisma and good looks, attracted my dad to her.

Her influence and personality were bigger than life. She was persistent, confident, driven and courageous. If she put her mind to it, you better believe it would get done or she would give it everything she had. Which is why her greatest gift was such a blessing and a curse. I believe her most powerful asset was her ability to forgive and keep seeing the best in others no matter the circumstance. There is an old saying I heard from an older gentleman, "When somebody shows you who they are, you better believe them." My mother didn't subscribe to this principle, she believed a person will show you what is in them, but what they show you is not all they are.

I believe this very conviction that she had in people caused her to keep fighting for her relationship with my dad. She kept seeing the best in him regardless of what he did or said, whether good or bad. Even to the point of my dad committing what some would call, the "deal breaker," by having a child outside of their marriage.

I wondered how our family dynamics would change. There was already tension in our house, would it cause more tension? Would my little sister, Ricketa, being introduced to the family equation change, shift, or alter our schedules and living arrangements? There already seemed to be a limited amount of time my dad had to spend with us. Would we get less time now that we have a little sister? We had a small house. Where would she sleep when she came to visit? Would my mom still be the same person and feel the same way when she had to deal with seeing my little sister when she came to visit? It's one thing to hypothesize what you will do when the situation is not in your face. Still, it's something different when you have to look at someone who is a symbol of that betrayal.

Ricketa's mom was a part of the same C.O.G.I.C. conference. Therefore, we would see them at least 2 to 3 times a year. Which consequently would be the only times we would get to see Ricketa. It would be five years before my father and Ricketa's mother could work out an agreement that satisfied both parties so she could visit us. I can imagine my dad and my sister's mom had some guilt, shame, and embarrassment that made it difficult for them to see how this would impact us the rest of our lives.

Later, my mother told me that she knew Ricketa's mother before my father got involved with her. They saw each other at many church events and would talk afterwards. She considered Ricketa's mom a friend. And despite feeling betrayed by both my dad and her friend, she showed her strength by choosing to forgive and not remain angry with either of them. She told me, there was nothing she could do about the past. However, she was in control of how she would decide to live in the present. And she made up her mind that she would make the best out of being a stepmom.

My mom made sure that she was not standing in the way of my father being a father to my little sister. Nor would she stand in the way of our little sister knowing us. For some people, they would see this as a sign of weakness. However, I believe in my heart I was watching superhuman strength and what it meant to fight for something and someone you believe in.

REFLECTIONS

Take a moment and think about the times you've watched someone show superhuman strength when it came to fighting for their relationship. It could be a mother, father, grandmother, grandfather, loved one, friend, or someone from a far. Did what you witness cause you to look in the mirror and wonder if you could ever do something like that? Perhaps you even debated on the inside if you ever wanted to fight that hard for a relationship. Regardless of how it made you feel or the questions you had, we all want a love that we believe is worth fighting for.

Take some time if the person is still around, and ask them why they fought so hard for their relationship. Ask them what kept them fighting when things got rough, and it seemed like it was over. Find out what love means for them. Then, maybe, you can start to formulate your own meaning of what love is. Just remember, love has a strange way of making you see things different when you're on the inside of it versus on the outside.

TWO

"If a child learns how to structure their lives based on what they see their parents do, I would have learned, family must settle for your leftovers"

BALANCE

Life is all about balance. The balance between family, work, and selfish desires. The balance between your dreams and your current responsibilities. Also, the balance between your spiritual, mental, emotional, and physical self. This balance is often measured in where and how much time we spend on anything. And the amount of time we spend on something also determines how much value it has for us. Value is not determined by what we say out of our mouths but by where we spend our time. People feel valued based on how much time we spend with them.

Regrettably, if most of us were to audit our time, we would see a deficit in the areas we claim are the most important. We may also see a surplus in the areas we say are necessary, but not our primary focus. For example, many of us would see a deficit in the time we spend developing a relationship with God and a surplus in the time we prepare for work.

Consequently, this practice causes the people in our lives we claim are important, to commonly get the least of us; and sadly, causing them to question their value to us. If you asked those people closest to you how much you value them based on your time with them, what would they say?

I began to question how valuable I was to my dad around six years old. His inability to balance work, church, pleasure, and family was apparent. If a child learns how to structure their lives based on what they see their parents do, I would have learned, family must settle for your leftovers. The family must settle for whatever you have left after work, church, and selfish desires. I believe my dad did this with a clear conscience because he thought his family would understand that the sacrifice for church was necessary and honorable.

One Sunday after leaving church, my dad told us he was starting his own church and asked us to make a major sacrifice. He asked us to be all in with him in starting this church. He presented it to us as if we were going into a family business. We all had roles to play. He reassured us that all of us would be a part in whatever possible way. He assumed we would understand what that meant and the sacrifice we would have to make. However, we had no idea what that would mean for our family or our future. I believe my dad thought starting a church was necessary for him and his spiritual calling. However, I don't believe he understood what it would take to have a church and a family.

We attended a church that had been established for many years and I had never heard of someone starting a church. My dad was an associate minister there for about five years. The church was part of the Church of God in Christ (C.O.G.I.C) denomination. The hierarchy in the denomination influenced many decisions about who would pastor certain churches. I don't believe my dad ever thought there was a chance of him pastoring there because of the influence of the hierarchy. Nor did he think the people at the church saw him as a future pastor. This was the only church he had been a part of since he became a Christian as a teenager. He felt like he had hit a glass ceiling there. He felt like he would never be considered to become the senior pastor. Therefore, he decided to step out on faith rather than let the church's hierarchy tell him when he was ready to pastor.

I don't think anyone is ever truly ready to transition when you've been somewhere your whole life. That church was the only church my brothers and I had ever known. Our friends were there. My siblings and I were heavily involved in the youth ministry. I was starting to play drums. I was not that good yet, but they were at least giving me a chance. I would get off beat and people would give me mean looks, but I was getting better. My sister was singing in the choir. My mom was an evangelist, which is what they called female preachers in the C.O.G.I.C denomination.

Our family was a significant part of the music ministry. My dad played the drums, organ, guitar, and he had a smooth first tenor voice. My mom's powerful singing would set any church on fire. All my siblings and I could sing and play drums. We had the makings of a fully equipped music ministry.

My dad was what some would describe as a total package. He was charismatic, energetic, a visionary, a phenomenal preacher, teacher, loved people, loved to encourage people, helped people, and people loved him. He had this amazing smile that would light up any room. He had this remarkable gift for drawing people. People just wanted to help him and do whatever he asked. There was not much he couldn't do.

If you talked to him for any length of time, you would see he was a dreamer. This is why I think he and my mom were good together in this part of their relationship. If he spoke it, she would come alongside, and they would make it happen together. She wasn't afraid to ask people for anything and he would convince whomever she asked for help, to come on board no matter the project. Together they were strong when it came to making the impossible, possible.

One of my dad's strong characteristics as a preacher was his ability to break down biblical passages so that everyone, including children, could understand. He didn't have any formal training in theology, yet, he used what he learned from other preachers, combined with his natural gift as a critical thinker, to expound upon deep theological principles.

He studied the word of God fervently by reading books, commentaries, and anything else he could get his hands on. He also studied how people thought and what motivated them. His charisma and ability to study the Bible and people would be a great asset. But those same gifts also served as a liability that caused him to be susceptible to the products of pride and ego. His lack of awareness for the balance of humility and keeping your pride and ego in check would serve to be a formidable challenge.

My dad risked everything, including his reputation starting the church. He did not have our former church's financial or leadership support, which made it even harder. There was an immense amount of pressure on him and my mom financially and emotionally. But to my surprise, they worked well together because both were determined to see it through.

For weeks, they searched around town looking for a building. Finally, they found a location within their budget that seemed to be an old, abandoned house. To renovate this building into a church would take some work. My dad had some handyman skills, but not enough to do all the renovations. When they started working on the building, people started coming from everywhere asking what they were doing. My mom suggested he ask some people in the neighborhood if they would be willing to help. People with all kinds of skills began to offer assistance. Within a few months, the church was up and running.

The church grew quickly. My dad was preaching and teaching his heart out every week. My mom was singing and leading the choir. People were giving their lives to Christ for the first time or coming back to church after years of being away. The way my dad preached was new and exciting. At that time, the town had many older preachers who made the Bible seem antiquated and irrelevant. My dad was 25 years old and full of energy. He made the Bible come alive by being creative and making the text sound inspiring and applicable.

The church was doing well and within months we were growing out of the building we were renting. My dad already had his eyes set on a larger building not too far away. It used to be some rich person's home. What one person saw as a home, my dad saw as a sanctuary. He was in his element, appearing to be firing on all cylinders.

At home, everything seemed to be going well. We had moved to a different house. The arguments, now, seemed to be about typical husband and wife stuff. More importantly, there were no physical altercations. We seemed to be doing so well financially that my dad bought this big, luxury van he had always wanted. But the more time my dad spent at the church, it seemed he had less and less time for anything else, including us. The church had become more important than family. What was on the horizon would alter the trajectory of the ministry and our family.

The church had just celebrated its first anniversary. It should have been a time of celebration; however, the arguing between my parents started again. My mom began questioning how much time my dad was spending at the church. My dad was now finding reasons to spend time at the church and not at home. He would say he was studying or working on something at church, but my mom was very suspicious of what he was doing with his time. Did he spend that much time at the church, or was there something else going on?

My dad's behavior began to change at home. He used to play with us when he had the time, but he began to have less and less time. Even when he was there with us it seemed like his mind was preoccupied. He would quickly lose interest in what we were doing, and he would go to his room. Unless it involved church, we did less as a family. He had more outside preaching engagements at other churches. He became good at doing all the things a good preacher does, by visiting with sick members, counseling those who were troubled and being present during peoples' most difficult moments in life. He seemed more concerned about being a good preacher than a good husband and father. We did not receive the same energy, time, or effort as the church members. Which I found ironic, because we were members too.

He may not have said it, but I think my dad thought his family would understand he had to do the work of the Lord. However, what we understood was that he was not there at the end of the day. If it wasn't a church-related event, my mom was usually with us by herself. When my sister, brothers, and I had sporting events or school programs, we would see my mom, but not my dad. What I understood, during this time was church must be more important than family and more important than me.

But I also believe there was something even more important to my dad than church and doing the work of the Lord. I believe that something was how the church members and people in the community responded to his preaching made him feel. He became addicted to the attention, love, and praise he received from the role of pastor and preacher. The more praise he received, the more it fed his pride and ego. He had all the praise without any of the consequences of past problems, like he did at home. At church he had fans who only knew the good he had done, but at home he had a family who knew the good and the bad he had done. At church, they only knew his history of helping people, at home we knew his history of hurting us.

The attention caused him to become increasingly obsessed with perfecting his performance for people rather than pursuing his purpose for God. Pursuing your purpose for God means becoming more clear and secure about what God has created you to be. It is getting closer to God so that God can continue to reveal his plan for you. Each revelation and layer brings your heart into a greater submission to God and inevitably shapes and molds your heart to help others. In other words, as my friend Shakura Fentress would say, "The mission becomes greater than the man." Ultimately, we follow and chase after what God wants rather than what we want. Pursuing his purpose would have led him to a place of humility because he would have been forced back to the God who gave him the purpose in the first place.

But perfecting the performance will always lead you back to the performer. And the performer's value is not determined by God, but by how great of a response the performance receives. A quick example would be a professional athlete. Professional athletes learn quickly that fans can be fickle. If the team is winning, they love the players, if they are losing, fans can be rude and disrespectful. The best athletes always know how to get back to the real reason they play. It was never for the fans, but because that's where their heart was, and they learn to reconnect with their love of the game. When connected to our purpose, people's responses are appreciated, but never relied upon to determine our value.

Do I think my dad was maliciously choosing church over us? No, I believe it was happening on a subconscious level. I believe he became co-dependent on the response of the church members. He needed that response to make him feel important and loved. Preaching invoked a response that filled a void that he felt like he desperately needed. Despite why he was preaching, people were still being blessed.

On the other hand, my mom was not receiving that blessing. My mom's response to my dad not being at home became more and more negative. She had lost her patience with his absence and had begun to confront him. The arguments grew worse than before, and the yelling got louder.

My parents' bedroom was on the lower level of the house. The lower level resembled a walk-out basement. The living room and kitchen were on the first floor, and two bedrooms were upstairs. My brothers and I shared a bedroom, and my sister had her own room. Even though a floor separated us, we could still hear the progression from yelling to physical abuse.

The fights were becoming more frequent. They would fight on Saturday night and then get up and go to church on Sunday morning like nothing ever happened. My parents were doing everything they could to save face in front of the church. Their fighting taught us that church and home were two different places. I learned that you don't have to practice at home what you preach in church.

One night, the fighting got so bad my brothers and I went to my sister's room because we were afraid. We were all huddled up in Racheal's twin size bed. Reuben and Ryan were covering their ears and Racheal had tears rolling down her face. I was shaking my head, angry and sad at the same time. I was so tired of the yelling and screaming. I wished there was more I could do. I felt helpless! I hated hearing my mom in that state. She sounded terrified. We had to do something.

Racheal decided to call the police. But before she could get to the phone my mom had come upstairs and told us to get dressed because we were leaving. My dad followed her up the stairs and started yelling at her not to leave. He grabbed my mom by the arms to keep her from moving.

My sister yelled at my dad, "I'm calling the police!" As she turned to pick up the phone sitting on the nightstand next to her bed, my dad let go of my mom and snatched the phone out of my sister's hands. As he was ripping the phone out of her hand, the phone hit my sister in the mouth. She held her mouth, cried, and looked at my dad in disbelief. I couldn't believe it. Was this really happening? I froze! My mind went blank. I didn't know what to do. I wanted to protect my mom and sister, but he was way bigger than me and was still my dad. My mother quickly ran to Racheal and started holding her. He then ripped the phone out of the wall and said, "Ain't nobody calling the police!"

My mom had finally had enough. She began screaming and yelling for him to leave her alone, and that she was leaving. Something about the way she said it caused my dad to physically take a few steps back. Maybe her seeing my sister get hit with the phone gave my mom courage that even my dad realized he shouldn't push her anymore. We all ran outside and jumped in the car. He came out of the house as we got ready to pull off and said, "You'll be back! You always come back!" and slammed the front door. My mom then stopped the car, grabbed a huge brick, threw it at his van, and busted the side window. The van, material things, and the church were all just reminders of what he valued over his family. That night, not only was the van window broken, but their marriage was broken too.

Weeks later, my mom filed for divorce, and we officially moved back to Indianapolis. When members of the church heard about the divorce, some members left the church. Some of them were key leaders who had been with them since the beginning. The leaders were hurt and disappointed in my dad. News had spread around town about the domestic abuse. His reputation was stained. Church members were also sad because they loved my mom and her personality. My dad was the pastor, but my mom was the heart of the church.

I often wondered if this could have been avoided. If my dad had learned the art of balancing and prioritizing. Perhaps he would have realized that everything he needed was not in others, but in God and his family. But when I look at the word *balance*, it means to have different things equal or in the correct proportions. Those correct proportions were not something that needed to start on the outside for my father, but on the inside.

Where my dad spent his time was directly connected to what he felt he needed and essentially what he valued most. The praise and approval became what he needed to feel whole. Because my dad had not done the work to identify why he felt like he needed the praise and approval; it controlled him rather than him controlling his desire for it. Therefore, the amount of energy it took for him to ensure he felt whole consumed any energy he had left to spend time with his family. And in the end, we felt less important and valuable to him.

REFLECTIONS

When our priorities do not align with where we spend our time, there is usually an internal balance issue. We are probably using something or someone we feel is necessary to fill a void, desire, deep longing, inadequacy, or hurt. If this internal balance is left unchecked it will lead to disproportions in where we invest our time, energy, and effort. Ultimately leaving the people we love wondering if they measure up or are good enough. Is your life well balanced? First, evaluate how much time you spend with the ones you love versus work, ministry, entertainment, hobby, or anything else. Who or what is getting most of your time?

Secondly, I realize sometimes work schedules do not permit us to spend as much time as we would like with loved ones. However, I encourage you to make time by planning how you can spend quality time with the ones you love. Talk to them and ask them how you can make your time with them more meaningful for them. Often, it is something simple and manageable like doing somethings with them that they find enjoyable. Third, schedule this time on the calendar as if it was an appointment that you must make. Your loved ones will feel and know they are a priority in your life when you make time for them instead of waiting until you get time for them.

THREE

"We were just pawns in his chess game to win back my mom"

I FINALLY LET GO, AND HERE WE GO AGAIN!

If you have ever had to relocate, there is this feeling that you are searching for. It's not a word or a particular thing that happens. There is no specific amount of time it takes to occur. You just know it when it happens. When you finally feel you are settled in your new place, city, home, job, or even a relationship. It is in that moment when you feel like you belong. The moment when you realize you fit, you are a member of a group, part of something bigger than yourself.

This is not an easy place to arrive. There is a natural process that happens where you, the people, or environment you have been introduced to need to evaluate each other. This occurs when those who are native to the place, are trying to see if who you are, what you believe, and what you subscribe to is compatible with those in the environment and space you now both occupy. There are no proverbial boxes you check off to see if you fit. You just know when it feels right. When you get that feeling, you can be total opposites or have different beliefs, but something in you and the people in that place go together like a puzzle piece.

However, one of the biggest stumbling blocks or delays to this process is when either or both parties are not open. This is often due to the fear of being hurt, vulnerable, or taken advantage of. Fear can prevent or hold you back from being open to fitting into any group or community. At the age of 7, my family and I found ourselves back in Indianapolis after my parents had divorced again. I thought it would be like the last time. Maybe we would be here a few weeks or a few months, and my parents would be back together. After all, this was their pattern. Therefore, I don't have to let myself get too attached to the place or the people here because we will be going back to Marion soon.

A few weeks turned into a couple of months, and we were still in Indianapolis. On top of that, school was getting ready to start. The summer before the second grade was quickly coming to an end. We lived with my grandparents, and I was having fun with the neighborhood kids. Kids kept asking me if we were staying to go to school. I told them, probably not, because we should be moving back to Marion soon.

But the truth is, there was no indication we were moving back. I had not even seen my dad since we left Marion to make matters worse. Then, my mom came home one day and said she had enrolled us into School 69, the school down the street from my grandparents' house. This was not a good sign. I had so many thoughts. Was my parents' marriage done? Was our family going to be separated forever? Would I see my dad again? Was this going to be our new home? With all those questions swirling around in my head, something in me still could not accept that this would be our new reality.

However, my sister and brothers seemed not to have any problems accepting and adjusting to this new life. My sister, who felt like Indianapolis was her real home, was living her best life. She reconnected with her friends, and they were all talking about school and boys in the neighborhood. She had already gone school shopping with my grandmother. She had no thoughts about going back to Marion. Marion was behind her, and Indianapolis was her life now. It was as if her life in Marion had been a nightmare, and now, she was awake and grateful that it was just a dream.

My brothers Reuben and Ryan showed no signs that they were sad about being in Indianapolis. They were sad that they had not seen my dad, but not sad about leaving Marion. Relocating was not easy on any of us, but Reuben and Ryan's advantage was that they were each other's best friend. Because they were so close, they always had each other. I believe they were each other's anchor. When you have a friend as an anchor, they become the one constant thing in your life while everything else seems to change. When you have a friend as an anchor you can share your experiences, confide in them, and you share memories that no one can take away. Regrettably, I did not have an anchor. I was always friendly at this age, but did not connect with anyone deeply enough as a friend to confide in. Therefore, leaving me to feel more shaken by the relocation than my brothers were.

I was always a loner. I felt like I was too mature to hang out with my brothers, but not mature enough to hang out with my sister, Racheal. I just loved annoying and messing with her to see her reaction. I got a kick out of it. Most of it was intentional. However, what it did was further isolate me from my siblings. I had friends because we would play together when we visited my grandparents over the years. But to them, I wasn't a kid from Indianapolis. I was a visitor; I did not belong. Racheal had my grandparents as her support, Reuben and Ryan had each other, my mom had family and childhood friends, but I didn't feel like I had anyone supporting me. I did not have a person or thing that allowed me to feel like I fit in.

My mom told us we were going school shopping because we were growing and couldn't fit any of our clothes anymore. Yes, it was always fun to go shopping. I loved having new clothes for the beginning of the school year. Something about new clothes felt like a fresh start. If I was going to be in a city and a school I did not want to be in, at least I would have new clothes to walk around in.

The first day of school had finally arrived. When we stepped outside, it looked like the whole neighborhood went to the same school. I had never witnessed anything like that before. The neighborhood where we lived back in Marion did not have that many kids. This was different. There were kids everywhere. Even the kids who normally didn't get to come out of their house to play with everyone was outside. It was a bunch of kids walking down the street and everyone was so happy. It looked more like a neighborhood block party than people going to school. Adults were hanging out watching the kids walk to school, which was two blocks away from my grandparents' house. But I didn't want to let myself get too caught up in this parade. I wasn't sure how long I would be there. There was still hope my dad would swoop in and take us back to Marion. But I had to admit...this felt good.

We had been in school for a couple of months and my siblings and I were doing well academically. We liked our teachers and enjoyed going to school with the other neighborhood kids. However, I had one issue—this guy who they called Buster. We were in the same grade, but he was much bigger than I was. On top of that, he was a bully. I had not played with him much over the summer, but I knew who he was. I had seen him pick on some other kids but did not think too much about it.

One day at lunch, Buster bumped into me. He looked at me and said, "Watch out little dude, before I hurt you!" I replied, "Whatever dude! You not gone hurt me!" A teacher quickly came over and broke us up. See, I had a slight temper of my own. I was usually the happy, smiling guy who got along with everyone. I also did not back down from a fight. I was usually the smallest one in the group, but I never saw myself that way. I knew people were taller or bigger than me, but I never thought they were superior to me. Some would say I had a Napoleon syndrome. That day, Buster would try the wrong person.

In elementary school, the word gets around quick about fights. Buster told people he was going to beat me up after school. My buddy, Bam Bam, who lived across the street from my grandparents asked me what I was going to do? He said, "Man, that dude is big!" I replied, "The bigger they are, the harder they fall." I wasn't scared. See, I needed something to hit. I was already angry because I had not seen my dad, I was still in Indianapolis and things had not worked out as I planned. If Buster knew that, he should have feared me.

School ended and all the kids were walking home. Buster, who usually goes the other direction walked my direction home. I heard the neighborhood kids hyping us up. My brothers, who were walking with me, were scared.

"Rickey, are you really going to fight that big dude?" my brothers asked.

"Yes, I'm tired of that dude talking crazy and bullying everybody. I ain't scared of him," I answered.

So, when we got to an alley where the adults couldn't see us, he ran up on me and swung at my head. I ducked, picked him up and slammed him. I then started punching him in his face and then his stomach. He, along with everyone else, was shocked. So shocked, in fact, that he got up and started to run, but I punched him in the head before he could get away and he flipped over a fence. He ran home and the neighborhood kids started shouting and chanting for me.

Kids were shaking my hands like I was a celebrity. Even some of the older kids there said, "You a bad boy. You kicked his tail." Something happened that day. After beating up the neighborhood bully, I was not just the kid from Marion anymore, I was one of them. I had not anticipated this feeling. The sense of belonging and peace. I started feeling like Indianapolis was home. It was easier to fight and hold on to the hope of my parents getting back together as long as the other kids saw me as an outsider; but now, they were embracing me. Maybe this wasn't all bad. Perhaps leaving Marion was the best thing for us all. But the question remained, could I see myself as one of them?

January of the next year my mom found a house to rent. We were moving into our own home. It was about five minutes from my grandparents' house. This was significant for several reasons. Although my grandparents' home was safe, it was extremely small. Their house had two bedrooms with a basement. My grandparents slept in one room, while my mom, sister, and my aunt's two daughters slept in the other bedroom. My brothers, my aunt and I slept in the basement. Needless to say, it was crowded in that house.

I enjoyed being that close to family, but that was too close, if you know what I mean. Therefore, it was a fresh breath of air to finally have some room to stretch our legs and walk around without running into so many people. The house my mom was renting was two stories with three bedrooms. It was a nice size house just for us. There was some work the landlord was still getting done, but it was great. This house represented us putting down roots.

Putting down roots was exactly what my siblings and I needed. A house with a space of our own. My sister got her own room again. Now she could kick us out of her room like before. She had a sense of ownership and independence. My brothers and I were just glad we didn't have to share the basement with my aunt anymore. We knew this was the beginning of something good for us all. We were all so proud of my mom.

Moving into this house also meant any hope I had of my mom and dad getting back together began to dissipate even more after we settled in our house. If I'm honest, I think the fact that my dad did not seem interested in being a part of our lives caused me to finally give up hope of a reunion. He did not call or come to see us turned me completely off. I decided to look to the future instead of the past. I found something new to be hopeful for. I was hopeful of us making it without my dad. I was hopeful that we could live in Indianapolis, and everything would work out. My hope was in my mom taking care of us.

We were almost at the end of the school year when my dad started calling out of the blue. It had been months since we had heard from him. I thought, "Why was he calling now? What was he trying to achieve? What angle was he playing?" And before we knew it, he was repeating his old pattern of coming to visit us for a few moments so he could spend some time with my mom. We felt used. My siblings and I knew he was showing interest in us to get to my mom. It wasn't authentic. We were just pawns in his chess game to win back my mom. And I could see her falling again.

I had finally let go...and here we go again. I finally let myself see Indianapolis as home and now I did not want to leave. Six months before, I would have been thrilled, bags already packed. But now things were different. I was different. Even though I was just 8 years old, I saw things much clearer than I did a year before. I was not as naïve about what was going on with my dad. I still loved him, but the blinders were off. I knew he had some issues and that going back to Marion may not be the best plan for us.

My siblings and I were already in conversation about what was going to happen next. We had our own little meeting. It was now summertime, and we knew if anything were to happen between our parents, it would happen before the school year started. This time, we all agreed with Racheal that we did not want to go back. However, we knew this would not be our choice, but our mom's.

My mom called the family meeting we were all dreading. She pulled us together to tell us she and my dad were getting back together. They were going to get remarried. I think she knew we were not going to be happy. I think deep down, even she knew she would have to give up so much to go back. Maybe she thought this was best for us to be a family together. Maybe tradition and watching her own parents remarry after they had divorced caused her to be hopeful it could work for her marriage as well. Perhaps she thought it would be easier to raise four children with a husband than without. Whatever she thought outweighed the negative history, my dad's proven patterns, and what her children thought. We were going back to Marion.

Everything changed. Even though we were leaving Indianapolis, Indianapolis would not leave us. Something inside of me would always call Indianapolis home. You see, hear, and experience things differently when a piece of you feels like it is somewhere else. You are there, but a piece of you is not all in. There's a small door or window of a chance that there is another option if things don't work out. It's hard to be all-in when a part of you enjoyed being somewhere else. Before we left the last time, I never thought of being anywhere else, but Marion. I never had a thought of living without my dad. Now that we had lived a completely new life in Indianapolis, could we ever be the same?

Ironically, when we returned, Marion now seemed like the foreign place. We were in Marion, but our hearts were in Indianapolis. No matter how long we would be in Marion, a small piece of my heart longed for Indianapolis, my other home. We were back as a family, but we would never be the same! Starting all over was going to be hard!

REFLECTIONS

Have you ever had to start all over? What impact did it have on you? I invite you to explore how relocating, moving, and even change has impacted you emotionally. Change threatens the very thing that those of us who have been through trauma, value and hang onto for dear life. Consistency, the same, and dependable things are what causes us to feel safe. When we experience constant change, it is very easy to develop a fear of losing control. When everything is consistent and the same, we feel like we are in control. When change is introduced into our world, we feel we do not have control and more importantly, we do not feel safe.

When you experience change do you shut out everyone and everything? Do you become angry? Do you have a habit of walking away or sabotaging opportunities? If so, perhaps you may need to seek some healing in this area of your life. One of the most constant things in life is change. Whether it is at home, on a job, or in relationships, things will continue to change. But seeking help to manage your anxiety surrounding change may bring you peace about what you experienced in your past transitions and how to manage expectations in the future.

Every time you make changes or relocate it may seem like you start over with less of you. Especially when you are connected to the people and place you are leaving. I believe a tiny piece of you never leaves the place you put down roots. Which is why I believe it is so important to mourn, grieve, or allow yourself some time to feel sad about what you are leaving. However, I also believe we were not created to be static or concrete. We are meant to be more fluid where we can grow, and our love and capacity can expand to include new places, people, and experiences. It all depends on the perspective you choose to take.

But here is a piece of advice if you must change or relocate. It is best to first consider for everyone if the change or move is right and talk about the impact of leaving with whoever is leaving with you. It is particularly important to include your children. I suggest even when a child does not have a choice in whether to change or move, you should at least give them a chance to share how they feel. Also, give them the honest reason you are moving. Kids are resilient, but they could become resistant if you don't take the time to help them understand. If this happens, they may just decide to not put roots down anywhere. It makes it extremely hard for them to communicate and connect with anyone anywhere in the future. So, take the time for yourself and your children to mourn the old, and embrace the joy of something new.

FOUR

"Relationships are not about winning and losing, but about cultivating and learning."

WHEN MY HERO TURNED INTO A MONSTER

What do you do when you see your hero turn into a monster? Heroes are the people we admire, respect, or idealize for their courage, bravery, or accomplishments. We see something great in a hero that we may not see in ourselves. Heroes seem to be dripping with confidence and certainty. It's not just what they do that we admire; it's who they are and what they represent. Heroes are faithful, loyal, and selfless. But even more than that, heroes represent the good in the world we all wish to embody.

I have always been a super fan of superhero comics, movies, and stories. What I love about superheroes is they always seem to be calm and under control. Even while the villain was attacking them, they would be concerned about the people in the surrounding area. The villain would try to knock over an entire building to smash the hero, but the hero was more concerned with getting the people out of the building than their safety. The hero could probably defeat their enemies quicker if they were not so concerned about the innocent bystanders. But this is what makes them heroes. Their job is not just to defeat an enemy but also to protect the innocent and serve those in need. When a hero's main objective is to win at all costs, what do they become?

Our return to Marion was amazing. It was storybook material. My dad was extra attentive to our needs as a family. He came directly home after work. If he wasn't at work or church, he was at home with us. The time he was home was quality time. We would go out for ice cream and have family dinners, especially Sunday after church. We even went on two family trips. One trip was to Six Flags in Ohio and the other was five days at a campsite in southern Indiana. Where we had the time of our lives, fishing, and hanging out.

My parents bought this little house with a big yard and a detached garage. It was the first time we had a garage. Although we never parked in it. We normally just used it as a hiding place when we played Hide and Seek. But on the outside of the garage my dad put up a basketball goal right above the garage doors.

My dad taught us how to play basketball. My favorite shot was the bank shot. I loved hitting the basketball in the square. It was almost always a guarantee I would make the ball go in the basket. My dad was doing all the things a good dad should do. He was present in our lives, teaching, talking, listening, and involved with us daily. It felt like we were a drama-free, normal family.

My dad was intentional about teaching my brothers and I how to be gentlemen. He said, *"Real gentlemen respect women in their conversation, actions, holding the door open for them, and waiting until they get their food before you eat. As men you are to protect your woman and your family."* My brothers and I took turns opening doors for everyone. It was exciting to run ahead of everyone to hold open the door. We would say, "After you ladies and gentlemen."

Things had really turned around for our family. Rachel was adjusting to the move even though she would have preferred being in Indianapolis. I must hand it to her; she was putting forth an effort to make it work. It helped that things were going so well with my parent's relationship. Racheal started making friends and hanging out with them. And from time to time she would even have a friend spend the night at our house. My sister never had friends spend the night before we returned to Marion.

I liked school and was excelling in my classes. I would not call myself a nerd, but school came easy to me. I understood what was being taught and tested in the top 10 percentile in math of all 3rd graders in the state of Indiana. I was also making new friends. Life was peaceful at home, and I could not have hoped for more. This seemed like a dream come true.

On the other hand, my brothers were not adjusting as well when it came to their academics. They had a hard time comprehending the 2nd grade material. The teachers could not identify if it was due to the change in environment or if it was a learning disability.

After many conversations and meetings with their teachers, my parents agreed they should be held back to redo the second grade. Later my brothers told me this was hard on them. They felt embarrassed and like something was wrong with them because they did not learn like everyone else. But thankfully, both my parents were very supportive and patient with my brothers.

They would have a long road ahead of them as far as education, but we were all willing to chip in and help them through it. Whether that meant helping with homework, studying, or just encouraging and celebrating them when they did well on schoolwork. We were going on this education journey together.

Alone was not a feeling I think any of us felt after returning to Marion. We all seemed to be in tuned with each other. We understood each other, were more patient with each other, and had similar interest in having fun as a family. We were not only building a family, but a team at home and church.

We all had our roles at church. My dad was preaching, teaching, and leading. My mom taught Sunday school, led the choir, and was very supportive as a first lady. My sister was helping play the drums and leading songs in the choir. I was the main drummer and helped my dad open and close the church building. My brothers were singing in the choir and of course still making fun of people. We all needed that comic relief from time to time. Together, we were unstoppable.

I always admired my dad. Not only because he was my dad, but also because of his many gifts and talents. However, I had started admiring him for something more. Over the year I admired him for the man he had become. My dad was my hero. I looked up to him. I loved his charisma, his smile, the way he always helped people. He would give people the shirt off his back. I saw him give away his clothes, shoes, and money out of his pocket to people who were in need. I saw the way people responded with such gratitude to his preaching and encouragement. He did whatever he could to help people turn their lives around. He had a way of seeing the best in people and showing them how much he believed in them. More than anything, he gave people hope that there was something better for them. That was what a hero was supposed to do and be.

But no matter how good things were, I could not help but have this nagging question in the back of my mind. *"Was all this real? And how long would this last?"* As bright of a light as my dad had been, my family and I knew he had a dark side. That dark side could spread across the house like the darkness of night. Causing the mood, atmosphere, attitudes, and everything in its vicinity to change for the worse.

My dad's dark side was angry, psychotic, and violent. It was as if he was Dr. Jekyll and Mr. Hyde. And believe me when Mr. Hyde came out, it was bad for everyone. But somehow, he had kept that part of himself locked away and hidden for just over a year. Unfortunately, when you try to hide the parts of yourself, you don't like, instead of seeking healing, whatever you are hiding will find a way out and wreak havoc.

A little over a year had passed and the honeymoon phase was over. Just like before, it started with more arguments, and more frequent shouting matches. My dad started spending less time at home and my mom was more upset. We did not have a floor in between our bedroom and our parents in this house. My siblings and I slept in the same room next to our parents' room. I was older now, and I could hear the contents of the conversation and understand them.

Was I hearing correctly? The arguments were not what I thought. These were not arguments about my dad being at church too much but about being with other women.

I was devastated. Could it be, the whole time I thought my dad had a problem with time management, his real problem was commitment. And even at 9-years-old, I could tell he did not seem apologetic. When my mom confronted him about being with other women, he went on the defense and became angry and aggressive.

One night my siblings and I heard our parents arguing again. I was hoping it wouldn't get out of control, but my hopes were quickly dashed when I heard something break. It sounded like glass shattering. We quickly got out of our beds and ran into the living room. My mother was shouting, "We're leaving!" My dad shouted back, "No, you're not! Not this time!" He then grabbed her purse.

Normally, he would try to calm down a little if he saw us, but not this time. This time was different because he looked right passed us like we weren't even there. He was in a complete psychotic rage, and we were very nervous. My siblings and I went and sat on the couch in the living room to try to be a presence in the room. We did not know what else to do. My mother trying to console us came to sit with us on the couch.

My father went into the master bedroom and to my surprise, he came out with a hammer. He started shouting, "You ain't going nowhere! Where is your money? I know you got some money hidden in here somewhere!" My mother shouted back, "I don't have any money! You have my purse!" You could see him getting angrier and angrier by the second.

He then started yelling, "Oh you not gone tell me? You better, tell me!" The next thing I knew, he started coming toward the right edge of the couch. He then stopped at the right end table, bashing the tables with the hammer. Glass was went flying everywhere. He then went to the left end table and asked again if she had any more money and she answered, "No!" He smashed the left end table with the hammer.

There was a coffee table right in front of the couch we were sitting on. My mom loved that coffee table. My dad saw her looking at it and just shattered it with the hammer. When those three tables were broken, he went into our room. All you could hear was the breaking of the glass from the TV. If that wasn't enough, he went to every TV in the house shattering the screens. My siblings and I would jump with every hit because we were so terrified. It was scary to see my father like this. It seemed like a nightmare, and I prayed I would wake up. However, it was real.

We were all horrified. I could see in his eyes that he was not himself. It was as if something had taken over him. That was not my dad, it was a monster! It was the first time I was afraid he might not stop until someone was hurt or dead.

All I could think was, *"What will he do when he runs out of things to break? Will he turn for my mom next? Will he hit her with the hammer?"* I had to do something. My mom had told me she had money hidden away underneath the TV in her bedroom. So, I blurted out, *"I know where the money is!"*

My dad stopped in his tracks. "Where is the money, Rick?" he asked while deviously looking at my mother. I paused for a second, and I told him exactly where my mom had stashed her extra money. "Thanks, Rick," he said. I then heard my brothers and sister underneath their breaths say, "Why did you do that? That was stupid."

He went into the room, threw the TV on the floor, and grabbed the money. Looking at my mom he said, "Now you ain't going nowhere!" He walked out the house got into his car and left. I remember the disappointed look on my mom's face when she looked at me. My brothers and sister kept saying, "You stupid! Why did you do that?" I didn't say anything.

Finally, my mom looked me right in the eyes and asked, "Rickey, why did you do that?" With tears in my eyes, I said, "Because I didn't know if he would hit you with the hammer next! I just wanted him to stop and leave!" She then grabbed me, and we all cried!! I remember her saying, "Don't worry about it. It will be all right."

That night after he left, my mom told us to pack some clothes. We got in the car and my mom had just enough gas to get us to Indianapolis. To this day, that night still haunts me.

You see, days after that incident, we were right back home in Marion. My dad had apologized to my mom and bought her a new car. In other words, he tried to buy her forgiveness. I don't know if my mom believed his apology or not. Later she told me she wanted to believe he was the man he had been the last year and a half and not the monster she had seen that night. Either way, we were back and so was my dad. He was back to his "good self." He was acting as if nothing had happened, cracking jokes, and making us laugh.

We were sitting in the kitchen, and I was barefoot, sitting on top of one of the broken TVs. My dad was getting ready to throw them out so we could get new ones. While talking and laughing, my foot slipped, and I cut my foot on the broken glass in the TV. The scar I have on my foot serves as a reminder that some things we break will cut others so deeply that even after it heals, it will still leave a scar.

My father may have thought he left that night behind him. But the memory would forever be cut in the recesses of my mind. That night, his goal was to win at all costs. And he may have won the fight with my mom. He may have accomplished his goal of trying to break my mom's spirit. He may even have won at scaring us and showing he was dominant. However, what he lost was far greater. He lost a little bit of our respect, our faith in him as the leader of our home, our trust in him to keep us safe, and he lost me looking up to him as my hero. The truth is a person must choose to be a hero or a monster. They cannot be both.

REFLECTIONS

Have you ever felt like you had to win at all costs? I implore, even beg you, to consider what you could lose when you take that attitude in relationships. You may win the argument and maybe even prove you are right, but your reward will be consequences versus a celebration. You may win the battle but lose the war.

You must always look at the bigger picture. You must ask yourself, "Will what I am planning to say or do cause this person to lose respect for me or trust in me?" If there is a slim chance your answer is "yes," don't do it and don't say it.

For some people right now, you are thinking this is copping out or perhaps not being you. However, I would invite you to think about it as using discernment or wisdom. Just because you have something to say or something you want, doesn't mean it has to be said right now or done right now.

Often, timing and how you say or do something means just as much as what you need to say or do. If you want to be received, the chances of that happening increases when you learn when and how to say what you need to say, in a way the other person can best receive it. It is better to think before you speak than think of an apology speech afterward.

You must choose if you will be a monster in competition or a hero in compassion. One leaves you feeling like a valiant winner, the second leaves the other person feeling valued and worthy. Relationships are not about winning and losing, but about cultivating and learning. Cultivate your relationship by improving yourself, giving careful attention to the other person, devoting time, and thought into the relationship. Learn to get knowledge and gain skills on how to navigate through difficulties with the people you are in relationship, through experiences and being open for them to share what they need from you. In turn you will begin to see difficult situations in relationships as opportunities rather than threats.

FIVE

"If you stay with crazy people long enough, you'll start acting crazy too. People won't be able to tell the difference because you'll both look crazy."

OUR CHILDHOOD TAKEN

What does childhood mean for you? Your childhood is meant to be the time you have fun, learn, experience, explore, and live carefree. It is the time when the only significant person or thing you should be responsible for is yourself. The heaviest burdens you carry are doing your best in school, completing chores, cleaning your room, and yourself. It is the time when you get the luxury of not knowing or caring about what is happening around you or to the people around you. Childhood should be a time of joy and making beautiful memories.

Childhood, on the other hand, should not resemble adulthood. A child is not a tiny adult, and they should not carry the same weight, worry, and concern as adults. Children may have the ability to handle more worries and concerns than we give them credit, but it is credit they should never be asked to utilize. A child should not be forced to learn how to be an adult while still a child.

More importantly, a child should learn how to navigate through the difficulties of relationships on their level with classmates, peers, siblings, and friends. And by watching their parents model a healthy relationship. Some children are subjected to watching unhealthy relationships between adults, causing irreparable harm. Children tend to model in childhood and adulthood the same unhealthy behaviors they learned from their parents. Since most children do not know how to separate their parents' relationship from their own, it is very easy for children to feel stuck between two parents who may be arguing or in disagreement. Therefore, leaving a child to feel responsible for whatever is wrong or worse, carrying the burden of fixing it.

At nine years old, I felt like I was stuck in the middle of my parents' relationship. I suffered carrying the burden of trying to fix their relationship. Things never went back to that fairytale we experienced when my parents remarried. Our lives were up and down. There were some good days and some bad days. It was not always bad. In fact, most days were good. One of my favorite gospel songs is "I Won't Complain." The first verse says,

"I've had some good days, I've had some hills to climb, I've had some weary days, and some sleepless nights, but when I look around, and I think things over, all of my good days, outweigh my bad days, so I won't complain."

And the song is true; we had more good days than bad. However, if I put the good days and bad days on a scale to weigh them, even though there would be more numerical good days, I think the depth and density of the bad days would tip the scales to the side of the bad days. Not erasing the good days, but just tarnishing a portion of their shine.

One of those tarnishing moments happened when my siblings and I woke up to my mom screaming in the middle of the night. This scream was high-pitched, like she was in a great deal of pain. Racheal, and I jumped out of bed. We looked at each other and said, "What are we gonna do?"

"We need to help Momma," Racheal Said.

"Let's get a knife."

Reuben and Ryan were too afraid to get out of bed. They were holding each other, crying softly. So, Racheal and I ran into the kitchen, opened the drawer, and grabbed the biggest knives we could find.

Dad was in the living room and had mom's arm hiked up behind her back. We ran to the living room, pointing our knives at him and shouting, "Leave our momma alone! Let her go!" Dad looked at us with disbelief and shouted at us to put our knives down. He said, "If you don't, I'm gonna break her arm!" And as he said it, he lifted her arm higher behind her back. Mom then shouted at the top of her lungs, "Put the knives down! He's breaking my arm!" The way she said it scared us. It looked like he was trying to break her arm. We quickly threw the knives to the ground on the side of each of us. After looking at the knives on the ground he let go of her arm. He and I made eye contact for a moment, and I could see shame and guilt written all over his face. He put his head down, walked in the room, grabbed his keys, and left out the front door.

We ran to hug our mom. My brothers then ran out of the room to hug her too. Mom was crying and in excruciating pain. Racheal asked her if she needed to go to the hospital. But she decided not to go to the hospital because she said, she would be too embarrassed to walk in because she worked there as a clerk. So, we all stayed in the living room huddled up on the couch with her that night as she iced her arm and shoulder.

It was hard pulling out a knife on our father. Because in a sense, it meant we were choosing our mother over our father and, more importantly, that we were willing to hurt our father to protect her. A little piece of our childhood died that night. We accepted the fact that we may have to inflict violence to protect our mother. We may have only been kids, but we made a pact to protect our mother. It was a heavy burden for two kids to carry, but we felt like we had no other choice. Racheal and I felt like my brothers were too young and not up for the challenge. I believe being forced to think of ourselves as my mom's protectors made us resent our father. Being the protector of our family should have been something he did as a grown man. However, it was hard for him to protect us when he was the one, we needed protection against.

My siblings and I started spending more time with my mom instead of going outside or hanging out with friends. I would go with her to the laundromat and hang around her while she would cook dinner. I even stayed behind and went to church with her instead of going early with dad. I would sometimes hover around like a bodyguard. I believe my presence, at least sometimes, deterred dad from abusing her worse than he did. Racheal would have me stand at the door or look at him, trying to make eye contact. Ever since that night we pulled knives out on him, I felt like he did not want me to see him like that again. I think the constant eye contact caused him to become embarrassed or ashamed of having his son see him physically abuse his mom. Whatever the case, at times, our presence seemed to dissuade him from continuing the abuse.

But our crime-fighting days would come to an end. Racheal and dad were not getting along. Dad barely spoke to her unless she was in trouble. He was extra sensitive about anything she did. If she made a mistake, he would complain to mom and make it bigger than it was. He was always making a fuss about how Racheal would respond to him if he asked her to do something. Dad was getting fed up with her.

On the other hand, Racheal was fed up with dad's abuse. She walked around with an attitude all the time. She let it be known she hated living there. She was very standoffish and rarely engaged in family activities. Sometimes she was short with everyone, including me. I did not take it personally; I knew she did not want to be around dad. And she did everything she could to stay away from him. She would stay with friends on weekends, ask our grandparents to pick her up on other weekends, or just stay in her room. It was apparent that things were getting worse and eventually a decision was going to have to be made if Racheal would stay or leave. Racheal was unhappy, dad was furious, and mom was frustrated because she was in the middle.

So, when her sixth-grade school year ended, Racheal spent the summer in Indianapolis with our grandparents. My brothers and I thought she would be back for the beginning of the school year. But, at the end of the summer, mom told my brothers and me that Racheal would go to school in Indianapolis. Mom expressed that it would be good for Racheal to be in a different environment for a while. That meant she wanted Racheal to be in a less toxic environment away from the drama that dad was creating.

43

I wondered if this was mom and Racheal's plan all along? But it wasn't a hard sell for dad to buy into. I'm sure dad thought it would be easier not having to deal with Racheal's attitude. But only because dad could not take responsibility for his role in her disposition. Ironically, everything Racheal was doing to upset dad was in response to his actions.

I was happy Racheal got a chance to get away. But I was sad that I lost my partner in protection. We tried to protect my mom together. Now don't get me wrong, Racheal and I argued on a regular, but when there was trouble and anyone attacked our mother, we were on the same team. It felt like she not only left my dad, but she left me. I felt more alone than I had ever felt before.

Dad was knee-deep in trying to be with different women, my mother was too consumed with trying to keep dad's attention, and my brothers weren't mature enough to understand what was going on or at least they did not respond the same way I did. It appeared like Racheal, and I were the only ones concerned about mom's welfare. It became our duty to watch over her. With Racheal leaving, I felt like the burden was now solely on me to bear.

I didn't hear much from Racheal when she left. We occasionally talked on the phone. But weeks after she left, I had to make one of the hardest phone calls I ever had to make. I had to call the police. The first time I had to call the police was not because of an intruder or because someone was sick. It was because dad was hitting mom. It seemed like that day, the only way to get him to stop was to bring in help from the outside.

My dad was so embarrassed when the police arrived because he was a pastor and community leader. He usually saw the police because he was speaking out against something, or they were at someone else's house. Now they were at his house and asking him to leave his own home.

I felt like I had snitched on my best friend. What was supposed to be a family secret was now public and in the open for people in the community to discover. The public would know things that were supposed to be private. We were taught what happens in this house, stays in this house. But that night, I was forced to betray that family principle. When the police arrived, they said, "Sir, a little boy called 911 saying his father was hitting his mother." My father looked at me with disgust. He looked at me as if I betrayed or stabbed him in the back. He tried to explain and lie his way out of it, but the police were not listening. They asked him to leave the house for the night. I watched enough gang movies to know if you snitch on someone, you are ostracized, kicked out, or worse, you may come up missing. Bottom line, you are no longer in the family.

Trust and loyalty are broken when you snitch. I didn't know if any or all those things would happen to me that night. I just knew I was not big enough to physically help mom, so I had to call someone who could. I felt disloyal to my dad, and at the same time loyal to my mother. Which one was more important, my mother or father? It's a decision a 9-year-old should not have had to make.

Sometimes the decision to stay in a relationship with someone who is not good for you can bring out the worst in you. If you stay with crazy people long enough, you'll start acting crazy too. People won't be able to tell the difference because you'll both look crazy. My mom would allow my dad to bring out the worst in her. Instead of divorcing him and leaving when she suspected my dad had been cheating on her, she became a detective and started following him when he left the house at night.

Some nights she would even wake me up, not my brothers, just me, telling me to put my shoes on. Sleepy and groggy, I would get my shoes on, walk outside, and get in the car. She would immediately tell me to put my seat belt on. And she would take off like she was racing in the Indy 500. She would follow behind dad like a private detective, just far enough that he would not see her. On one particular night he stopped, and a girl got in the car. She then sped up to confront him and he sped off in the car. She took off after him. They were speeding through streetlights and swerving in between traffic. Eventually, dad made it to an old country road. Dust was flying up everywhere. It was hard to see because there were cornfields on either side of the road and the stalks were high. Dad must have taken a quick turn somewhere because the dust began to clear, and he was nowhere to be found. Mom kept looking for him for a few minutes and decided to go back home. She said, "See, I knew he was up to something! I knew he was messing around!"

The late-night escapades were crazy and unsafe. Mom not only put herself in danger, but me as well. I thought that my mother catching my father with another woman would at least lead to something meaningful. I thought it would be the straw that broke the camel's back. However, it led to more arguments, not my mom's action to leave. Mom was becoming as irrational as dad. Their relationship was consuming her sanity. Everything else got pushed to the back burner because their relationship consumed all the air, space, and time in our family's life.

* * *

I was excited about turning 10-years-old. I was finally going to be in double digits. It was a big thing to me. I researched ahead of time what bike I wanted for my birthday. When I went shopping with my mom at Kmart, I saw it. It was a big bright red 12-speed mountain bike. Was it too big for me? Yes, but I wanted it. I never backed down from a challenge. To my surprise, after sharing with my parents what I wanted, they both said yes. All I had to do then was count down the days until my birthday.

The week of my birthday, mom nor dad, had mentioned the bike. I thought they were trying to keep it a secret. A couple of days before my birthday, still not a peep about the bike. I thought they must be trying to throw in a surprise birthday party, too. I had already prepared myself for the bike and the celebration.

My birthday had finally arrived and that morning, no one said "Happy Birthday;" not even my brothers. I thought they must be messing with me. They will say something when I get home from school. They will jump out and say, "Surprise!" and sing Happy Birthday. But when I got home, not a single word. Nobody jumped out, nobody sang. All that evening, at dinner, and afterwards, no one said anything about my birthday. I went to bed crying. How could they have forgotten my tenth birthday? I told them how important this was to me. My brothers' birthday was just five weeks before and we celebrated their birthday. How did they forget about mine?

The following day, I went into the kitchen and both my parents were standing there looking preoccupied with their own agendas. I said, "Mom and Dad, y'all forgot my birthday. My birthday was yesterday, and no one said, 'Happy birthday!'" Both of their mouths dropped to the floor. They began to apologize profusely. They both said, "We're sorry! We're gonna make it up to you...we promise! Do you still want that red bike? We will get you that bike today!" That day they did take me to get the red 12-speed mountain bike I wanted. I was happy to ride it, but a piece of me was still sad. I was sad because I began to think my parents were so consumed with their drama that there was not enough space for anyone else, not even me.

Birthdays are supposed to be significant. But if my parents could easily forget my birthday, was I important to them?

A couple of months after that incident I started having stomach pains. The pains felt like I had been punched in the stomach. And sometimes it felt like I had a huge knot that was contracting or like someone was squeezing the knot in their hand. My mom took me to the pediatrician, they ran some test, but could not identify what was wrong. Eventually, I went to a doctor in Indianapolis. It was there where I first heard the doctor ask if I had any stress. I had not heard of that word before. The doctor began to explain that stress was being overwhelmed or unable to cope with mental or emotional pressure. As soon as he said it, I knew that was what was going on with me. I felt like the weight of the world was upon me. The pressure of feeling like I had to keep mom safe was causing me to worry and lose sleep. The emotional toll from the drama happening at home had manifested itself into physical pain in my body.

Despite agreeing with the doctor that this pain was stress related, I did not say anything. I learned a lesson from calling the police that it would not be a good idea to tell other people about what was happening in our home. From my mother's silence, I could sense that she may have suspected our stressful home life was the contributing factor to my stomach pains. Neither one of us said anything. But the doctor did teach me some breathing exercises to practice when I felt overwhelmed.

We left the doctor's office, and I knew that my parents' relationship was suffocating me. The joy a child should feel about life had fled. I was not dreaming about the future or imagining life in the future. I was concerned with what was going to happen that night. I was in survival mode.

My biggest concerns at night should have been going to sleep and having nightmares. However, my biggest fear was being awakened to a nightmare of my mother's screams. My father's actions forced my siblings and me to miss out on a piece of our childhood, and I wondered if we would ever get it back.

REFLECTIONS

Are your actions taking away from something that is valuable to someone else? It is easy to think of how our actions affect us, but how often do we think about how our actions affect those we love. Create two lists to identify how your actions positively or negatively impact your friends and loved ones. How do your actions add or take away sustenance or value from your friends and loved ones? Be honest with yourself and open to seeing it from other people's perspective.

Then, take some time asking friends and loved ones if they agree with your list. If there are some things that you are doing that add value to people's lives, keep doing it. If there are things that negatively impact people's lives, find out from them what you could do differently. Go into the conversation willing to listen more than defend!

Remember, you can't add value to a relationship while you're defending your subtraction.

SIX

"There seems to be a fine line between what is considered acts of being in love and acts of being naïve"

THE LAST STRAW

How do you know when you have reached your breaking point? Oxford dictionary defines "breaking point" as *the moment of greatest strain at which someone or something gives way.* It is when you are pulled or pushed beyond your capacity to hold something together. At that point your hold breaks, the thing you are holding breaks, or worse, something in you breaks. When this happens whatever care, thoughts, concerns, and fight you had remaining, is completely drained from you.

In this moment you no longer have anything left to give. You have no energy for hope, for thoughts of the future, nor conversations about it. Moreover, consequences and what you may lose are no longer a deciding factor for your decisions. That breaking point is the moment when you don't just know cognitively that you're done with that relationship or situation, you act on it and leave. Finally, surrendering, giving way to whatever destruction has been trying to pull you and that person or thing apart.

This breaking point is reached at different times for everyone. That point is not usually one incident or a certain number of times you are hurt that signals you have arrived at that place of breaking. The breaking point is usually a culmination of many different factors converging all at once. The equation equals a breaking point when you have the time put into the relationship multiplied by disappointment, hurt, helplessness, hopelessness, revelation, and courage. For some people getting to the breaking point doesn't take much. If they are hurt just a few times by another person, they will leave, and never look back. However, other people have a greater capacity that allows them to endure continual hurt from a person and that end seems to almost never be in sight.

I often wondered if being in love is a major factor in determining how long a person has before they reach their breaking point. And at what point does being in love look the same as being naïve? There seems to be a fine line between what is considered acts of being in love and acts of being naïve. Interestingly, the opinion that outsiders of the relationship form is always based on what they think they might do if in the same situation. For example, at a family gathering, I saw a wife making her husband a plate and overheard other women saying, "Girl, I wouldn't be doing that. Ain't nothing wrong with his legs. I ain't no slave or his maid. I wouldn't do all of that to keep no man!" For them making a plate for their husband seemed naïve, but to the wife it seemed like an act of love. The difference is the person watching is not playing with the same stakes as the person in the relationship. People on the outside don't have the same emotional investment. Therefore, the differentiation between what is love and what is naïve seems clearer for them, versus the people in the relationship.

But many times, the people in the relationship can only see their need or desire to be with that person. Justifying whatever actions as necessary to being in that relationship. But the question becomes, how long can a person justify their illogical actions in a relationship before they can see their own actions as completely devoid of wisdom and judgment? In other words, what must happen to help a person see that they can no longer justify their actions because their actions are harmful to themselves and others?

I am curious as to how mom would have answered the question, "Was your decision to stay married to your husband, even through all the abuse, because of love or naïveté?" I'm sure mom had her reasons that her breaking point was much further away than most people, had they been in her shoes. Mom and dad both, grew up in a home where there was abuse. Our family has suffered from a generational curse of abuse in the home. For that reason, I believe mom knew abuse was wrong, but possibly it was a normal dysfunction in her idea of family dynamics.

After being confronted by his own children, my grandfather was reminded of the feeling of helplessness as a child when he watched his father abuse his mother. He accepted the challenge to change and become a better man. When I grew up with my grandfather, he was the gentlest man you could meet. Perhaps my mother's breaking point was where it was because she hoped that my father could and would change like her father.

Mom also witnessed; my grandparents have irreconcilable differences and get a divorce. My grandmother started a new life and remarried. And after a year or so of marriage, she divorced her then husband, and remarried my grandfather. Perhaps mom's breaking point was also where it was because she believed that if her parents were able to get back together after a divorce, it could happen for her.

My mom's breaking point could have been where it was because she was avoiding the embarrassment of going back to Indianapolis after failing again in her marriage. This would make it the third marriage and third divorce to my dad. She had family members and friends who advised her not to go back after the last divorce. She even had us as her children who tried to discourage her from going back. But despite all the advice, she went back anyway. Maybe she wanted to save herself from having to face all those family and friends. And I'm sure she didn't want to move back into her parent's house again.

The religious community my parents were a part of was strict. The C.O.G.I.C. (Church of God in Christ) denomination frowned upon divorces. They believed you should stay married no matter what. Through prayer, fasting, and counseling from the pastor, they taught that you could save your marriage. She even heard an old evangelist say that the person who leaves the marriage is not saved, not a true believer. Other church women encouraged her that things would get better. She just had to hold on and trust God. Perhaps my mother's breaking point was where it was because she believed her faith would turn it all around, and if it could not, she would be shamed by the church.

But maybe her reason for staying so long was that she wanted to keep her family together. Her family was everything to her. She just wanted to save it at all costs. Even if that cost meant her suffering abuse and losing her own identity. However, would that price prove to be too steep to pay. And what would it cost us as her children to watch her stay in this marriage? Would she ever reach her breaking point? What would be the straw that would break the camel's back?

My fifth through seventh grade years would test my mom's resolve. They were the years of transitions, change, responsibility, and revelation. Our family dynamics changed the summer of my tenth birthday. My aunt Tammy and her newborn baby girl Noel, moved in with us for the summer. Aunt Tammy was the youngest of my dad's siblings. There was seven of them altogether. Aunt Tammy was a firecracker and a pistol. She didn't mind standing up to my dad. She would speak her mind; and would never hold her tongue. I don't think my dad knew how to handle her. She was quick with the verbal comebacks.

Consequently, dad rarely disrespected mom around Aunt Tammy. Because he knew Aunt Tammy would say something to defend my mother. Dad was more hesitant with his actions around Aunt Tammy because he didn't want her to verbally embarrass him.

Mom and Aunt Tammy really hit it off. They bonded instantly. They were always talking and laughing. Aunt Tammy was hilarious, she could make anyone laugh by making a joke out of any situation or about anyone. She was petite but her laugh was big, high pitched, loud, and cut through any noise in a room. Mom didn't really have friends because dad kept her isolated and paranoid about other women. I also believed this caused her to be sad. She was a people person, it gave her energy to be around people, but it was hard when dad was always watching her every move in public.

I was glad to see mom smiling and laughing again. To the dislike of dad, in those few months, mom and Aunt Tammy became best friends. When the summer was over Aunt Tammy moved out, but her and mom's friendship remained. I wondered if that summer with my aunt somehow served as an oasis for mom. Perhaps it was the reprieve she needed. Yet and still, an oasis tends to also cause you to forget you are in a desert, a dry, barren, desolate place. But how long would it take before mom was reminded that she was still in a desert?

To my surprise, right before my fifth-grade school year started, my sister Racheal came back. I was so glad to have her back home. She had been gone a whole year. We all missed her, even dad. Whether she would admit it or not, she was happy to be with us too. But I don't think this was her idea. I think mom was longing for us to all be together again. Regardless of how crazy things could get, mom wanted her family all under the same roof.

A few months after that school year started, we got some good news. Our little sister Ricketa was coming to visit us for the first time. My siblings and I were so excited to see her. She was five years old, and she was so pretty. She had this beautiful dark, long, and curly hair. She looked like the women on my dad's side of the family. She had finally come to visit, and I was hoping her visiting would become a regular routine.

We all played outside, running around with her. She smiled and laughed just like my dad and me. It was amazing how much her mannerisms and idiosyncrasies were like ours, and she had not even been around us often. She tilted her head like us when she was thinking, and she had a whole lot of personality even at that young age.

You could tell Ricketa was thrilled to be with us too. She giggled almost the whole time. Everything made her laugh. Except when my brothers and I were playing cops and robbers. My brother Ryan was playing the role of a cop and tied a rope around her because she was playing the role of a robber. But when he went to take the rope off, she took off running and she got a rope burn on the side of her neck. She of course began to cry. My mom asked us what happened and then cleaned her neck off and put some Neosporin on the burn. She told us we must be more careful; she is not a little boy like us. After a few minutes Ricketa was better, and we were back playing. It seemed like a minor incident with kids. She seemed fine, and there was no malicious intent to harm her.

However, after my sister went home and her mother saw the rope burn, she made a big deal out of incident. She accused mom and dad of neglecting to watch Ricketa. I think she thought mom harbored ill feelings toward her and perhaps had taken it out on Ricketa by not watching her. Mom tried to reassure Ricketa's mom that it was just an accident. Nevertheless, it got so bad that Ricketa's mom decided she could never come to visit again. And unfortunately, dad didn't put up enough fight and Ricketa's mom kept her promise. It would be years before we saw Ricketa again.

We were miserable. We had just connected with her and just like that, she was gone. My brother Ryan felt responsible, but my mom expressed to him that it was not his fault. She said, "Sometimes things like this happen and you have no control over how people will respond. Ryan, this is not your fault. This is no one's fault." This drama with Ricketa's mom was just another reminder of what mom had to put up with to be with dad. But not even baby mama drama was enough to cause mom to hit her breaking point.

For a while, things seemed to be stable between my parents. Mom and dad weren't arguing and fighting as much. The church was growing. We had moved out of our 3-bedroom house into a big new house with 5 bedrooms. Everything seemed like it was finally coming together. On the surface everything looked like we were going to have the family I always wanted. We had a new house, new cars, and I had new hope. However, little did I know, new things do not equal a new person.

Several months after moving into our new home, everything began falling apart. My mother and father started arguing more and more. There were several physical altercations where I had to call the police on my dad. The police would show up and make him leave. It was embarrassing, because twice, the police officer was from our church. Things went from great to worse than it had ever been.

My mom accused my dad of having more affairs. Yet he would do all he could to deny them. She even caught him driving at night with a woman in the car a few times. She thought she was going crazy. She confronted several of the women, who also denied the affairs. But she knew something was going on because she answered the phone one night when a man's voice said, "Tell your husband, if he gone be with you, he needs to leave oh girl alone!" Apparently, my dad and this man were involved with the same woman. The physical and verbal abuse got more intense. My dad hit my mom in the head with a glass bottle, pushed her down the stairs, and pushed her out of a moving car. And yet she still had not been pushed to her breaking point.

With all the strain between mom and dad, mom and Racheal began to have issues too. Racheal was now in high school, and she began to express her frustration with mom's choices to stay with dad. She began coming home after curfew, talking back to mom. It seemed like mom was always yelling at her for something. Her grades began to slip lower and lower. Between mom and our grandmother, they decided my sister needed a change of location. At the end of Racheal's freshman year, she moved back to Indianapolis with our grandparents. It might have been the right decision for Racheal, but it meant my brothers and I would be alone again with no big sister there to help us through that difficult time.

Just one year after we moved into the new house dad moved out. He got a one-bedroom apartment on the outskirts of town. He was trying to take care of both households while also maintaining his expensive lifestyle. Unfortunately, he found out quickly how impossible this would prove to be. The financial strain became too much. Mom was forced to get a better paying job. This in turn forced her to look for employment outside of Marion. Eventually she found a really good job. The only problem was, it was in Indianapolis, an hour away. Some days she would have a two-and-a-half-hour commute because of the traffic.

Our household became even more unstable after mom started traveling back and forth for work in Indianapolis. She commuted for about a year. There were days when mom couldn't make it back from Indianapolis because she was too tired, or the weather wouldn't permit. This meant I was responsible for taking care of my brothers. It was a big responsibility for a 12-year-old. But I took it on with stride and did my best to make my brothers feel safe. Even though at times I was scared to death of making a mistake or not being able to protect them. I know mom did not feel it was safe for us to be alone either. Yet she had to do what she felt was best at the time. But not even this could push her to her breaking point.

I think mom thought dad would help more. She was thinking he would pick up the slack and be there with us when she could not, but that was not the case. Sometimes he would make promises that he was going to come to the house or pick us up and we would be at the door, bags packed waiting on him. However, he would not show up. He wouldn't even call and say he was not coming. This made mom furious. It was obvious that they were on two different pages.

I remember in the 7th grade I decided I wanted to wrestle. Mom thought for sure dad would step up and help with wrestling. Seeing my dad was a great wrestler and was even undefeated his junior year in high school. I was excited about wrestling. Dad had told me stories about him having one of the fastest pins at 7 seconds. I thought I would make dad proud if I could be as good as him.

So, I asked dad to help me learn some wrestling moves. He sounded excited about helping me. He told me how good I was going to be. He promised me he was going to teach me some moves that would help me win. But again, dad's promises turned into nothing but empty words.

Because mom felt sad for me, she practiced with me at home. She couldn't stand seeing the disappointment on my face. One day, I overheard her on the phone saying to dad, "These are your sons! They deserve more than that. You could at least to be there for them. What kind of man would do his own sons like that?" But even when my dad continued to disappoint his children, it was not enough to push mom to her breaking point.

As a matter of fact, it started looking like dad might come back home at some point. He started spending the night once or twice a week for about a month or mom would spend the night with him. Then everything came to a head early one morning outside of our house. I was in my bedroom when I heard the commotion outside. As I opened the blinds, I saw a car parked in front of the house. A woman with whom dad had an affair was standing outside the car yelling at him, while mom was just standing there. I couldn't hear the conversation that well, so I lifted the window to hear and get a better look.

The woman was screaming at dad saying, "What are you doing here! I thought you were done with her." He replied, "Get out of here! She is still my wife!" At that point things quickly escalated. She walked to the trunk of her car and pulled out a large pipe. Dad told her, "Put that down before you get hurt!" She began swinging it at my dad's head. He grabbed the pipe from her and swung it back at her. He hit her in the head, and she was bleeding everywhere.

Mom was now yelling at dad. "Why did you do that!? Why did you do that!?" The woman was screaming, "My head! My head!" Surprisingly, mom was more concerned about the other woman than my dad. Mom found a rag to hold against the woman's head. Out of fear, dad quickly ran and jumped in his car and took off.

While mom was helping the woman, she began to tell my mom everything. She shared how she had been having an affair with my dad for years. She confessed that it was her in the car a couple of times when she was chasing them. She also told mom that it wasn't just her that dad was having an affair with. There were many other women. She said, "That's why I was so mad. He told me he was done with you and all the other women, and he was now going to just be with me. I'm so sorry for doing this to you!"

By this time neighbors were coming out of their houses pointing and talking. My mom helped the woman into her car, and she drove away. I later heard the woman went to the hospital and received several stitches. She did not press charges against my dad, because he convinced her it was self-defense. Briefly his actions seemed to not have had any real consequences. He seemed to have dodged another bullet. However, what he did, would later prove to have cost him everything.

My mother had finally hit her breaking point! Seeing my dad hit that woman and listening to her confession about not just her affair, but how there were many other women, was the last straw for my mom. She was done with her marriage to my father. The truth this woman shared with my mother was the catalyst that caused mom to realize what she was fighting for was not worth her sanity nor her life.

After all that time! After all the abuse! After all the broken promises! After all the affairs! Mom had finally had enough after all the drama, heartache, pain, and disappointment. What about that incident caused her to say, enough is enough! I Can't stand it anymore! I have to leave?

Seeing dad hurt another woman like he had hurt my mother was the proverbial straw that broke the camel's back. My mother realized that dad was lying to these women the same way he was lying to her. She realized she was fighting a losing battle. She was tired of seeing everyone around her get hurt because she had decided to remain married to my father. The culmination of the hurt that she had experienced dad inflict on her, our

Dr. Rickey McCray

family, the church, and others was too much. She no longer had the energy to hold their marriage together. Mom had to let go of the thought of having her family together because the threat of her being broken was greater than the threat of a broken marriage.

Mom told me it wasn't just a breaking point for her. That incident with my dad's girlfriend was a release for her. She no longer had to wonder if she was crazy. It was all real. Everything she suspected and more, was real about dad. The truth that woman shared served as a pulley device that allowed the weight mom carried for years, to be lifted off her. In the end her breaking point became her releasing point. She was now free to walk away knowing she had done all she could.

REFLECTIONS

What is your breaking point? Who are you hurting because you choose to stay in a hurtful relationship? If your sanity, health, peace, and God forbid, life is at stake, it is time to leave. Don't put yourself in a situation that causes you and your loved one's severe traumatic mental harm because you stayed too long. Ask yourself: "Am I staying because I choose to accept them just the way they are right now or because I believe they can change to become something better?" If your reason for staying is the latter, you are staying for the wrong reason. You should stay with someone because even if they don't change you accept them for who they are now. If you are banking on them changing one day, you may be wasting your time and theirs.

If you are in a position where you are trying to decide whether to leave or stay in a relationship, I suggest you first take some time for self-care. Take some time to do something for yourself. Take some long walks, get a massage, spend time praying and meditating, or do something fun. Also talk with trusted friends about what is going on and ask them to pray with you. Trust that feeling you have on the inside. I would call it the Holy Spirit, some call it a gut feeling, but either way, the most important thing is listening to the voice inside of you telling you to choose you.

SEVEN

"my anger always seemed to hide in the shadows"

HOW CAN I STILL LOVE HIM

Is love an emotion? Can it increase and decrease based on the actions of others? Does it diminish with time? Does hurt, pain, and disappointment somehow decrease loves validity, potency, or power? Does distance dampen the longing or desire to be with that person you love? Does love evaporate into thin air when you are no longer around the person you love?

Karla McLaren wrote, *"Every emotion has a specific function and a specific action for you to complete so that it can move on and make room for your next emotion, your next thought, and your next idea... When an emotion is healthy, it arises only when it's needed, it shifts and changes in response to its environment, and it recedes willingly once it has addressed an issue.* [1]

If love is an emotion that is waiting on a specific function or action to be completed before it moves on, then why does it stay after relationships end? Why doesn't love move on when you move on? Why does it seem like love does not want to listen or respond to hurt and disappointment? Love seems to come and tends to stay no matter what you tell yourself or what you try to do behavior wise to oppose it. Love tends to stay even when the one you love has rejected, failed, lied, and walked away from you. Is love really an emotion?

After my parents got their final divorce, I would find out that love was not an emotion that I could easily get rid of and leave behind. And no matter how angry I was or how much I blamed my father for every bad thing that happened to us, love stuck around and would not leave me alone. But if love was going to stick around, it would have a fight on its hands. I was determined to resist love with all the anger and hate I could produce. I had made up my mind I was not going to love my father anymore because that love always ended with me emotionally broken and disheartened. This time I would not have hope that my father would change. I was going to accept that this was all his fault. Furthermore, the pain and sadness my family was experiencing was caused by him.

Emotionally, I was all over the place. I did not know if I wanted to cry or scream because I was so angry at dad. I was angry because I felt like all he had to do was get himself together, get some help, and fight to keep us together. All he had to do was choose us instead of other women. But instead, he went out like a coward and let his family walk away. And now everything would be different.

Emotionally I didn't know if I was coming or going. Yes, I was sad my parents' marriage did not work out, but happy that we were done with all the drama. I felt discontentment because we were not a complete family anymore, but I felt satisfied that it was still the right decision for mom to leave. A piece of me was glad to be back with some old friends from my

---

[1] *The Twisted Love Inside Hatred, Revisited!* Karla McLaren. (2020, March 27). Retrieved February 16, 2022, from https://karlamclaren.com/the-twisted-love-inside-hatred-revisited/

grandparent's neighborhood but scared of trying to fit in at another middle school. Especially in the eighth grade where those kids already had established relationships. I was afraid I would be looked at as an outsider. I was nervous about trying out for sports. Would I be good enough to play with the kids in Indianapolis or were they much better than me?

Going back to Indianapolis proved to be an even more difficult task than I thought. We moved back in with my grandparents. But this time, things were different. Six years ago, where my grandparents lived, it felt like a neighborhood, a close-knit community, but now it felt more like the hood. There were new kids, new dangers, and new threats. I had to worry about gangs and which territories belonged to who. My grandparents lived in an area ran by a gang called the Gangsta Disciples or "G's." But just three blocks away from us, the area was ran by a different gang called the Vice Lords. If you were caught walking in the wrong neighborhood, a group of guys would all fight you at one time. This was not the same Indianapolis I left six years ago. And I was angry and blamed my dad for putting us in that situation.

One thing that was familiar about this situation was poverty. Every time my parents got a divorce, we were thrown into poverty. We went from a two-income household down to one income. And it was my father who made the most money. And when they separated, my mom had to scrape together what she could to keep food on the table and clothes on our backs. I later found out that my dad's child support was minimal at best. It wasn't enough to help take care of four children. But my mom made it work. My mom was not concerned about getting us the latest and the greatest brands of clothes, shoes, or electronics, she was focused on making sure we had the basics. I must give my mom credit, we may have gone without what we wanted, but we never went without what we needed.

Mom had a fierce determination. She was hell bent on getting us out of my grandparents' house as soon as possible. We only stayed there for about two months. Mom needed a better paying job, so she applied and was hired at the United States Postal Service. She took on the hardest job there as a mail carrier. She started in the middle of the extreme heat of the summer, fighting off dogs and working sometimes 12 hours a day to support us. She saved her money and was able to convince a lady who lived across the street from my grandparents to rent out a house she owned, one house over from my grandparents. She told mom that she didn't usually rent out her house to single moms with kids because she was afraid, they would mess up her house and she would have to do a lot of repairs when they left. However, God gave mom favor with this lady, and she went against her own rule to rent to my mom.

It was a tiny house that only had two bedrooms and a creepy basement. When you walked into the front door you could see a straight shot through the living room, dining room, and kitchen. Off to the right of the dining room was a small entrance way. Through the entrance way was a narrow hallway. Straight ahead through the entrance was the only restroom in the house. Turning right down the short hallway was mom's room and on the opposite end of the hallway was my Racheal's room.

My brothers and I slept in the unfinished basement. The stairs were just wood planks, and the bottom step had a cylinder block under it to keep it stable. The basement was dark, cold, with exposed wood ceilings, cement walls and floors. The washer and dryer were down there as well. It was one big, open, dark space. And it had a place where people used to store coal for an old coal furnace. The lighting was horrible. There were only three light bulbs in the whole basement. My brothers and I hated staying down there because it was a little scary at night. Like a scene from a horror movie. It reminded me of a dingy dungeon in a prison. But more importantly, it reminded me of how things were going to be different.

And as if moving to a small house in the hood wasn't bad enough, dad lost his job and did not pay child support. This could not have come at a worst time. I was growing and my clothes and shoes were too small. I only had 3 pairs of pants, 4 nice shirts, and one pair of shoes I could fit. Mom let us know she would do what she could, but we would not get school clothes until she could save up some more money. She told us she would get us a few school clothes at a time starting a few months after school started. All I could think about was how embarrassing it was going to be for me. Middle school kids can be cruel. They usually talk about the kids who keep wearing the same thing over and over again. This was the first time I would start school without having new school clothes. For me, new clothes represented transition and a fresh start. But because everything was different, we were stuck with old clothes and an old reminder that we came last.

We were struggling financially and now we were expecting a new addition to the family. Racheal told mom she was pregnant. Mom was upset because she had asked Racheal if she was having sex a year prior.

Mom even told her she would go with her to get birth control. Racheal kept saying, "No, I'm not having sex."

Later, Racheal told me she did not feel she could trust mom enough to share with her that she was sexually active. Racheal felt like she would be judged or punished by mom. Apparently, she had gotten pregnant right before we moved back to Indianapolis. Now, mom was concerned about feeding six people rather than five. This added to the financial stress my mom was already under.

But I had my own stress to deal with. Forest Manor Middle School would prove to be one of my most difficult school transitions, yet. It was a new school for me, but I did remember Racheal going there when she was in the seventh grade. I visited her one time when we were still living in Marion, and we went with her to something called a jamboree. It is where all the public middle school's football teams came together and played each other for one quarter each. Racheal told me that game was always packed with people in the stands. I couldn't wait to make the football team so I could play in the jamboree.

My first year playing football was in the seventh grade in Marion. I may have occasionally seen a football game on TV if I was over someone's house, but I don't remember dad ever watching any football games on TV. In seventh grade I learned the basic idea of the game, if you're on offense, you block to help your teammates run to the opposing team's end zone for a touchdown. If you are on defense, your job is to tackle the person with the ball. But there were many things I did not know about the game of football, like the strategy, rules, positions, and purpose of those positions. I knew I liked playing football because I felt like it gave me an opportunity to use my speed and strength to hit people.

The first week of school they announced football tryouts. I couldn't wait to get out there and show them what I could do. After school, I walked to the football field only to see a sea of kids wanting to try out like me. It was intimidating, and I was a little nervous. Everyone seemed to know each other, and it was obvious by the stories they were sharing that many of them had played together before. But I was still determined that none of that would stop me from making the team.

The coaches called everyone together. It was sunny and hot. They introduced themselves and then had us line up in rows. They taught us some stretches and then had all of us line up on the goal line all the way across the field. The head coach said everybody is going to race to the other end of the field to the other goal line. This was right up my alley. I was a much better runner than football player. I was the third fastest seventh grader at my last school. I just knew if the coach saw how fast I was, I would be a shoo-in for making the team and soon, I would be playing in the jamboree. He said, "On your mark, get set, go!" I took off! It was just me and three other guys competing for first place. About halfway, all three of them flew right past me. But I finished fourth. That had to mean something, right? I came in fourth out of all the kids out there. I felt good about my performance. We went on and did some drills and they divided us into groups, and we started learning different positions.

For the next couple of days, we learned plays and I had a chance at running the ball. I realized I liked hitting people, but I also liked running away from them to avoid being hit. But Friday was the big day. It was the day they would decide who would make the team or be cut. I wasn't too worried about it; I knew I was fast and had some flashes of running the ball well. On that Friday, the coach asked me and another guy if he could see us on the sidelines. I thought he might be pulling me over to tell me he wanted me to start taking more reps with the first team offense. However, what he said would sting for many years to come. He said, "I'm sorry fellas, y'all didn't make the team. Y'all are just too little to be on the team. Thanks for trying out. Leave your pads here." I was stunned! I wanted to ask questions, I wanted to say something, but nothing came out. I thought I was having an outer body experience. Maybe this was a dream.

It felt like I was standing in the same spot for an hour before I finally moved. The other guy and I looked at each other with disbelief. I don't know why the other guy got cut, but I couldn't understand, if I was the fourth fastest person on the team, how could he cut me? I may have been small, but I was tough. He didn't even give me a chance to prove how tough I was. When I was in Marion, my height was not a hinderance. It never kept me from doing anything. Now suddenly, I get to Indianapolis, and I get disqualified and cut from the team not because of my lack of skill, but my lack of height. This didn't make sense to me.

That walk home was the longest walk ever. At first, all I could think about was how disappointed I was that I would not play in the jamboree. Then, I started thinking how embarrassing it was going to be to tell my mom I did not make the team. But I went from being hurt and disappointed to being angry. I thought, if only my dad would have kept his stuff together, I wouldn't even be in Indianapolis right now. I would have made the team in Marion. And the hard part about it was I couldn't even call my dad and tell him. He had moved to Memphis, and we hardly ever spoke. He couldn't be there to comfort me or to encourage me that it would be alright. This sent me over the edge, and I decided that day that I would prove to my dad that I didn't need him. I was also adamant that I would prove to anyone and everyone that if they said I couldn't, I would do everything to prove I could. It became an obsession that was fueled by other people doubting me. I would fight like hell to prove myself even if that meant taking on bigger guys, bigger challenges, and bigger risks.

My mom responded the way I thought she would. She consoled me and told me it was going to be okay. She told me that I always have wrestling and track. She said, "That coach don't know what he is missing. That's alright, you gone show them in wrestling and track. You got this. Shake this off, there will be other opportunities." I admit she always knew how to encourage me. She was like my coach at home. She knew how to give great pep talks. I felt better after talking to her, but there was something that I just couldn't seem to let go of. Was it me? Was I not good enough, tough enough, strong enough? And what would I need to do to prove I was all those things?

In response, I started developing this chip on my shoulder. I was constantly looking for a challenge and an opportunity to prove myself. Whether it was out talking to people, athletics, or just being competitive about any and everything. I wanted to win at all costs. And it started to affect my behavior at home and at school. Yes, I always got into trouble at home because I was always antagonizing my siblings, but before we moved back to Indianapolis, rarely did I get in trouble at school. But things changed and I was disrespectful to my mom and teachers. Mom didn't know half of the time if she should discipline me or feel sorrow for me. I know she could see I was having a rough time dealing with the disappointment of not making the team, their divorce, and not talking to my dad. She once commented after I had gotten in trouble again at school, "Rickey, you're changing. This is not who you are. You are better than this. I know you're angry and hurt, but we will get through this."

She was right, I would get through this, but my plan for getting through it was different than hers. She wanted me to be respectful and follow the rules. However, I was tired of being emotional and feeling vulnerable. I was tired of worrying about pleasing everybody else. So, I decided I needed to change to survive in my new reality. I decided I was going to become hard, closed off and not let anyone or anything affect me emotionally anymore. I decided to be selfish and do what I wanted. It was all about me.

I began to take things out on my mother. I manipulated mom into giving me lunch money. Because mom's income was low, we qualified for free lunch. My siblings did not have any objections to it. They thought they were getting the hook up. My brothers were excited about getting free lunch. They acted as if they were getting a gift. But I refused to carry one of those little blue cards that indicated you got free lunch. You had to show your card at each meal, and the lunch person would stamp it. It was humiliating. And I told my mom she had to give me lunch money every day or I would refuse to eat. At first, she told me, "If you don't eat, that's on you. You the one that's gon' be hungry." But after a few days of me not eating, she realized how stubborn I was, and she gave me lunch money while my siblings kept eating free lunch. It was selfish and inconsiderate. I was adding to my mom's stress and not helping to take it away.

At school my behavior got progressively worse. I was openly and very loudly cracking jokes while the teachers were giving their lessons. I had become a distraction and irritant to teachers. What I quickly picked up on was the other kids who got in trouble gave me respect because of how I would clown in class. Therefore, their approval became the reason for me taking my antics even further. I kept pushing the boundaries to see how far I could go. I wanted to find out how much I could I get away with. Once some kids dared me to take the teachers grade book and rewrite the grades. I said, "Man, that's easy." I knew this teacher wrote her grades down in pencil. So, I waited for the right moment when our teacher was distracted, and I took an eraser and changed a few of the students' grades. After class, the kids who knew what I did, gave me props, they said, "Man, you're crazy!" and for me, that was acceptance. That day, I decided if I was going to be accepted, I had to play the role of being the "crazy guy who would do anything."

In short, I was a mess. I was hurting and I didn't know how to express my hurt. I realize now that testing all the boundaries was like a rush for me. It made me feel like I was in control. I couldn't control my parent's divorce. I couldn't control whether my dad and I talked. But I could control me taking risks. I enjoyed trying to get away with doing something wrong because it took my mind off the pain and feelings of abandonment. Pushing the boundaries helped push the feelings of vulnerability and powerlessness to the side, even if it was only momentarily.

The second semester of eighth grade year, mom started doing everything she could to keep me out of trouble. After my midterm grades were all C's and D's, she grounded me for three months. There I was, feeling helpless, because I was on punishment again. I was ready to do something reckless. Mom was working late, and she specifically told me not to leave the yard. A friend from school came over riding on his moped. I had always wanted to ride on a motorized scooter. He asked me to ride with him to see his girlfriend. At first, I told him I couldn't, but he let me know his girlfriend was over her friend's house, a girl I liked from school. That quickly changed my mind. I thought it might be worth getting into trouble to see her friend. I hopped on the back of the moped and we hung out with the two girls.

At first, everything was fun. We were all laughing and joking around on the front porch. But, then, my buddy asked me to go around the corner with him for a quick minute. I agreed and we walked up to this house that looked suspicious. This house looked like it was abandoned on the outside, but the guy who answered the door looked more like he was guarding Fort Knox. He barely cracked the door, and I could see his gun tucked in the front of his pants. My friend and this guy exchanged words, then slapped hands. I could tell they gave each other something. I couldn't quite see it, but the situation didn't feel right.

When we left to go back over to see the girls, I asked him what he got from that guy, and he told me it was weed. He told me he sold weed on the side. At this point, I was scared. I had never been around drugs before. I had heard about kids in the school selling drugs but had never witnessed it with my own eyes. I immediately thought, *I have to get out of here. My momma will kill me if I get arrested because of some drugs.* The situation had just gotten real. I wasn't having fun hanging out anymore. I was ready to go. I just needed a clever excuse to get my buddy to take me home.

As we sat there talking on the porch, I saw a group of guys standing on the corner watching us. The crowd started with just a few and then more guys kept coming. I got really nervous and told my buddy, "We need to go. Them dudes keep staring at us." He replied, "Ok, let me take my girlfriend home first and I will come back and get you." "Naw, bruh!" I said. "The only way we are getting out of here is if we all go or none of us go."

The guys on the corner started walking toward the house yelling, "What's up? What y'all doing over here!" So, my buddy jumped on his moped, with his girlfriend on the back and me behind her. But because it was too much weight on the moped, we were barely moving. I felt like we were only going about 10 miles per hour. I just kept praying, "Please Lord, let this moped go faster! Please don't let them catch up with us!" Then all the guys started running toward us at full speed. One of them caught up with us and punched me in the face. I fell off the moped and the moped took off. As I was getting up, I could see my friend getting farther and farther away.

He left me. I couldn't believe it. But I had bigger troubles on my hands. This guy was swinging at my head again. I started fighting this one guy and saw all these other guys still coming towards me. So, I took off running. I jumped one fence and the guy was right behind. I then ran to another fence and as I was jumping over it, I saw him slow down. I wondered why he was slowing down, but I realized that I never looked to see what was on the other side of this fence because all I could see were some tall weeds. I soon found out why he stopped. The other side of the fence was a creek, deep enough that I had to swim across to get to the other side. The water was cold, and I had never swum fully clothed. But I was so glad I knew how to swim. I had to walk two miles to get home, and it was already pitch-black outside. I knew my mom was going to be home waiting for me. I knew it was getting ready to be all bad for me.

When I opened the front door, my mother was sitting at the table waiting for me. I tried to explain what happened and how these guys were trying to fight me, and I had to swim across Fall Creek. She showed no sympathy and said, "You would have never got jumped or had to swim across Fall Creek if you had stayed your butt in this yard like I told you. You brought that on yourself!" Then, she took out a belt and began whipping me. She tried to act as if she was angry, but I think she was probably more scared than anything. Especially not knowing where I was for so long. I could see I was breaking my mom's heart. But I was in too much emotional pain, and I didn't know how to stop.

What became interesting was the worse my behavior became, the more my brothers tried to do right. I admit I was not thinking about being a good big brother. I was consumed in my own world. And therefore, my brothers would scold me on the things I was doing. They would tell me I need to start making better decisions and stop making mom so upset. They would say, "Rick, you know better than that. You know we weren't taught to act like this. Quit trying to act like you're so hard." I knew what they were saying was right, but I was on a different path. I was guided by anger and not what was right.

While I was out trying to act like a thug, my brothers were getting into something new. My brothers and a couple of their friends started their own dance group. They created their own hip hop dance routines and competed in local talent shows. And to my surprise, they were phenomenal. They really had talent. No, they were gifted. They spent all their time dancing, talking about dancing, and practicing new moves. I gave them a hard time about it at first. I made fun of them for wanting to dance. But the truth is, I loved watching them practice and dance because their movements were smooth, calculated, rhythmic, in sync, and always kept you on the edge of your seat waiting for the next creative motion. They had found their thing, their passion, and was pursuing it. Unfortunately, I was pursuing the approval of my peers versus a passion.

My need for approval from my classmates kept me in the hot seat with my mom. She was watching me like a hawk. I couldn't sneeze wrong without her being right there. But, as Racheal got closer to the time to have her baby, my mom shifted her attention off me and onto Racheal. One night, I was asleep on the couch in the living room when I heard my sister calling my mom's name. My mom was on the phone and must have thought my sister didn't want anything important, so she stayed in her room. Then, my sister yelled at my mom, "Get off the phone! I'm having the baby!" My mom jumped up, grabbed the baby bag and they flew out the door. It would be a couple of days before we saw Racheal again.

I didn't know how to feel about Racheal having a baby. I knew she was young, and it seemed like she was not ready to be a mom. She barely took care of herself. I always thought moms had to be older. I also didn't know how she would finish high school while being a mom. I guess I always thought of Racheal as a little girl, but now she was becoming a woman.

When Racheal came home with my nephew, Dominique, it was amazing. It was awkward holding him for the first time because he was so tiny. I looked into those little eyes, and I was hooked. I knew I would do anything for that little guy. I was an uncle. And I took it seriously that he would one day look up to me. I would hold him, and he would sleep on my chest. It's amazing how new life can somehow give you a new way of thinking.

We were all preoccupied with taking care of Dominique to be busy with much else. We all chipped in to help feed, change, and put him to sleep. Having Dominique around helped give me something positive to focus on while changing my perspective. I felt like I had to be a little more mature and responsible.

Even my behavior at school improved. I was being respectful to my teachers and even doing well in sports. I found something I was good at. I made the wrestling team, went undefeated in the regular season, and lost my final match in the championship round at the city tournament. However, I was so angry that I threw away my second-place ribbon. I hated losing. Even as I was trying to do better with my behavior, my anger always seemed to hide in the shadows. It never really went away; it was just quieter at times. But when things did not go my way, it roared loudly and was destructive to anyone in its path.

The anger seemed to be more powerful than I was. It was controlling me instead of me controlling it. And I knew it was birthed out of my relationship with my dad. I was angry that he had not come to my wrestling meet. I was angry that I was doing well in something, and he was not there to see it or support me. After all, he was the one who first got me excited about wrestling. But this would just be another moment I had to experience without him. I thought living without him would get easier the more time passed. I thought I would not miss him or think about him as much as time went on. However, I found myself thinking about him even when I did not want to. And this made me even more mad because I felt like I had too many emotional scars to prove he was not worth me missing him.

But the person I was missing the most was me. I was not myself, but somehow, I made it through the eighth grade, and I was looking forward to high school.

It was the first semester of my freshman year at Arsenal Technical High School. I was excited about going to high school. And because many of the kids I went to middle school with chose different schools, I felt like it was my chance for a fresh start. I could reinvent myself. I did not have to try to be the class clown, the crazy one, or the thug; I could just be me. I had made some new friends in the neighborhood. Some went to other schools, and some went to the same high school as me. One of my new friends was, Keith. He was a year older than I, but we started hanging out a lot. We met one day while some of us played tackle football in the neighborhood. He was real cool. He knew everybody in the neighborhood, and everybody knew him. Him and his older brother, Nathan, who we called, "Junebug" were known for fighting. They were both much bigger than I was, but they looked out for me.

Keith and I hung out probably about four to five days out of the week. When he would come over to our house, my mom would always invite him to church. But he would respectfully decline. Sometimes he would spend the night on Saturday and when we got up to go to church on Sunday, he would leave and go home. He did this for months until my mom finally wore him down. Then, he started going to church with us on a regular basis. It felt good to have a reliable, trusted friend that I could depend on. It was also good to have someone close to keep me accountable. If I did something wrong, he would not hesitate to tell me the truth and vice versa. His friendship helped me to be a better person and make better decisions.

One of the greatest decisions I made was going to Arsenal Technical High School. We had a choice of what high school we wanted to attend based on whatever magnet program we chose. The magnet program was where each high school had different concentrations or tracks for professional careers. There was a performance arts high school, culinary art, auto mechanics, and a few others. I chose the health professions magnet program because it had a dental program that would allow you to work part-time at a dentist's office during your senior year. Once I read that, I was sold. I was all for going to school part-time.

Everything was going great. I kept my head down, did my schoolwork, and did not talk much. I heard about football tryouts, but I did not go. I didn't want to risk being embarrassed again. However, I knew I was going out for wrestling and track. I was staying out of trouble, and everything finally seemed settled for me. I had found my new normal.

Little did I know, one phone call and a visit could send me into an emotional tailspin.

While sitting on the couch playing video games, one day after school, my mom handed me the phone and said, "Your dad wants to talk to you." I hadn't talk to him in months. I thought, *what does he want? Why was he calling?* I got on the phone, and he said, "What's up Rick!? How you doing man? I'm gone be stopping in town next week. I have to be in Marion for something, so I thought I'd stop through Indianapolis and come see y'all." I thought, *why does he want to come see us now? He hasn't seen us in a whole year.* It seemed like he had completely forgotten us and now, he wants to come and see us on the way to somewhere else. I felt like saying, *"Man we don't need you to show us no pity. We don't need you! We've made it over a year without you. You can stay in whatever hole you have been living in for the last year. We got this without you."* But instead, I said, "Ok, Dad. We'll see you when you get here." Why couldn't I say what I thought about saying? Perhaps the truth is there was a part of me that did want to see him. There was a part of me that did miss him. But how could I miss someone who had abandoned and forgot about us?

Dad had given me a time when he would be at our house. At an hour past that time, my brothers and I thought he had forgotten about us again and ditched us for someone or something else. I was not going to allow myself to get sad, instead I became angry. Two hours later, my father showed up driving a two-door, manual transmission BMW. I was angry because he was late, but I was happy to see him when he smiled. He just had this spell on me. I could be hot fire mad, and he would just smile and say, "Rick, what's up, man?" and I found myself not being able to hold on to my anger around him.

My dad could be fun to be around when he was in the mood. We laughed and joked for a while, and then he took us to get something to eat. I liked riding in his BMW because it looked like luxury. And luxury was one thing we were short on in our lives. After we ate, we went back to our house. Keith had come over and was sitting on the front porch. I asked my dad if he could teach me how drive stick and to my surprise he said, "Yes!"

If I was honest, I just wanted to show off to Keith and the other guys in the neighborhood that my dad had a BMW. I asked if Keith could come with us, and my dad said yes. So, Keith got in the back seat, my dad in the passenger seat, and I got into the driver seat. I felt proud that my dad was there, and he was teaching me how to drive. My dad instructed me on how everything worked and how to shift the gears. So, I practiced the motion of shifting for a little while before we headed down the street. I was thrilled! I was flossing, showing off. I deliberately drove past a few of my friends' houses and honked the horn. I was stunting and profiling. I just wanted everybody to see me driving a BMW. After about thirty minutes of driving through the neighborhood, we returned to my house. Dad had to leave for Marion after only spending a few hours with us, but I must admit we did have fun and I learned to drive a stick shift.

I was grateful to see him, but something wasn't right. When he left, something kept bothering me. I couldn't place my finger on it right away. But I knew something felt off or wrong. That night it finally hit me. What was troubling for me was he was riding around in a BMW, and we were struggling. He was somewhere in Memphis, TN living his best life and we were barely making it. I wondered; how could he do this? How could he spend money on expensive cars, suits, boots and clothes and he knew we were struggling? I was grateful that he had come to visit, but something wasn't right about him riding in luxury and we were almost living in poverty. At the age of 14, even I knew that your family should come first.

I was conflicted and had so many questions. How could I still love a person who did not put his family first? How could I still love someone who left his kids to struggle while he drove around in a nice car? How could I still love a person who did so many hurtful things to my mother? How could I still want to be around him and still admire him? At times I felt like I was betraying my mother. Often, I hated myself and felt guilty for still wanting to be around him. I thought, *what is wrong with me?* This man hurt my mother, my biggest supporter, my biggest cheerleader, my best friend in the whole wide world. This man clearly put you last on his priority list, and completely abandoned you and your siblings. How could you still love him?

I believe this is when I discovered that love was not an emotion. Love is not something you can turn on or off when it is convenient. It does not dissipate once you have some distance between you and that person. It's not something that moves on just because you stop talking to that person. Love is something in its own category. It doesn't diminish or disappear because that person you love has disappointed you, abandoned you, rejected you, moved 600 miles away, or has broken promise after promise. Love doesn't respond to our hurt; it listens to our heart. Our hurt can say stop loving that person because we need to protect ourselves from getting hurt again. However, our heart says, "I can't stop caring for them because the bad part of them hurt us; I made a promise to love all of them, not just the best parts." Love is constant and steadfast. Karla McLaren said it like this:

"If emotions repeat themselves endlessly or appear with the same exact intensity over and over again, then something's wrong. Yet real love is a steadfast promise that repeats itself endlessly through life and beyond death. Love does not increase or decrease in response to its environment, and it does not change with the changing winds. Love is not an emotion; it doesn't behave the way emotions do. Real love is in a category of its own."[2]

I was going to have to figure out if I was going to keep fighting and ignoring the fact that I still loved my dad or embrace it. Fighting my feelings for my dad was becoming too much of a battle. The anger I felt and the blame I was placing on him for every bad thing that happened to us was not hurting him, it was hurting me. I was the one who was suffering the consequences of getting in trouble, being defiant, and losing the trust of my mother and siblings. Perhaps I was learning how powerful love was. Maybe I still loved him because love was stronger than any hate I could ever conjure up against him. I had a decision to make, embrace loving my father or continue to find reasons to hate him.

REFLECTIONS

Is the blame you are putting on the one who hurt you causing you to suffer even more? Yes, they may have hurt you and that incident left you feeling vulnerable and powerless. However, blaming them for every bad thing that happens after the moment they hurt you only assigns them more

---

[2] *The Twisted Love Inside Hatred, Revisited!* Karla McLaren. (2020, March 27). Retrieved February 16, 2022, from https://karlamclaren.com/the-twisted-love-inside-hatred-revisited/

power over your life. Stop punishing yourself and those who love you because you are blaming someone else for where you are. Take back your power by making the best out of the situations you have been dealt. See the opportunities for growth, new experiences, and new relationships.

Hate is toxic to us emotionally and can manifest into physical pain as well. If you are angry about what a person has done, have a conversation with that person or write them a letter expressing how you feel. The goal is not for them to necessarily admit their wrong or guilt, but to free yourself from the weight and consequences of anger. Choose to let go of the hate and focus on who and what you love.

EIGHT

"Am I good enough?"

SEEKING HIS APPROVAL

Have you ever wanted to hear someone say to you, "Good job!" "Well done!" "I'm proud of you!?" Words of affirmation have a way of making you feel worthy, accepted, valuable, and satisfied. They represent the moment when you feel recognized for your achievements, accomplishments, and hard work. Affirmations take on an even greater meaning, depth, and weight when they come from someone you admire. From the right person, the words can make you feel like you have been seen for who you are on the inside and for your true worth. It makes you feel like you are valuable to the person speaking those words. But more importantly, when you hear declarations from those you desire it most, you know you have their approval.

Let's also define approval. The dictionary defines approval as the belief that someone or something is good or acceptable. You know they think well of you when you have someone's approval. You also have a sense of significance because you know they believe in you. And that belief shows up not just as words, but they manifest in the supportive actions of the person who approves of you.

But why do we need the approval of others? We inherently have a desire to know what others think about us. What they think often influences what we think about ourselves. Generally, we evaluate our value based on the merit of other people's opinion. The problem is that other people's opinions can be subject to their own experiences and biases, often limiting what they see in us to what they want to see, or not seeing in us what is right before their very eyes. For example, when a person is an athlete and people only see the athlete, they may dismiss that athlete's passion for civil rights. When people only see what is on the surface, they miss the depth of who we are. People tend to place us into neat little boxes that they find acceptable for them, but not necessarily big enough for all that we are.

Yet, when we don't have the approval of those we are seeking it from, it can leave us feeling as if we are not good enough, strong enough, or smart enough. Dr. Frank Thomas, in his book "The Choice," says it like this:

"Looking outside in for approval and affirmation, we ask, "Am I good enough? Am I pretty enough? Will they like me? At the core we are not confidant as we ought to be. We follow the crowd because we do not trust our own thoughts and feelings. We never really developed a true sense of our inner self and the ability to stand on our own. Seeking approval from the outside in, we reach outside of ourselves to fulfill the missing core."[8]

At the core, we seek approval from others because something inside of us is missing. And when we have something missing from our core, it can lead to us engaging in unhealthy practices and habits. We become overachieving perfectionists, taking on too much responsibility and not knowing how to say no. The need for approval can even drive us to perceive negative attention as sufficient attention. Ultimately, causing us to try to fulfill a deep complicated void with simple words of affirmation that are meaningless if we don't first believe them for ourselves.

---

[3] Thomas, Dr. Frank. *The Choice: Living Your Life Inside Out... pg 4-5*

There was something missing in me, and I struggled, fought, wrestled, ran, and rebelled to find it in my father's approval. I did everything I could, good and bad, to inspire, push, coerce, manipulate, and compel my father to pour into me to fill the void actively. But much to my dismay, it appeared that my attempts were unsuccessful. Instead, what I got was broken promises, ulterior motives, and visitations that felt more like a cameo appearance than a main character in the story of my life.

In the fall of my freshman year of high school, I tried out for the wrestling team. I was determined to make the team. We had a lot of kids who tried out, but just a few guys near my weight class. I weighed 119 lbs., but I wanted to wrestle 112 lbs. varsity. I would have to cut 7 lbs. to make that weight class, but I was up for the challenge. I sweated a lot in practice because I worked hard, so I believed it was possible. The coach held wrestle offs for anyone who wanted to wrestle varsity; and more than one person wanted that varsity spot. A wrestle off is when you must wrestle a full match with three 2-minute rounds, and you had to win either by scoring more points, or by pinning the other person.

I wanted the varsity spot, but I had to wrestle three guys to win it. One guy was a freshman, another a sophomore, and the third was a junior. I was a little more nervous about the junior. In conversation, he told me he was 17 years old. I was intimidated because I was only 14 years old. But I was going to have to wrestle him if I wanted the spot.

The coach had the other freshman and I wrestle first. I beat him easily by pinning him in the first round. The sophomore was a little harder. I could tell he had more experience than I did. However, I was quicker and stronger. It took me two rounds to pin him. The third guy was the junior who was strong and quick, but his skill set was not that advanced. We went all three rounds and I finally won by a pin in the last seconds of the match. I was so happy, I jumped up and down and screamed, "Yes! Yes! That's what I'm talking about!" I couldn't wait to tell my mom I made the varsity wrestling team as a freshman!

I got home and my mom was cooking. I ran in the house and started screaming, "I did it! I did it! I made the varsity wrestling team. I beat out three guys and two of them were older than me. Mom, one of them was 17 years old. I did it!" I was jumping up and down and she was just excited as I was. She said, "Boy, I'm so proud of you! You did it! I told you they can't handle you! You can do anything!"

Her words were powerful. But then again, she always had my back. I never had to question if she was supportive or not. She held it down for me. She was my anchor. The one person who constantly reminded me of who I was even when I doubted myself and told me the truth when my behavior didn't align with that. She was the one who was cheering me on when no one else did. And as loud and as important as her voice was, it could not make up for the one missing voice. I did not say anything to her, but I also wished my dad was there to join the celebration. Regrettably, his voice had been absent since the last time he had visited.

I went on to do decent in wrestling my freshman year. I may have beat the guys on my team, but I would find out that the competition outside of my team was much steeper. I had some flashes of greatness, but I had more humbling, learning experiences than I had hoped or expected. I ended up winning as many matches as I lost. But the friendships I gained were even more important. Me, James Brown, who we called "JB," and who also wrestled with me in middle school, Aaron Thomas, and Lyndal Tipton, all became close friends. We also agreed to go out for the track team together.

There were some very talented athletes on the boy's track team. The junior and seniors were extremely fast. I couldn't compete with those guys running. I thought I could run fast until I ran against them in the 100 and 200-meter dash, and I came in 7th out of 9 people. My legs moved fast, but my running mechanics needed much work. Regardless, I was determined to be on the varsity team. But if I was going to be on the varsity track team, I would have to do something other than run sprints.

One day during the tryouts my coach asked if anyone had heard of pole vaulting. Pole vaulting is an event in which competitors attempt to vault over a high bar with the end of an extremely long, flexible pole held in their hands and used to give extra spring. Another guy and I raised our hand in response. Ironically, my coach in 7th grade gave me a couple of lessons so I could get some extra points for our team in the city tournament. No one else on the team was crazy enough to try it.

The coach said, "You two, with me." He took us outside and we went to a shed, grabbed some pole-vaulting poles, and started going over the basics. He then told us that because we were the only two learning pole vaulting, we were now pole vaulting on the varsity team. It happened again!

I was on varsity as a freshman! What are the odds. It wasn't running, but it was still competitive, a little crazy, and at the varsity level.

The sprint coach worked with me on my running mechanics. He had me stretch out my stride to cover more ground. As a result, I gained more confidence and became much faster. Halfway through the track season we had the Freshman City Track Meet. My coach chose me to compete in pole vault, 4X100 and the 4X400 relay teams. I won first place medals in all three events. Our freshman team was very talented. Our success that day was a sign that we would have a good team for the next few years. But also, little did I know, the head varsity football coach was at that track meet. No doubt scouting out new talent he had not seen.

A few days later, the track team worked out in the weight room. Unbeknownst to me the head football coach was in the room watching. I had not met the head coach and did not know what he looked like. That day, I squatted 400 lbs. Afterward, he came over to me, said hello to everyone, and introduced himself to me. He told me how he had seen the Freshman City Track Meet.

"I've seen you wrestle and run. Have you ever thought about coming out for football?" he asked.

"I don't know if football is my thing or not," I replied. I was too embarrassed to tell him I had been cut from the 8th grade team because the coach said I was too small.

"I understand. But you never know until you try. I want you to come out for the football team next season. Just come out and give it a try. You might find you like it."

"Ok, I'll come out and try it."

Wow! I couldn't believe that the head varsity football coach personally invited me to come out for the football team. What a turn of events. It was just one great thing happening to me after another. It was better than a dream! It was all that I could hope for and more. And yet, something was missing.

I hadn't talked with my father in months. The home number I had for him always just rang until the answering machine picked up. I was tired of leaving messages and not hearing back from him. But I was sure if I told him about me wrestling and running track on varsity, and now the head varsity football coach wanting me to play, it would make him proud of me. If he only knew, he probably would be more involved. If he only knew, he would probably want to see me play. I just needed to talk to him.

Toward the end of the school year, my dad finally called me back. I told him about everything that had happened, and he said, "Rick, I'm so proud of you. Great job, man! I'm gone come see you play football, wrestle, and run track. I gotchu. Your dad is gonna be there." I replied, "Thanks, Dad! I really hope you can make it! I'll get you a schedule!" Even though those were the words I wanted him to say, I didn't feel the way I thought I would feel. Something about his words felt empty and weightless. I heard the words, but it felt like he was saying what I wanted to hear, rather than making a promise he would keep. But I gave him the benefit of the doubt and thought to myself I will see if those words are true when the season starts.

All summer I had been going to football workouts and it was a month out before school started. It was gruesome! We were working out in the weight room, running outside, running the stairs in the stadium, and running plays. I reached out to my dad about coming to spend a couple of weeks with him. I thought it would be a good opportunity to connect with him more before the season started. I figured if we spent some time together right before the season it would be more likely that he would come to some of my games. He had recently moved from Memphis, TN back to Marion, IN. After some pleading on my part, he finally agreed. I intentionally asked if I alone could come visit him because I had been thinking about exploring my options of living with him.

Mom had finally introduced us to someone she had been dating privately for a few months. He was a good guy, but I just wasn't excited about my mom dating. It was nothing against him, I just had a hard time trying to wrap my mind around mom being with anyone else besides my dad. And on top of all that, mom and I had a few more incidents where we didn't see eye to eye. I felt like she was being overprotective and too strict about some things. This was all too much for me.

In one incident, mom set my curfew for the summer at 11 P.M. At 11 P.M., I had to be in the house, or I was going to be grounded. Well, I thought that was too early. Most of my friends at least had a 1 A.M. curfew. It's not like I was a little kid. I was going into my sophomore year in high school, and my 15th birthday was a month away. I felt like I was old enough and responsible enough to stay out late.

One weekend a major event called "Soulfest," which was a big outdoor carnival and concert, was being held in the park about three blocks away from our house. It was an annual three-day event that drew a huge crowd of people from all over the city. A few of my friends all met up around 8 P.M. at my house. It was me, Keith, Junebug, JB, and a few other guys from the neighborhood. We went to the park and walked around for a couple of hours. It was a great night, the weather was perfect, it was warm, but not muggy. They had several carnival rides like the Ferris Wheel and even had bumper cars. They had elephant ears, vendors set up all over the place, and they had a huge stage. The music was loud, and the crowd was loving it. The group SWV was performing. They had a few nice hits out at the time. We saw people from school, and I even saw some people I hadn't seen since middle school. It was like a mini state fair.

While we were walking, we all bet each other that we would get a girl's phone number before the night ended. We thought it was cool if we talked to a girl and got her phone number. Many times, we were too scared to call them and talk to them; or at least I was. We all started conversations with different girls we saw that night. Unfortunately, we all struck out and didn't receive not one number. But we had fun listening to the music and eating the good food.

We left the park at about 10:30 P.M. We were walking in the neighborhood toward JB's house, who lived about five blocks away from me. We were told that there were people hanging out near his house. At around 10:45 P.M., Keith says in front of everybody, "Rick, you better get home. It's getting ready to be your curfew." He said it in front of the other guys to be funny. But he was also trying to keep me out of trouble because he knew how strict my mom could be. Him and his brother, Junebug, did not have a curfew, so they always made fun of me because I had one. I laughed it off and came back with a smart comment. I said, "Boy I ain't worried about no curfew. I'll go home when I feel like it!" Keith replied, "Alright, you gone get in trouble trying to be stupid! You need to take your butt home." Keith was always trying to look out for me, even when I didn't want him to. But against his advice, I stayed. We walked around for a couple of more hours. The whole time I was nervous. I knew I was going to get in trouble, but my pride wouldn't let me stand down in the face of embarrassment. But I really couldn't enjoy myself because I knew it was going to be bad for me when I got home. So, if I'm gone get in trouble, I figured I might as well stay out as late as I can and make it worth it.

I finally decided to go home around 1 A.M. I was hoping my mom was in a deep sleep and I wouldn't have to deal with her until the morning. I slowly put my key in the door, and I started turning the knob ever so slightly as to not make any noise, but as I tried to push the door open, I was met with some resistance. The chain lock was latched at the top of the door. I quickly thought, *The chain latch is never on, what is going on?* And that's when I heard momma's serious, stern, "you in trouble" voice.

"Do you know what time it is?"

"No, ma'am!" I answered. Knowing good and well I knew what time it was.

"Oh, so you don't know when to come home at night?"

"Momma, I'm sorry. I was walking around the neighborhood with Keith and them and I lost track of time. I don't have a watch on."

"Oh, so you think I'm stupid!? Ok, I'll show you how stupid I am. You wanna be grown? Stay your grown butt out there on that porch tonight. And you better not leave to go over your grandparent's house! Goodnight!!"

She slammed the door in my face, and I heard the door lock. That was a rough night to say the least. That concrete porch was so uncomfortable to sleep on. But that was the price I had to pay for not following my mom's rules.

That next morning, I was still mad at my mom. I felt like that punishment was extreme. A week later, I called my dad and told him what happened, hoping to get some sympathy and support. And just like I thought, he said, "Man I'm not sure if you staying with your mom is the right fit for you. You're old enough to choose who you want to live with." Once he planted that seed in my head, I began to act different. I felt like I didn't have to listen to everything mom said because I had options to leave and stay with dad.

I told my mom, not asked her, that my dad was going to pick me up for a couple of weeks. She said, "Good, I think it would be good for you to spend some time with him." She probably thought it would also be a nice break for her to not have to deal with me for a couple of weeks. But I felt the same way. Maybe getting away from her strict rules and overreacting would be good for me.

Part of my frustration was the house we were living in was too small. I didn't have my own space. I was sleeping on the couch where there was no real privacy most of the time. The other part was, I knew my dad would be more lenient with rules. I knew he would be too occupied with his own life to worry about the details of punishment and rules. And I would soon find out just how preoccupied he would be.

My dad came to pick me up about three weeks before we started back to school. I missed my dad because I hadn't seen him in about 8 months. I was looking forward to getting some one-on-one time with him. When he arrived, he spent a little time with my siblings and then we hit the road. I always enjoyed the road we took to get to Marion. State Road 37, was a long two-lane highway filled with nothing but a few houses and corn fields. I don't know, something about it was peaceful to me.

If I'm honest, it was usually more peaceful going in the opposite direction than going to Marion. Often because there was so much turmoil, fussing, and fighting between my parents, it was usually great to get away from Marion. Marion represented my pain, disappointment, and dreams that turned into nightmares. But it also represented my roots, my start, and so much of my foundation. Many family members on my father's side was still there. My father's parents, a few of my aunts, uncles, and cousins were there also.

I was the oldest grandchild on my father's side. Some of my cousins were young when I left. They were now starting to get older, and I wanted to check in on them. I loved my dad's sisters and brothers. The older I got the more supportive my aunts were. My aunts Tammy and Rita were amazing. They would drive from Marion to support me if I had something going on. My aunt Gloria, "Sissy" as we called her, lived in California, and supported from a distance with phone calls. My uncle Tony was the jokester. He always had everyone laughing. He also taught me how to play piano before I left Marion the last time, to which I continued to practice and hone in on those skills that would later pay great dividends. We were always glad to see each other.

Going to Marion was like going to a different world. Most people called me Rick in Indianapolis, but in Marion, my family called me Rickey Jr. It was like going back in time. In Marion, people knew me based on them knowing my father. I was more of an individual in Indianapolis because people did not know my family.

Getting closer and seeing certain landmarks, I was flooded with memories. Riding in the car reminded me of dad's mom, Grandma Tot. As the old folks would say, "she was something else." Grandma Tot was a firecracker and fire starter who never held her tongue for anyone. But Grandma had a big heart, and she gave us grandchildren birthday and Christmas gifts.

One time we were taking Grandma Tot home from church and my father said something she did not like, and she cussed my father out. It was shocking because of all the things my parents did, I never heard them use foul language. So, my brothers and I were in the car, covering our mouths with amazement and laughter. I never heard anyone put curse words together like she could. But this time, my dad never said anything back to my surprise. Normally he would try to defend himself. However, he didn't disrespect or yell at her this time. When she got out of the car and slammed the door, he looked sad. I later realized he just wanted his mother to approve of him, too.

I didn't know much about my dad's childhood because he never talked about it. But I could imagine if my grandmother disrespected him while he was an adult, it probably was much worse when he was a child. Something was going on, but my dad held it close to the vest. You could just sense the weird energy and tension when dad was around his mother. He was extremely timid and quiet. It was almost as if he was a little boy again when she came around. I wanted to know, but it would take years for my dad to open up about what happened in his life when he was younger.

I knew more than anyone what it felt like to have that weird energy when I got around my dad. From a young age, I wanted my dad's approval. Growing up, even when my parents were together, I don't have many memories of dad being home. I know he was there, but I don't remember many times where we were just sitting there watching tv or doing activities outside. He was often gone to work, or church, or at least I thought it was church until I later found out he was out having affairs with different women. As a child, the most memories I have were seeing my dad in church. I feel like I have more memories seeing him in the pulpit than I do seeing him at home.

But whenever he was at home, I was always trying to do things to get his attention or impress him. Usually, it ended with me being disappointed or in trouble. Like, the time I tried to scare dad as a practical joke. When I saw him and mom pull up in the driveway, I ran behind the front door. I could hardly contain myself; I knew I was going to scare the living daylights out of them. And I was already picturing what their faces would look like. I heard the keys enter the door and the door slowly swing open because they were talking, and while they were looking at each other, I jumped out from behind the door and screamed, "Raaaarrrr!" I saw my dad's fist and the next thing I know, my dad was waking me up. I heard him say, "Man, Rick, don't you ever do that again! I thought you were a burglar! Boy, I swung because I didn't know what was going on! Don't you ever try to scare your father again! Now get up and go to your room!" He was so irritated with me. I tried to scare the living daylights out of them, but I ended up getting the living daylights knocked out of me. He didn't realize that it was my way of trying to play with him and spend time with him. But because I didn't know how to ask him for some of his time directly, I tried to do something I thought would make him laugh. Unfortunately for me, I ended up hurt physically and emotionally.

The drive had finally ended, and we arrived in Marion. This was the first time I had been back since we moved two years before. The streets, buildings, and everything seemed to be the same. Except, this time, I was visiting. This was no longer my home. In the back of my mind, I was hoping that this time with my dad would convince him to allow me to live with him. Perhaps I longed so much for what was familiar that I forgot how flawed familiar was. This trip would remind me.

We arrived at my dad's apartment, which was smaller than my mom's house. It was a one-bedroom apartment with the kitchen and living room separated by a half wall covered with a countertop, which sat just above the kitchen sink. My bed was the love seat that backed into the half wall. I jumped out of the pot into the frying pan. His apartment was at the edge of town which was far away from family and friends. However, I was willing to make it work. It had been a long time since we just hung out. I finally had him all to myself. Or so I thought.

My dad worked from 6 A.M. to 3 P.M. We would eat dinner together when he got off work, and then, most nights, he would leave until late in the evening. I think, to keep me occupied and pacified, he let me drive his work car—a small four door Chevrolet Chevet. It was gray with red cloth interior, and it was amazing on gas. After a day or two of me driving him around, he released me to drive on my own. He told me I could drive it after he got off work and we finished eating.

This was interesting to say the least because I was only 15 years old, and I did not have a license. I will admit, I did not complain. As a 15-year-old with a car to drive, I was the man! I reached out to a couple of my friends whose numbers I still had and let them know I was in town and driving. I went by and picked up a friend and his little brother. They gave me directions to some other guy's house we went to school with. I had to show off a little bit. They looked at me like I was super cool. They said, "You went to Indianapolis riding a bike, and you came back driving a car and you don't have a license." I felt like I was on top of the world. I drove them around and we had a blast. But even with as much fun as I was having, I knew my dad did not allow me to drive because he wanted me to feel the freedom of driving. I really felt like he wanted to find a way to keep me occupied while he went out with different women.

After driving for about a week I did some very irresponsible things with my dad's car. Instead of slowing down the car to go over railroad tracks, I sped through them as fast as I could. I put the car in drive and then after driving about 15 miles per hour I threw the car in park. The car came to a violent stop, and it almost gave us whiplash. Then, I let my friend throw a firecracker in the car and it burned a hole in the back seat. When I went back to my dad's apartment, I put the floor mat on the seat to cover the hole created by the firecracker. The next day when my dad came home from work, he called me out to the car and asked me what happened? I told him a friend accidentally threw a firecracker in the car. He looked at me disappointed and said, "You should have just told me instead of trying to be deceitful and cover it up. Now I'm not gone let you drive for a couple of days."

I wondered why I did those things to his car. Why did I allow my friend to throw the firecracker in the car? Why didn't I just tell my dad it was an accident from the beginning? I wanted to hurt him for abandoning us. I wanted to hurt him because he brought me all the way to Marion, and he still wouldn't spend his time with me.

I was also okay with the punishment of not driving because I thought it would cause him to stay at home with me. Sad to say, it did not work. He still went out, and I was left all alone in his apartment. After a few days, he gave me the keys again and I was back driving and wanted to make the best out of my last few days in Marion. I made sure I didn't mess that up because I didn't know when I would be able to drive again, because I knew no one else in my family would allow me to drive their cars.

In the two weeks I was there, we did not spend the time together I imagined or hoped we would. I felt more alone in those two weeks, than I ever had before. It was like that vacation you go on and although you had fun, you know it's not home. Deep down inside, I knew this could never be my home again. Not just Marion, but a home with my dad. The fairytale I had of what it would be like living with my dad was given a cold-hearted ending by the reality of how lonely I would be because I would not be his priority.

I think more than anything I wanted my dad to think I was good enough to come live with him. I wanted him to see me as good enough to spend time with and make me a priority. I realized that approval for me was not just the words, "I'm proud of you" or "Great job." It was time spent with me. The time spent with me far exceeded any words that he could have uttered. I wasn't looking for my dad to say the right things, I wanted him to be the right thing for me.

I don't think I was angry as much as I was sad. I gained a new perspective. It was great to visit my dad. He was still incredibly fun, when we did spend time together. However, his life was not set up for a long term, structured environment for me. As much as I enjoyed having fun and all the autonomy he gave me to do whatever I wanted, that was not what I needed. I did not need someone who would let me do whatever I wanted, I needed someone who would care enough to "not" let me do whatever I wanted.

Although my mom's rules could sometimes be strict, I realized in those two weeks with my dad, those rules were because she cared about what happened to me. I think my dad was parenting out of a place of guilt rather than a place of guidance. My dad wanted to make sure I was happy because he felt guilty for all the things he did to my mom and not being present with us. As a result, those two weeks would be the longest time I ever spent with my dad at one time.

REFLECTIONS

Sometimes the things we think we need from others to fill the void on the inside are impossible for them to give us. Sometimes people don't have the capacity to be what we need for them to be. I once heard Bishop TD Jakes say, "Sometimes, we are 10-gallon people who need 10 gallons of love to be full. However, sometimes we only have pint size parents, who even when they give their all, it will never be enough to fill your 10 gallons because they just don't have the capacity to fill it. There is not enough in them to fulfill what you need."

Perhaps we need to stop expecting others to give us what they do not have the capacity to give. Perhaps it would be helpful to accept that what a person is giving is all they are capable of giving at that time. And it is insane to think we can inspire, compel, push, or manipulate them into giving more. Insanity is doing the same thing the same way yet expecting different results. Maybe we need to stop practicing insanity by expecting people to give us more than they are already giving us. Maybe this is all they have to give for right now.

The next time you are with your family member, friend, or loved one identify and focus on what they are trying to give you. Pay close attention to what they are giving such as their smile, a listening ear, a laugh, good advice, acts of service, gifts, or just their time. Everyone has something to offer. Even if it's not much, it can be valuable if you learn to receive it as their act of love for you. Appreciate your family member, friend, or loved one for contributing their best to the relationship.

NINE

"I did not have the emotional maturity it took to express what I was feeling."

REBEL WITHOUT A CAUSE?

One of my favorite movies in the 90's was "Boyz in the Hood." It was a movie for us black youth who felt like nobody was telling our story. It wasn't just about violence and drugs, it was about surviving in a world that wanted to take us out. But one of the things that stood out to me the most was the main character, Tre, who moved to live with his dad because his mom could no longer handle his behavior. He needed his dad's guidance to help him navigate through the difficulties of life. And because of that, Tre was one of the few in the neighborhood who survived and went on to go to college. It was what I dreamed of happening to me, but that dream seemed out of reach because Tre's father took pride in being a father in the movie. In real life, my father did not take that same pride.

Two years after "Boyz in the Hood" released in the theaters, one of my other favorite movies in the 90's came out.. "Menace to Society." In this movie, the main character, Cain, had a father who took pride in being in the streets. Cain lived with his grandparents because his father was killed in a drug deal gone wrong and his mother died of a heroin overdose. Cain rebelled against everything his grandparents and other positive influences were trying to teach him. He became a rebel without a cause. He had no real direction, he just followed what he saw others doing. He was selling drugs, stealing, and fighting. He was still trying to live by the rules his father and another street hustler had taught him.

But in the middle of the movie, his grandfather warned him that if he didn't change his life and get out of the streets, he would end up in jail or dead like his father. Cain would have to decide to continue to rebel or listen to the positive influences in his life and get out of the street game. If he listened to the advice, it would alter the course of his life, but if he did not take heed, he would fulfill his grandfather's prophecy.

Like Cain in the movie, there are times when we must choose between following what we have seen or what we cannot yet see. For me, it was the decision between the streets or school; to follow my dad's advice or to follow what I saw to be true. My sophomore year in high school was the year I had to come to terms with what future I wanted for myself. The future that ends in jail and death, or success and satisfaction. To make the right decision I needed to listen to the right people and receive the right advice.

After coming home from spending two weeks with my dad, my mom told us that she was getting married to Irie, whom she had been dating for several months. I felt like we had only known Irie for a short time. How could they get married already? I'm not sure I knew how to handle that announcement. So many different things went through my mind. For the last two years I had been the oldest male in the house, which kind of made me feel like I was the man of the house.

There were many questions that I wanted answered. Was he going to try and be our daddy? We already had a daddy. Were we going to have to move in with him? Would I have to change schools. I thought, *I can't change schools again. I have a good thing going at Tech. This is ruining everything.* I knew my mom was happy, but I couldn't help thinking, at what costs to me. And on top of that, they were getting married the next month, which would mean a month after school started, I could be moving to a whole new neighborhood. I was not happy about them getting married. Not because I did not like Irie, but because I did not like the idea of me having to uproot my life again because of some man.

I called my dad and told him mom was getting married. He asked if the guy was alright? I told him, "He's ok, but he ain't my daddy!" My dad then told me something that would set me on a course of rebellion for the next year. He said, "Make sure that dude knows he ain't your daddy and he better not put his hands on you. You got a daddy, and that's me. You make sure you let me know if he lays a finger on you or your brothers." As my grandmother used to say, "The pride in me swelled up, my chest poked out, and my ego enlarged ten-fold." I just knew Irie couldn't tell me nothing and he couldn't do anything to me. Because I was protected by my daddy. This attitude would later prove not to serve me well but further isolate me and set a bad example for my brothers.

I began to rebel against everything and everyone. I was back to being reckless and making stupid decisions. When I wasn't at football practice, I hung out in the streets with my friends. Most of them had slowly started getting into selling drugs and smoking weed. Some of them were even into committing small, petty crimes. The street life began to seem appealing to me. I hadn't come from that world, and quite frankly, I didn't want to live in it, but it seemed like a good place to visit to escape from my own. Especially since my world was forever changing and looking more and more unfamiliar.

After school, one day, Keith and I were walking and talking, and he said some guys we knew from the neighborhood had stolen several cars from a car lot. We went over their house, and they were bragging about what they did. One stole a handicap accessible van, two other people stole regular cars. It sounded exciting. They said they were going to meet up the next day and ride around.

As we walked home, Keith looked at me and said, "Man, don't hang out with those dudes. Them dudes gone get caught because they talk too much."

"Man, you ain't my daddy," I responded.

"Man, ok, you better be careful."

The next day I skipped school and met up with the guys who stole the cars. I got in the car with one of them and we rode around town for a little bit before someone suggested we go to Broad Ripple High School. Which was on the other side of town from my high school. We parked on the street to get away if we needed to. We walked right into the school like we belonged there. We roamed around the halls for a while trying to talk to some of the girls until the bell rang, and everyone went to class. When that happened, we stood out like a sore thumb. Security quickly realized we were out of place. They started asking us to come to them, but we took off running. We ran into the parking lot. The security guards were right behind us. I ran faster than I had ever run in my life. I slid underneath a van, grabbed the van's bottom, and pulled myself up so they couldn't see me. I was so scared. I couldn't do anything but pray, "Please Lord, don't let me get caught. If you allow me to get out of this, I promise I will never do this again!"

By the grace of God, we did not get caught. After they got in the cars, I met the guys around the corner, and we took off. I was so afraid I was still shaking. All I could hear was my momma's voice, "If you go to juvenile, you gone stay there, because I'm not picking you up!" I knew I was done with that type of life. I wasn't cut out for it. I asked them to drop me off at school. Later that night, I heard on the news that they got caught and a couple of them ran and got away but a few of them got locked up. I was so grateful I did not get caught. But had I listened to Keith in the first place, I would have never been in that situation.

I would like to say that I was done with trying to do foolish things, but I wouldn't be telling the truth. My sister was dating a guy at the time who always came over to the house in nice cars and nice clothes. All his cars had custom paint jobs and gold rims. He wore the latest expensive hip hop gear. I wanted to know what he did so I could do the same thing. One day, I got the courage to ask him. He told me he moved weight, which was slang for selling drugs. I never really saw myself as a drug dealer, but I wanted what he had and if that's what I had to do get it, I would do it. I already had a few close friends who were selling on a small scale. I asked him if he could help me start moving some weight so I can start making money like him. He told me I just needed to start with $50. If I could get him $50, he would put me on and give me some weed to sell. I was excited because I was on my way to making some money.

However, I could never get $50. When I got money, I was eating it up by going to the store or the McDonald's that was right around the corner. Perhaps it was because, deep down, I knew the streets looked appealing, glamorous, and fun on the surface, but the truth was it was cold, dangerous, and could end in death. But even more important, I believe this was God's way of protecting me from doing something even more stupid than all the other things I had done.

God had mysterious ways and good people helping to keep me safe in that season. One night, I was walking with Keith, and some other guys from the neighborhood and they were all smoking weed. Up to this point, I had never been tempted to smoke. I considered myself an athlete and it never made sense to smoke something that would make me choke. And all the people I had seen who smoked, looked sickly. But that particular night was different. I wanted to fit in and do what everyone else was doing. I was tired of feeling like I was still an outsider. I was ready to not just be a visitor to this street life, but fully participate.

Consequently, that night I spoke up and said, "Yo, let me hit that! I want to smoke." They all started laughing and one of the guys said, "You can't handle this. You know you square! Do you really want to try this?" I said, "Whatever! I can handle it. Yes, I want to try it! Let me get a hit!" As I was reaching out my hand to grab the weed, Keith smacked my hand away. He said, "Man, you better not smoke this weed. As a matter of fact, I bet not hear about any of you giving him any weed or I'm gone kick ya tail." I said, "Bro, you not my father! Quit acting like you can tell me what to do. Why you trying to keep me from smoking weed? You smoking it, too!" His answer shook me to my core. He said, "Because you're different than us. There is something different about you. You not like us. You can't go down this road. There is something better for you." I just paused. Something inside of me agreed with him. Something inside of me stood up and said, "He's right." I knew in that moment he was speaking the truth. More importantly, I knew it was not him, but God speaking through him.

For some people, weed was not a drug that would cause them any addictions. However, weed was a gateway drug to deeper, more serious addictions for people in my family. I had uncles who were on hard drugs and others who were alcoholics. It would not have been wise for me to take that kind of risk. That night, I decided to listen to what I believe was God's voice using Keith as an instrument. I didn't smoke weed that night, nor have I ever afterwards. Not because I thought it was bad, but because I knew it would be bad for me. When you get a warning like that, if you listen, it could be the difference between life and death. I believe that decision that night saved my life.

I also believed being in sports saved my life. My time was occupied, and I had a good group of friends around me, and we kept each other accountable. The football season had finally started, and I was on the junior varsity team as a running back and also a back-up defensive back on varsity. I even got a chance to be on the local news channels for high school football highlights. I scored my first varsity touchdown when I picked up a fumble and ran thirty yards into the end zone. I was learning the game of football and had some good coaches.

In the middle of the football season, my mom and Irie got married. They did not have a wedding because both had been married before and did not feel that it was necessary. So, they went to the justice of the peace to get married and immediately went on their honeymoon. Upon their return, it was decided that we would move in with Irie. I was happy that my mom was happy, but I was not happy about the move.

Irie lived in another school district. My brothers did not want to change schools, but they weren't like me; I had sports teams I was a part of. They didn't have anything but friends tying them to their school. Therefore, my mom pulled them out of their school and enrolled them into a new school district. Racheal had recently graduated from high school, so school was not an issue for her. She would only stay with us for a short while because she was looking for her own place.

However, my mom agreed to allow me to stay at Arsenal Technical High School. She would have to take me to my grandparents in the morning or I would have to ride the city bus from our new house to my grandparents' if she was not available. I was willing to do whatever it took to make it work. I did not want to leave my school, friends, or sports teams I was a part of.

But one of the things we did change was the church we were attending. The new church was across the street from our new house. The first Sunday we attended, the pastor stood up and announced they were looking to hire someone to play the organ for the youth choir. My mother found out what I needed to apply for the position. I was still practicing regularly since my uncle taught me some songs when I was in Marion. We set up a meeting with the pastor and the minister of music. They heard me play and asked me some questions and told us they would get back with us. A couple of weeks later they hired me as the organist for the youth choir. It was a great part-time job for me because they only had choir practice twice a month and sung once a month. It worked out perfectly with my sports schedule. This would be easy, but unfortunately, other transitions would prove to be much harder.

I had a hard time in the beginning of my mom's marriage. Not only was I rebellious, but I was stubborn, disrespectful, and a downright jerk. I created stress and tension with everybody. I disrespected Irie and my mother. At times when she was angry because of what I said to him or the attitude I gave him, she would say, "You don't have to like him, but you do have to respect him."

Once, Irie asked me to take out the trash. I responded, "No, I don't feel like it."

"Hey man, I need you to take out this trash right now!"

"I told you I ain't taking out no trash. I don't feel like it. You can't make me do anything! Man, you ain't my daddy!" I told him.

I could see the fury in his eyes. But, instead of him saying something crazy back to me, he said, "I'll let your momma know how you feel."

I knew my mom would chew me out, but I didn't care. I didn't feel like I owed him anything.

I did start to feel bad because I could see my brothers following in my footsteps. I heard them make some comments to him that were disrespectful. But I was also angry that every time my mom talked to us about what we said or what was disrespectful, she would bring up the fact he didn't have any biological children, yet he took us in and renovated his basement to make it a living space for us. He had two bedrooms, living room, and a full bath built in the basement just for us. It was like we had our own little apartment down there. It was a huge leap compared to the last basement we lived in. However, I hated feeling like we were indebted to him because he did that. I felt like it was kind and generous, but it should not have been used as a weapon to make us feel guilty about having some apprehension about this new living arrangement. And definitely not held over our head to make us comply or adjust any faster. I never wanted to feel like I was for sale if I'm honest. If our relationship with Irie was going to grow and we were going to fully accept him, it would be because it developed over time, not because of how much money he spent or gave us.

I did not have the emotional maturity it took to express what I was feeling. I felt like if my mom could replace my dad, perhaps she would replace me, too. My anger was misplaced. I was not upset with Irie or my mom; I felt threatened and insecure. I was afraid that I would not be important in my mom's life. I felt like I was being replaced by Irie. I already had one parent who didn't make me a priority in their life, I did not want it to happen again. And just like I discovered with my dad, even negative attention was still guaranteed attention. So, in a way, my acting out was me trying to force the assurance that I would still be a priority in my mom's life. However, just like many of my plans, it backfired and blew up in my face.

My mom was tired of taking me to my grandparents in the mornings. But I also believe she was tired of my attitude and disrespect. Therefore, she came up with the plan with my grandparents that I would stay with them during the week and come home on the weekends. It seemed to satisfy everyone. I was rarely even at my grandparents except to sleep. I left for school early in the morning and had practice, whether it was football, wresting, or track until 5:30 pm. Then, the after-school activity bus did not drop me off until around 6:30 at night. At first, I was thrilled about the idea. I wouldn't have to keep getting into arguments or disagreements with Irie and my mom, and I could keep going to the same school. But it also gave me some time to do some necessary thinking and watching and put things into its proper perspective.

What I observed was how Irie treated my mother. He treated her with respect. He honored her and held her in high regard. He was always attentive to her needs. I never heard him raise his voice at her or disrespect her in anyway. I could tell my mom was broken, but happy. Meaning, she was still traumatized by her marriage with my dad. Sometimes she would go on defense and go off on Irie about stuff that seemed small or insignificant. For example, when Irie suggested we do things, my mom would come back with a quick remark asking, "Why do we have to do what you suggest?" He was not being controlling, but with her lens of abuse, she saw his suggestions as a threat to her newfound freedom. Even when my mom did snap off or misinterpret what he said or did, Irie just tried to explain where he was coming from. Interestingly, she would get on us about our attitude and how we spoke to Irie, when often she was guilty of doing the same thing. We were all hurt, regrettably, attitudes and disrespect were ways we expressed our pain.

I learned in that time, when my dad told me, "He's not your dad, I am," that was not a totally accurate statement. Over the course of that year, Irie showed up to almost all my football games, wrestling meets, and track meets. He talked to me about going to college. No one had talked to me about that except my mom's uncle, Dewitt. Irie helped water a seed that was planted years ago. Knowing he had gone to college made it feel like college was something that I could do, too. And whether he knew it or not, his encouragement was what I needed to begin to draw my attention away from the streets and more towards school. I was now starting to see something different in my future than I had seen before. I didn't just see myself doing some trade like barbering. I could see myself as a college graduate. It wasn't that barbering, or any other trade was not good enough, I just started seeing there was something else for me.

I had this sense that the dream that I could be like the character, Tre, in the movie "Boyz in the Hood" was becoming real. Tre was able to escape the hood environment because he had a father who took the time to pour into him and teach him about life, success, and how to take advantage of opportunities. I felt that having Irie in my life gave me a chance to see myself outside some of the negative influences I had encountered. I began to see my future with possibilities and hope.

I didn't see my dad my entire sophomore year in high school. He proved that all those words he said about coming to watch me play were nothing but empty promises. But I saw Irie show up when my brothers were dancing, or my sister was singing somewhere. He even showed up for my nephew, Dominique. I saw him come to events even after working 10-12-hour shifts. He knew all my friends by name and was known for dropping knowledge to them. I saw a great model of what fatherhood looked like; and it wasn't shown to me by the man who had the title, but by the one who had no biological reason to.

I surmised, yes, a man can have the title of being a dad because they conceived a child with a woman. But the true definition of a dad does not stop at a title, but at the work it requires to show up physically, emotionally, mentally, and spiritually. Being a father is not just a right, but a responsibility. My dad had the right to be called father, but it was Irie who was carrying the responsibility. Irie was not perfect by any means, but he kept showing up and he stayed consistent. He did not try to force himself onto us. He just gave the gift of his presence. He showed up to games, picked me up, took me places, talked to me about responsibility, and taught me about life. He was the one I could depend on for whatever I needed. I talked to him more than I ever talked to my dad. I realized I needed to give him respect not because he married my mother, not because he remodeled his basement for us, but because he fulfilled a father's responsibility.

Irie reminded me of the grandfather in "Menace to Society" who tried to sit his grandson down and talk to him about life and responsibilities. He tried to warn him that life can be hard. Cain left that moment not choosing to listen to the voice that was trying to get him to change the direction of his life. In the movie, Cain went outside and almost beat another guy to death in front of his grandparents' apartment. Later, after he survived a shooting, he finally was ready to leave the streets behind and go with his girlfriend to another city. The day he was loading the car to leave, it looked like he would finally be able to get out of the hood. But our choices always have a way of catching up to us. And the very man he almost beat to death in front of his grandparents' apartment drove by and killed him and his friend.

I know it was a movie, but I must believe that if Cain had taken his grandfather's advice and decided to accept the help and change his life, things would have ended differently. Perhaps he would never have gotten shot the first time Maybe he would have never beat up the man in front of his grandparents' apartment and the guy would never have come back to get revenge, and Cain would have gotten his happily ever after ending.

REFLECTIONS

I believe there are times in our lives where we are being warned about impending dangers that are unseen with the naked eye. You won't have a choice about hearing the warning, however, you will have a choice whether you choose to listen or not. You will have a choice to take it seriously, make different choices, and change your trajectory. But whichever decision you make, it will lead to new life, a new chance, or repercussions and consequences.

God has a way of getting our attention. It may be through a person, an event, a dream, or some other sign. Many times, it won't be screamed at you; it will be subtle, but core shaking. You will know when it is happening because it will seem like everything around you has stopped. In that moment, you will question why you are rebelling. You will realize that whatever reason you are rebelling does not measure up to what you may lose if you continue in this direction. If you find yourself here and don't know what to do, always err on the side of caution. It is better to listen and change what you were doing than dealing with irreparable consequences of a decision already made. Because once you go too far, you can't turn back without suffering more than you had to.

For someone, this is your moment. This is your fork in the road. This is God getting your attention and warning you to change directions. If you continue on the same path, it will end with regret or destruction. However, if you change directions now and say no to what you have been chasing after, it will lead to success and may even save your life. Don't miss this opportunity to live a better life.

I want to pray with you:

God in Heaven. Our creator and sustainer. We come to you now acknowledging that we hear you calling out to us. We hear your warnings. We acknowledge that we have sinned and fallen short of what you have planned for us. We admit we have been too angry to realize we aren't just fighting and rebelling against those who have hurt us, but we've also been fighting and rebelling against you. But God we submit to you now. We submit to the plans you have for our lives. Your word tells us in Jeremiah 29:11, "For I know the plans I have for you; plans to prosper you and not to harm you. Plans to give you hope and a future." We want to move forward walking into the future you have for us, not the one we planned for ourselves. Shape us, make us, mold us, into whoever you want us to be. Thank you for the people you have placed in our lives that are a positive influence. Give us a listening ear and a humble heart to hear them as they are guiding us into greatness. We surrender our all to you today. Show us your plan and your way. In Jesus name we pray! Amen!

TEN

"good things happening were a trigger for me"

YOU'RE JUST LIKE YOUR DADDY

Has some one ever said to you, "You are just like Aunt Tammy?" Or "You act just like your Uncle Bobby." What do they mean when they say you are just like someone else? Does that mean you are an exact copy and there is no difference between you and the other person? Does it mean you are parallel and therefore you both have the same size, value, importance, or meaning as someone or something else. Perhaps it means you are simply similar to another person but not exactly the same in their eyes. Or is it that they see something in you that they also see in the other person.

The more I ponder the question, the more I believe the answer is much deeper. They not only see something in you that they see in the other person, but they have experienced an echo of emotions. Meaning, something you have said or done causes them to have the same emotional reaction or response as they had with the person they are comparing you to. It's like a sister who hears her brother tell her, "Don't stay out too late!" Immediately those words and tone trigger an emotional response that reminds her of how she felt when her father used to say it to her before she went out. And she responds by saying, "You sound just like Dad!" She is not talking about her brother's voice audibly sounding like her father's, she's talking about how she experienced the same feelings as when her father said it. Certain actions or words from others evoke emotions that send us back down memory lane.

When that statement was directed toward me, I thought, did my actions or words trigger a good or bad emotional response in that person? Sometimes when people have said, "You're just like so and so," it was because whatever I did sparked a positive emotion that they felt with someone else. However, more times than not, whatever I did was a trigger that sparked a negative emotion they felt from some trauma they experienced in their past. And that trigger caused them to abruptly alter their mood or state. Pushing them into fear, sadness, or anger.

Healthline.com says, "An emotional trigger is anything - including memories, experiences, or events — that sparks an intense emotional reaction"[4] Many times, it is not something we are aware of, it just takes over and runs the show for a short instance. All actions, words, and your disposition are now controlled by that intense emotional reaction to that trigger. The flip side of that coin is the person who is getting compared to someone in your past, is left wondering how much of this is truth.

I felt like I was a bad person the first time I heard my mom utter those words to me in anger, "You're just like your daddy!" When I heard her say those words, I felt instant shame, guilt, and sadness that my actions caused my mom to emotionally be thrust back into her trauma from my father. Yes, dad had some good qualities about him that made him great in some areas in his life. However, he had some demons that caused him to be a horrible person at times. There were parts of dad I never wanted to imitate.

But I know you're asking the question, "What happened? What led to your mother saying those words to you? I'm sure they didn't come out of nowhere. Did you provoke your mother to speak those words?" Yes, you're right, I did give my mom good reason to declare those words to me. But before I tell you what happened, I need to tell you what I believe led to this infamous moment. Also, what I had to change and ultimately what I learned was most important about relationships.

---

[4] *https://www.healthline.com/health/mental-health/emotional-triggers*

I had a full fledge chip on my shoulder by my junior year in high school. I was trying to prove myself in sports, relationships with females, and friends. When it came to sports, it started with football. My junior year was my opportunity to become a starter on the varsity football team. I wanted to play running back, even though I had played very little on junior varsity the previous year. The person who was in line to take the starting position was the back up the previous year. However, that did not scare me. I had something to prove. I worked out all summer. I even got faster after working more in depth with my track coach.

When we went into two-a-day practices in the beginning of the season, I told the head coach I wanted to start at running back. He said, "Ok, McCray! Let's see what you got. Go prove it!" That was all I needed. I tried to make sure that the coach saw me run faster, block harder, and catch the ball better than the other guy all training camp long. And at the start of the season, coach named me as the starter. But, I wasn't done. I learned as a freshman, it's not enough just to earn the starting spot, you have to do something while you're there. So, I was determined to prove I didn't just earn the starting spot; I was going to produce some good work out there on the field.

For a young team, we were pretty good. Even if we didn't win, we gave teams a run for their money. All my friends who came in with me as freshmen were now starters. This was our team, and we were learning how to lead. I did well running the ball and was still learning as the season progressed. I got the catalyst I needed to take my game to a higher level about halfway through the season. We played Manual High School, which was a school in our conference.

The beginning of the week is when we went over our scouting reports and watched film on the team we were playing next. I saw a name I recognized at the top of the scouting report, which gave examples of the other team's top plays. The head coach of Manual was the same coach who cut me from the eighth-grade football team because he said I was too little. Steam was coming off my head that day. I told my head coach who the guy was and what he had done, to which my coach replied, "You should be chomping at the bit to get out there and prove him wrong!" I had no idea what he was saying, but I knew what it meant. And he was right! I was ready to get out there and run all over them to prove that coach wrong.

I was so excited the night of the game that I couldn't sit down on the sidelines. It was a home game, and the crowd was full of energy and screaming loudly. They kicked the ball off and I returned the kickoff for a touchdown. But it didn't stop there, I had my highest stats of the season that game. I had over 150 yards rushing, 30 yards receiving, and 3 touchdowns. We blew them out. The score wasn't even close. At the end of the game, we always shook the other team's hands in the middle of the field. When I got to Manual's coach, he said, "Boy, you sure can run! Good job #25!" I responded with a laugh and said, "Too little, huh!? I bet you don't think that now!" As he kept walking, looking back at me, he looked puzzled, and I kept walking with a humongous smile on my face. I'm sure he didn't recognize me, but it didn't matter, I proved I belonged on the football field and could play with the best! Maybe, just maybe, this football thing was really for me.

That coach didn't remember me. I'm sure I was a faint memory in his mind. However, I held on to the memory and pain that came from that rejection. Yes, it gave me an edge as an athlete, but little did I know it gave me a jagged edge in my character. I didn't know how to turn it off. And as a result, I was holding on to pain and trying to prove myself to everyone. Maybe my mom saying I was just like my dad, was because I held on to pain caused by others. Inevitably it influenced me to justify using that same pain back on them?

Sometimes in my pursuit to prove myself, innocent people would get hurt. Coming off a really good football season, we had a two-week break before I started wrestling. I had a different level of swag and confidence, and I was eager to wrestle that year. The first half of the season was unreal. I was undefeated at 17-0. I was so excited about what was going on that I reached out to my dad. I shared with him how the football season went and how I was now undefeated. He said he was going to come to my next big tournament which was two weeks away. I thought, I will believe it when I see it, but secretly hoping he would make it. Maybe somewhere in me I thought, if he saw what I could do, he might want to be more involved in my life. But I would not let myself go all the way with those thoughts. I had been there before and didn't want to set myself up for disappointment.

To my surprise and delight, my dad showed up. He actually showed up to the tournament. I must admit my chest was stuck out because I got to introduce my coaches and friends to my father. I could see my mom was happy for me. Her and Irie, who were almost always there, were in their usual place in the stands. Dad sat on the floor right behind the wrestlers. It was a dream come true. This was what I always wanted. I now realize I was a little too excited to prove to dad that I was good like him. He had once told me he went undefeated his junior year in high school but quit before the season ended because none of his family members would come to support him.

After all these years, he was finally there to support me. I was dead set on putting on a show for dad. I was easily pinning opponents left and right. I was super aggressive and quite frankly, felt invincible. The wrestlers were already scared of me before they got on the mat because they had heard of how well I was wrestling. Dad looked so proud of me. He was cheering me on, and for the first time, I heard my dad's voice on the sideline and not just my mother's. It was a phenomenal feeling.

I was on the third to last match when I got too aggressive. I put this guy on his back and while I had him in a pinning position, he kept bridging up extremely high. Meaning he was rolling to the top of his head to keep his shoulders from touching the mat. I kept kicking his legs out from under him and lifting his head up to get him to lay flat so I could pin him. However, I got so frustrated that I lifted his head high off the mat and slammed it to the ground. He screamed really loud. The referee blew the whistle signaling for me to get off him. His coach ran to check on him. I could see he was in pain. His coach told him to stay down. They called an ambulance. They had to put him on a stretcher and take him out of the gym. Consequently, the referee declared that I was disqualified from the match for unsportsmanlike conduct, handing me my first loss of the season.

I was devastated. I had never done anything like that before. Truth is, most days, if I was wrestling someone like that, I would be patient and just keep them on their back. He wasn't going anywhere. I was already up on points. It wasn't like he could have gotten out and beat me. But this was not most days. I was trying to prove something rather than just wrestling. Anyway, I ran to the locker room upset. I was bawling crying. I had never gotten that upset or emotional about losing a match. Especially, since the guy didn't beat me, I beat myself.

My dad came into the locker room to console me.

He said, "Rick, it's gone be alright. You did good. You don't have anything to be embarrassed about."

But I just kept saying, "I lost! I was undefeated, but now I have a loss!"

I was more upset that I lost in front of my dad than just losing. This was my one big shot to impress him and I felt like I blew it. Eventually, I got myself together and came out of the locker room. I finished up my last two matches by pinning the last two opponents, in a sportsmanlike way. I went on to win the tournament and ended up with 24-1 record at the end of the first half of the season. My dad, again, expressed how proud he was, but I had a hard time hearing it because things did not go the way I had planned. And if I didn't already think I disappointed him, it felt like it was confirmed in the fact that he never came to watch another wrestling match. It would be his first and last match he would watch. However, that year I ended the rest of the year with a 30-6 record.

I, too, had a record now of hurting innocent people because of my selfishness. I was so engulfed, obsessed with winning to prove myself to my dad, that I did not stop and think about how I hurt that guy's neck for a long time. He eventually got better, and I wrestled him later that year in the city tournament. I was usually better at being sensitive to other people, but my infatuation with proving myself dulled that part of my character. Maybe my mom saying I was just like my dad because I had innocent victims who were hurt unnecessarily. Like with my dad, the people at his church, people in the community who looked up to him, and his own children. I wonder how many other innocent people would be hurt by my selfishness.

My selfishness came honestly. My dad was the king of acting as if the world revolved around him. Four months after he came to watch me wrestle, he moved to Bowling Green, Kentucky. He called me and told me he had to go to Marion, and he wanted to know if my brothers and I wanted to hang out with him there. I was down for it. My brothers, on the other hand, were not. Not because they didn't want to, but because they had started dancing more and things were really starting to take off for them.

They were now getting into gospel mime dancing. It was a combination of hip-hop dance, with choreographed mime movements. It was amazing to watch. They took gospel songs, old and new, and choregraphed these energetic movements that took the song to a higher level. They had won the big state talent show competition in Indianapolis; now, people were booking them locally and all across the nation. They were growing into a huge success. They performed at Bishop TD Jakes', Potter's House, and with Kirk Franklin, and other people in the gospel industry. They were even on TV performing on the Bobby Jones Gospel show on BET network. My mom was traveling everywhere with them as they performed. Eventually, they had so many gigs and traveled so much that my mom had to hire them a manager. They were truly budding celebrities. Their schedule was so booked, they could not get away to go with my dad because they had a scheduled performance that same weekend.

My brothers were disappointed they couldn't go. But they were angry that my dad hadn't made time to come see them dance. Later, Reuben told me he was mad at dad because he abandoned them when they needed him the most. He wasn't there to teach them about life, girls, how to handle success, and being in the public eye. He was also resentful that dad left his fatherly duties to Irie.

"Dad wasn't there for us, and we talked to him way less than even you did."

What Reuben did not know was ninety percent of the time, I initiated the contact with dad. But my brothers did not feel like it was their responsibility to reach out to him, because he was the adult and father. They felt dad should have done more to initiate a relationship with them.

My sister was a little different. She was off in her own world and could not care less at the time what dad was doing. She had other things on her mind. Her main priority was raising Dominique. She was out on her own, living in an apartment. She was independent and doing well. I was really proud of her as a single mother. She later told me that she didn't have anything against our father, but she was at full capacity between working, taking care of Dominique, and singing in a local gospel group. She didn't have time or room to think about a relationship with him. Yes, she would have enjoyed if they had a consistent relationship, but it was what it was. She hadn't seen him in a couple of years, hadn't heard from him, nor had she reached out.

With my brothers not being able to go and my sister being busy with life, it was just going to be me and dad. I didn't mind, it would give us a chance to catch up. I was excited because I hadn't been to Marion in almost two years. I had my bag packed and ready. He told me he would be there around 6 P.M. I was at the door a little early just in case, I didn't want him waiting on me. 6 o'clock went by...7 o'clock... 8 o'clock...and I was still waiting for him to show up. I kept asking my mom if the phone ringer was on for the house phone. I wasn't sure if something bad had happened to him or if there was traffic. I wanted to make sure he hadn't called. I asked my mom how long it took to get from Bowling Green, Kentucky to Indianapolis. "3 and a half hours, she said." By that time, it was 9 o'clock. Even if he left at 5 P.M., he could have been there by 9 P.M.

At 9:30 P.M., I was still waiting outside. Not because I thought there was chance that he was still going to show up, but because I was embarrassed that I fell for his lies again. My mom finally opened the screen door while looking at me and said, "Rickey, just come on in. You know he's not coming." With my head held down and my bags in my hand, I did the walk of shame back to my room.

Heartbroken, I picked up the phone and started calling the only number I had to reach him: his home phone number. No answer. I called for the next few days, but no answer. A week or so went by and I got a call from him. He acted as if it was no big deal and I should just get over the fact he didn't show up. I was always amazed at how he didn't seem to realize how his broken promises hurt me. Did he think my heart was made from steel and did not get hurt? He said, "What's up Rick!? Man, I'm sorry I didn't get by there last week. I was so tired, I decided to just go straight on through to Marion. I'll catch up with you next time." I was dumbfounded. If he was really that tired, it would have done him some good to stop and get some fresh air at least. He could have taken a nap in front of our house in his car. He knew I had my license. I could have drove the rest of the way. He could have taken advantage of so many options if he really wanted to see me. I knew it was a lie. I couldn't prove it, but I knew it was a lie. It just didn't make sense.

The other thing that didn't make sense was the fact that he never called. He could have pulled over and used a pay phone to call me and say he wasn't coming if he really was tired. But it wasn't about proving he lied, it was about how angry I was because he didn't show up again. Yes, I was disappointed in him not keeping his promise. But for the first time I was more disappointed in myself for believing it again! For the first time I felt like the fool. I felt weak and vulnerable. I felt like I was the stupid one for allowing myself to trust him again. Why did I keep doing this? I couldn't explain it. If it was anyone else, I would have cut them off and stopped talking to them. Why couldn't I do the same to him?

My mom tried to talk to me, and I just walked away from her. I isolated myself and shutdown communication with almost everyone. I just didn't want to be bothered with anybody. I was short with everyone, including my brothers and teammates, for a few weeks. I turned into a little jerk for a few weeks. Eventually, I came back to myself and started engaging with everyone again. But I allowed what my dad did to affect who I was as a person.

I was not my jovial, happy, joking, trying to make everyone laugh self. When I was myself, I was the extrovert, life of the party. But when I got upset, I would pout, have an attitude, and ruin everyone else's mood. I had the gift to change the atmosphere in a room to fun and high spirited. However, when I was upset, I also had the power to change an atmosphere to gloom and depressing. Maybe my mom saying I was like my dad was because I was like Dr. Jekyll and Mr. Hyde. You never knew which Rickey you would get from time to time.

I wish I could say it stopped there. However, I started developing a pattern of going back and forth, being wishy washy. I was uncertain and afraid to commit to anything, mostly relationships. I had met this girl at a track meet. She was beautiful, smart, witty, and had great conversation. She was what old school guys would call, "a good girl." Her mother was phenomenal. I got along with her mother as well as I did with her. I started looking at her mother as a second mom. As we started talking on the phone, we realized we went to the same church. She went to the early service, and I always went to the second service. It was such a small world. My mom loved her and thought she was good for me. We even went to the prom together. Everything seemed perfect.

But I was discovering something about myself. When things started feeling too good to be true, I would become anxious. I felt like the bottom was going to eventually fall out, so I should protect myself, and at least, let it fall out on my time rather than being surprised and getting hurt. I didn't realize it at the time, but good things happening were a trigger for me. It caused me to think about when things were good with my parents at first and then all hell would break lose and I was left disappointed. Good times felt like a set up for a letdown.

Therefore, although everything seemed flawless, I started backing away from her. I became distant and talked to her less. Eventually, I broke up with her and came up with some lame excuse that it was not her, but me. Which was true, but at the time, I couldn't fully grasp why I felt the way I did. We agreed to remain friends, and I also remained close to her mom. But I realized, I was probably a better friend than boyfriend. Still, I know I left her with a broken heart because I was broken.

Senior year, I would learn more about just how broken I was. That year, was the year of should've, could've, and would've when it came to sports. It was the year I started feeling myself and thought I was bigger than I was; and it was the year of triumph and failure. But most importantly, it was the year I made a decision about what would be more important to me,

All of my football buddies and I took Economics and Government together in summer school. It was something everyone did, so they did not have to go to school full time during the second semester of senior year. After class, we would sit around and talk about how good we were going to be when the season started. We had most of our starters returning and we were also getting back one of our players that did not play the previous year. He was the missing piece. We were set to go all the way to the state finals. Except, we did not get this plan approved by God first.

Two weeks before the first game, our teammate who had not played the previous year, could not play again. We were all sad about that. But we were confident that we could still do this. We all knew we had to give it all we had. I was so focused that year that I decided that when the season started, I would not take my helmet off on the sideline. I was not worried about being seen. It was my way of being focused on the goal we set out to accomplish.

We started the season doing exactly what we set out to do. We started undefeated 4-0. But it came at a cost. In the fourth game of the year, my buddy Aaron, broke his arm. That was the blow that set us back. He was the glue for the offense and the defense. He was the fullback on offense and the nose tackle on defense. He was so good that everything on both sides of the ball started with him. We were not the same team without him.

We ended the regular season 6-4. We finally got Aaron back for the sectional playoff game. He, of course, was not the same after missing 7 weeks. However, in the first half, we hung in there with the number one team in the state. But we lost due to a second half of bad calls by the referee and not having the chemistry with each other we needed. However, I feel good about how that team went on to win state. I can at least say we lost to the state champs.

I made the All-City team, All-Regional team, and All-State honorable mention. I also received other honors like, Player of the Week for the state of Indiana, and I had over 800 yards rushing, 200 yards receiving, and 18 touchdowns. One of the greatest honors was being voted team MVP. And for the first time, I started receiving letters from schools wanting me to come visit and play for them. I started going on a few recruiting trips and narrowed my options down to two schools—St. Joseph's College and Indiana State University. It was November, but the big signing day for sports wasn't until February of the next year. So, I decided I would take my time and make the decision in a few months.

This was more than I could have hoped for. I did not think I would play well enough to get a scholarship. I was just out there playing. What was funny to me was, one day I was in class with some other students and a discussion broke out about #25 and whether or not he was the MVP. I started laughing and said, "I'm number 25 and yes, I won MVP." They started laughing and said, "Yeah right, you!?" I said, "Yes, that's me." They replied, "We never knew. You never took your helmet off." To some extent, I can say my plan worked, but maybe a little too well.

But what I also did not anticipate, was the attention I would get from girls who knew who I was. Usually, I was the one approaching girls about getting their phone number, but things started changing. One girl in particular, who was popular and an athlete as well, approached me. I saw her at a party, and somehow, she and I were sitting on the couch together and she told me she had a crush on someone. She said she didn't want to tell me who it was. I asked who it was and told her that maybe I could talk to them and hook her up. She said, "Naw, I can't tell you. You might laugh at me." "What? I'm not gone laugh at you," I replied. "Is he a little weird or crazy or something?" She said, "No, nothing like that. I'm just shy and don't want to say." I kept asking and finally she whispered in my ear, "It's you." If I was in a cartoon, my eyes would have popped out of my head. I thought, *how can she like me?* She is beautiful, tall, athletic, popular, and seemingly out of my league. But I wasn't going to blow this opportunity, so I went for it. I had no idea what I was in for.

I was what people call, "wet behind the ears" or green when it came to dating. I had only had two real girlfriends before her, and they had only lasted about 4 months. In those relationships, neither one of us knew what we were doing. However, that was not the case with this girl. I came to find out she was very experienced and ahead of her time. It was like she was from the city, and I was from some country town down south somewhere. I was head over heels infatuated with her. I started spending more and more time with her and I hung out with my boys less and less. Then, I started lying to my mom about where I was going. I would use my boys as decoys in my deception. I would tell my boys that I told my mom I was over their house just in case she asked. Nevertheless, I was at my girlfriend's house.

I had lost interest in one of my favorite sports, wrestling. I was burned out because I had been playing sports all year round for four years. The football season took all I had. I was exhausted and could not take a break. Within two weeks of losing the last football game, my coaches were looking for me at wrestling practice. Reluctantly, I went to practice, but my heart wasn't in it anymore. I had lost that love for it. I was there, but I was only going through the motions. It didn't help that I also had someone pulling for my attention in a way I had never had before. This was new territory for me. I was breaking all kinds of personal and home rules to be with her.

One night, I did not come home because I spent the night at her house. My mom was furious. I came up with this ridiculously detailed lied. When I came home, my mom started yelling, asking me where I had been. I told her that I had got lost trying to take a friend home late at night who lived out in the country. It was a dark county road in the middle of nowhere and while trying to avoid hitting a deer, I ran off the road and was stuck in a ditch. There were no gas stations or anything near me. I waited all night until someone came by with a big pickup truck and I waved them down. They had a chain linked to their truck and they pulled me out. I had the face and emotions to go with the lie. My mom looked me dead in the eye and said, "I know you're lying. I just can't prove it." Those words sounded eerily familiar. She, then, let me go to my room. I was shocked! I wanted it to work, but never in a million years did I think it would. I got off that day, but I was too stupid to quit while I was ahead.

I had taken a job working at Long John Silver's. I only worked every other weekend and sometimes one day during the week. My mom knew my schedule. That particular week, I was scheduled to work to close. Which meant I wouldn't get home until late. I decided I was going to call in sick at work and stay late over my girlfriend's house. I had everything set up to get away with it. But I didn't anticipate my mother paging me. These were the days when someone would page you on your beeper and leave their number. Then, you would call that person back.

So, I told my girlfriend, "Be quiet, I gotta call my mom back, otherwise, she might get suspicious." I called my mom and held a pretty regular conversation for about 2 minutes. Then, I told her I have to get back to work because customers were coming in. We said goodbye and I thought it was over. But in the moment, I forgot that my mom was notorious for using *69, which allowed you to call back the number that just called you. She always forgot something and had to call back and tell you. The phone rang, and my girlfriend answered, "Hello!" Then she screamed, "It's your momma!" and threw the phone down. I knew my mom was going to be hot. Why couldn't the girl just play it off? She panicked and put me into a situation where I had to answer to my mother.

I picked the phone up off the ground and answered." All I heard was, "You are a liar and you're just like your daddy!" Then, I heard the dial tone. She had hung up. My heart sunk deep in my chest. I was so embarrassed. Not because I got caught. Not because my girlfriend heard my mom. I felt instant shame for my actions of sneaking, lying, and deceiving my mother. She was right, I had become just like my father.

This girl had become more important than everything and anyone else. I had made this girl a priority over my mother, sports, friends, and my future. I had lost myself. I had become the very thing I hated about my dad. I hated how he lied, was unreliable, put women in front of his family, and hurt whoever he had to get what he wanted. I put everything at risk to spend time with this girl. I violated my trust with my mother and made my friends accomplices to my foolishness.

Contrary to what it may seem, it was not the girl's fault, it was mine. I did not know how to handle the attention she was giving me. I did not know how to put it in perspective. I had never been taught the art of balancing my romantic emotions with everything else I had going on in life. I operated on this either-or mentality versus both-and. Meaning, I thought it had to be either her or everyone else. Moreover, I kept choosing her over everyone else. I never stopped to think, it possibly could have been both-and. I could have balanced being with my family, friends, and her. It did not have to be all or nothing.

I don't think my mother disliked the girl. I think she did not like my behavior and the person I was becoming because of the girl. The girl also got the short end of the stick because it wasn't really about her, either. The truth is, I was intoxicated with the attention she gave me. It became like a drug. And when a person becomes addicted to a drug, it is no longer even about the drug, it is about what the drug can do for them. It wasn't fair for the girl that I used her for what she could give me.

My mother, who has always been very spiritual and into her Bible, gave me some scriptures to read. The scriptures talked about a young man who was foolish because of his decisions and the consequences for him not heeding wise counsel. And, in addition, how his punishment would be death. Something about that story and those words pierced my soul. It was the same feeling I got two years ago when my friend told me he didn't want me to smoke weed because I was different. I knew this was one of those life changing moments I had to listen to. I called the girl a few days later and broke up with her. I let her know it was not her, it was me. And again, it was the truth. I still liked her and there was nothing wrong with her, but I knew she was not right for me.

My mom's words rocked me to my core. I wanted to be different than my father. I wanted to be better than he was. As I reflected on what that looked like, I wondered if he was that kind of father to us, what kind of father was he being to my little sister, Ricketa? And more importantly, what kind of big brother was I being to her? I hadn't seen her in years. I understood I was old enough now to reach out to her myself. I was driving and had my own car; nothing was stopping me from reaching out.

I talked to my mom about the best way to find her. I did not have her number and did not want to wait and depend on my dad to give it to me. So, my mom suggested going to her grandfather's church where her and her mom were members. One Sunday, when I didn't have to play for the children's choir at my church, I went to visit. Her and her mom were there. My little sister had really grown up. She was 13 years old and still so pretty and sweet. She was musical like us. She sang and played the drums! She had a lot of me and Dad's features, and our demeanor.

After church, I walked up to Ricketa and her mom. Ricketa turned around with the brightest smile you could ever see and gave me a great big hug! "Brother!" she yelled. I wasn't sure she would recognize me or not, but she did. The first thing her mom said to me was, "Boy, you look just like your daddy! I mean, just like your daddy!" I laughed and said thank you. I considered that a high compliment. I told her I was there because I wanted to reconnect with Ricketa. I asked her mom if I could call, pick her up and take her out to eat. She said she didn't mind at all. She thought it would be good for Ricketa to connect with her other brothers. I told Ricketa I would call her that week to set something up.

I wanted to be a man of my word. So, that week, I reached out and went and picked her up. We went out to eat and talked. She talked about school and church. We talked a little bit about our dad. But there was not much to say because she had only seen him about five times in the last eight years, and the majority of those times was because they were at the same church service. I told her I was making the commitment to be a better big brother. We no longer had an excuse for not staying in touch with each other. I told her she could call me directly if she needed anything. We stayed in contact with each other as we promised. It felt like the beginning of something great.

But I believe my reconnection with Ricketa was birthed out of the hard, cold, truth my mom shared with me about being just like my father. It caused me to look in the mirror and make a decision about who and what I wanted to be. And I decided I did not want to be like the bad parts of my father. Yes, I wanted to be like those good parts of him— charismatic, with a big heart and a big personality that could brighten the mood in any room. But, I also wanted to be me. Someone who cared deeply for people, practiced what he preached, was a man of his word, and someone people could depend on. I knew all those things would require me making many changes in my life. Especially, when it came to what I prioritized.

I started dating someone else. This time I was determined to not allow myself to be consumed with them and lose my priorities or myself. This girl was different. She did not want, nor require all of my time. I learned to have a healthier balance of family, school, athletics, work, and a girlfriend.

My track season was amazing. We had the two fastest times in the state in the 4x100 and 4x400 meter relays. Again, that year we were set up to place high in state, if not win. We made it to the state track meet, but one of our teammates got hurt. Therefore, we ran with our alternate, who was fast, but not as fast as the injured teammate. Instead of us placing high or winning, we got 8th place in both relays. It was an unfulfilled dream of having that first-place medal, but I never thought I would make it to state in track two years before. The experience alone was electrifying.

Track, for me, was more of a secondary sport than a main sport. My main sport was football. And I had finally come to a decision on what school I was going to attend. I spoke with my mom and Irie, my coaches, and even my friends, but the conversation I had with my uncle, Dewitt, sealed the deal for me. Uncle Dewitt called me and said he had heard I was trying to decide what school to attend. He was the first African American male from Indianapolis to attend Notre Dame. He was a highly successful CPA and his wife, Aunt Deloris, was a school principal. I valued what he had to say.

Interestingly enough, he didn't talk about the athletics of the schools, nor the coaching. He didn't talk about the pros and cons of each institute or the education. He talked about which one could I graduate from with less distractions. He told me his suggestion was St. Joseph's because it was a small school, and I would not be as tempted with everything outside of school and football. He said, "Nephew, the most important thing is that degree. You're going to school to get a degree. Football is just what you have to do to pay for it." This sounded right to me. It agreed with my spirit. I had a sense of peace about it. Therefore, I chose St. Joseph's College. What made the decision even that much greater was my buddy, Aaron, had committed to the same school; therefore, we were going to be teammates for another four years.

I called the coach at St. Joseph's and let him know I was committing to his school. The coach was thrilled, but I was even more thrilled because I was on my way to college. And with a football scholarship of all things. If someone would have told me after I got cut from the 8th grade team that I would get a football scholarship to college one day, I would have told them they were crazy. But God works in mysterious ways.

As much as I was trying to change into a better person, some mysterious parts still remained about me. While everything was going well with my new girlfriend, I started feeling a little claustrophobic about how close we were becoming. I couldn't understand it, because everything was going great. She was attentive and caring. But I just felt like I needed to get out, break free. The idea of commitment for me was scary; and I just did not have the maturity to identify what caused it and how to remedy it. Following suit, I took off running. I made things awkward and pushed her away, eventually telling her I needed to break up with her because I wanted to focus on training for football in college. As much as I wanted to change for the better, there was still this part of me that would not comply. I felt horrible, but I did not know what else I could do at that time.

My mom's words about me being just like my dad would remain true in this area of my life for a while. I ran from commitment and sabotaged good romantic relationships, and it left me with a trail of women who were hurt. In the beginning, I drew them in with my kindness and thoughtfulness, and ability to listen well. Everything I did said I was a good guy who they could trust and become vulnerable with. However, when things started getting too serious, I ran and left them standing there wondering what happened. One girl put it like this, "You keep girls on an emotional rollercoaster."

One emotional rollercoaster I was on was my high school graduation. It had finally come! I was sad about leaving high school because I knew I would be leaving so many of my friends. However, I was ecstatic because I was on my way to college. I reached out to dad and let him know the graduation date. I asked him if he would come. He said he would, but I told myself, I'm not going to hold my breath. I'm not going to have any expectations either way. He would either come, or he wouldn't. Yet, deep down inside I was hoping he would make it.

The big day came, and all my family was there, including dad. I was the happiest person in the world that day. I was grateful because I knew things could have gone differently. There were kids in my old neighborhood who weren't graduating. A few of them were locked up. I was thankful to God who had brought me a mighty long way. He kept me and covered me. I understood that graduating high school was a right for some people, but it was privilege for me. It was not something that had to happen, it was something God allowed to happen.

As much as that statement my mom made about me being just like my dad caused me some shame, it caused me some good. It was a wake-up call that set me on a different track. I was now headed down a path that would lead to me walking into my own identity. Yes, some pieces of me would always resemble my father, but I learned I did not have to be my father. I could be an upgraded version of him. I could take what he did well and improve on what he did not do well. Some of the best discoveries and inventions were built upon failed ones. My future was wide open and would be whatever I wanted to believe and put in the work for it to be.

REFLECTIONS

My challenge to you as a reader is for you to think about your wake-up call. What is it? What path or person have you been following that is not leading you to the best version of you? This is the time to reflect on who you have been and what about who you've been that you do not like. No matter if you are young or old, you don't have to remain who you've been if you don't like who you've been. It is not too late for you to change those parts about you.

But where do you start? It starts by identifying those character flaws and making the commitment to change. You must be honest with yourself and with others. Share with a trusted friend or family member what those things are and ask them to help keep you accountable. Give them permission to be honest and speak truth into your life. Know that this is a process that won't happen overnight, but if you stick with it, positive results will come.

Lastly, make sure you are changing, not because you want to please someone else, but you are doing it for you. Therefore, the changes will be a lasting character change and you will be at peace!

ELEVEN

"Who I wanted my dad to be and who he was did not line up"

DECEPTION

Have you ever been tricked by someone? When my siblings and I were little, if we wanted a certain spot on the couch and someone was already sitting there, we would trick them into getting up. We would tell them, "Momma wants you," or "Your friend is outside looking for you." And when they got up, we took their spot and yelled, "Ha ha! I tricked you!" It was funny at the time, at least to the person who took the other person's spot.

As we grew older, the term for doing something like that evolved into what we called lying. The word lying seemed to be harsher and more serious. According to the dictionary, a lie is to make a deliberate false statement. It is to tell someone something as if it is the truth, when in reality, it is false. Being lied to leaves you hurt, and it erodes your trust in that person.

But I learned there was something even more hurtful than a lie. Deception is one of the worst things you can do in any relationship. Deception is the destroyer of relationships. Oxford English Dictionary defines deception as making someone believe in something that is false as the truth. This goes a step further from lying as it distorts the truth by verbal or non-verbal actions. When a person lies, they want you to believe what they said is true. However, when a person deceives you, they want you to believe they are truthful. In other words, a liar wants you to believe what they said, and a deceiver wants you to believe in them. For example, if a person fakes being injured for a period of time so another person will feel sorry for them and then they start asking that person to take care of them, that is deception. The person being deceived not only believes what that person said, but they become attached to the person, defend them, and invest in them. There is no greater betrayal than the moment you realize you have been deceived by someone you love.

While in college, I experienced what I would call one of the worst deceptions in my life. That deception left me with feelings of distrust, anger, and sadness for many years. And the fact that it came from someone I loved, magnified it ten-fold. There is no hurt like the one that comes from someone you expected to help you.

Going into my freshman year in college, I had many things to get worked out. Especially, when it came to my tuition. The college football recruiter promised that I would get a partial football scholarship, but I did not know how partial until I arrived on campus and met with the financial office. I also received the 21st Century scholarship (a scholarship program I signed up for in the 8th grade for Indiana students to go to an Indiana college) and I also received a Crispus Attucks Alumni scholarship, compliments of one of our church members. After all of that, I was still short on paying the full tuition. My mom told me I needed to call my dad because she believed his job at General Motors offered scholarships. I reached out and told him what was going on and he checked on it. He called me a few days later and told me they did have a scholarship and he just needed the school's information. I gave him the information and he told me they would send the check to the school.

Having my dad involved in the scholarship process was memorable for me. He had never been involved in my education in the past. He was also not involved in financial affairs outside of the child support he paid. I learned my lesson in high school about asking my father for money. I once asked him to help me buy my first car. He told me he couldn't because he was paying child support. As if child support took the place of him being there for our life moments. After that, I was adamant about not asking him for anything. But, this time was different. I had to get him involved so I could get my education paid for. My mom always said, "A closed mouth don't get fed!" I was persistent about getting in school and getting my degree. And I am grateful my dad did the footwork to get the GM scholarship money. It was important and I felt like he was a part of that college experience. I learned that my dad could come through and help me out every once and a while.

Things started out rocky in the beginning of the football season. I had a little trouble adjusting to my new position as wide receiver. However, I eventually caught on and played a few games. Playing football in college was a little more challenging, but the camaraderie with the other players was amazing. We truly developed a brotherhood on and off the field.

One night after practice, I got a phone call from my mom saying Irie was on his way to pick me up because my Grandma Tot was really sick in the hospital, and she was asking for me. My Grandma Tot and I had been writing each other ever since she heard I was going to college. In her updates, she never said she was sick. I quickly packed a bag, and when Irie arrived, we drove to Indianapolis. I walked in the hospital room, and she smiled and said, "Rickey Jr." I held her hands and told her how much I loved her and appreciated her Christmas gifts and her letters. After talking to her for a while, I noticed she was tired, so I said goodbye to her and walked into the hospital's lounge. I asked my auntie where my dad was, and she said he was supposed to be on his way. However, shortly after I left my grandmother's room, she passed away. My dad did not make it in time to see his mother before she passed. He later told me not seeing her before she passed was one of his greatest regrets. He told me he was upset with her because she said some harsh words to him, and he hadn't returned her phone calls for months. He was angry with himself for allowing something so small to come between him and his mom.

When we got the news, my grandmother had passed, my aunt said to me, "Rickey Jr., she stayed alive long enough so she could see you. She kept calling for you." I broke down crying. I didn't get to spend the time with her like I wanted, but we had some meaningful moments together. I remembered how I went to visit her about a month before I went to college. My buddy, Aaron, and I drove to Marion, and I got a chance to hang out with her. I was so grateful that I took that time to spend with her. It made her death that much more meaningful for me.

My brothers and I saw my dad at the funeral for the first time since my high school graduation. By his actions, you would think that we saw each other all the time or he at least talked to us on a regular basis. Around people, he was acting proud of my brothers and I as his sons. He was bragging to family members and friends about my brothers dancing and how I was playing football in college. Maybe he was; however, to us, it seemed faked. As a matter of fact, it was deceitful. His over-the-top affection felt like he was putting on a show to save face in front of family members. His behavior was irritating and insulting to us. But we smiled and put on the show right along with him. I think we didn't want to draw more attention than we had to. That moment was uncomfortable for us because we mostly only saw our dad at public events now.

Furthermore, we were sad that he wouldn't even take advantage of the time we had together because he was too focused on seeing everyone else or him being seen. I wanted to spend some time with him and tell him about all that had been going on, but he came up with some excuse why he had to get back to Bowling Green. Just like that, he came in, preached the funeral, stayed shortly at the repass, and he was gone. I was probably just as eager as he was to leave, I was ready to get back to school, my friends, and football.

After I got back to school from the funeral, I finished the football season strong. My coach noticed my progress and offered me an increase in scholarship money. I gladly received the increase and let him know I wanted to try out for the track team and change positions from wide receiver to running back. He gave me permission to try out for track and told me he couldn't promise me anything about changing positions, but he would see how things go in training camp the next year.

That spring, I tried out for track and made the team. I had so much fun running track. The women's and men's team practiced and participated in meets together. I gained a whole new family when it came to the track team. We had a good coach and an environment where we could thrive. I ended the season running really well and even placing second and third in a few track meets. At the end of the season, my coach awarded me with a track scholarship. I almost couldn't believe it. I went from not thinking I was good enough to play a sport in college, to having two athletic scholarships. I was so thankful to God for the favor he had given me.

That summer before my sophomore year, I worked out harder than I ever had before. I was determined to start at running back. I went into training camp sixth on the depth chart. I out worked all the other running backs in training camp and by the grace of God, I was named the starter by the first game. I had a phenomenal season, and our team was 7-4. I did well in track also. I won some track meets and got faster. I had one of my best years academically, as well as, athletically. Amazingly enough, I received scholarship increases in both sports. I was walking on cloud nine.

I wanted to share some of the good news with my father. I reached out to him right before I got out of school. He was really excited for me and all that I had accomplished in the past year. After talking a little more, he told me that when I got out of school, he would come and pick me up in Indianapolis and I would spend a week with him in Bowling Green. By this time, my brothers had graduated from high school, moved out of the house, and they had stopped dancing. They felt like they wanted to transition from dancing to singing. However, they had not had the same success they had with dancing. They also decided college was not for them. Their plan was to work a regular job until they make it with singing, songwriting, and producing. When I mentioned to them that Dad was coming in town, they weren't excited at all. Honestly, they were over trying to have a relationship with him. But for whatever reason, I was still open for trying to have a relationship with my dad.

He was coming to pick me up on a Monday at 1 P.M. I was sitting at the door waiting on him. Of course, I was nervous and was really going out on a limb to trust him to come through this time. I saw how my mom was trying not to pace the floor and check on me. But you could see the front door from the kitchen island. So, she kept acting like she was getting something from the cabinet under the island. But I knew she was checking to see if he was really going to show up. It was an extremely sunny warm day in June. That being the case, I went outside to avoid my mom trying to walk by and see me. As I stood out there, 1 P.M. came and went.

At 2 P.M, I went in the house and called my dad and there was no answer. My anxiety at that point went through the roof. I couldn't believe he got me again. I was almost 20 years old, and my dad still had me standing by the door with my bags packed, waiting on him. I went back outside looking down the street, jumping at every car that drove by. My mother finally walked outside and said, "Not again! What time did he say he would be here? Rickey, you know he's not coming. Why do you do this to yourself?" I was sad and angry at the same time. I did not want to hear those words from her. It was like throwing salt in an open wound. I said with a stern voice, "Mom, I know I got played again! I already feel bad enough. Don't do the 'I told you so' dance!"

But in that moment, I decided this time would be different. I told my mom, "If he is not going to come here, I'm going there to see him." The difference was, this time, I wouldn't take a "no call, no show" as an excuse. I was not going to let him off the hook that easy. I kept calling and did not get an answer. I then decided to call from my mom's business line. I knew he didn't have that number. He picked and was surprised to hear my voice.

"Dad, what happened to you?"

"I'm sorry, Rick, I just couldn't make it. I had some things I needed to take care of."

"Dad, don't even worry about it I'm coming there."

He was shocked. He paused, started stuttering and asked, "What do you mean?"

"I'm driving my car to come see you," I answered.

After going back and forth for a few minutes, he reluctantly agreed. I could be pretty convincing when I wanted to be—a trait I got from both of my parents. My mom lived by the motto, "No, is really just a yes that hasn't manifested yet."

My mother was so angry. She said, "You ain't got no business going way down there when he was supposed to come get you. That's not right! That's not fair! Why are you doing this? You know how he is. Why are you going through all of this? Why are you fighting so hard for this?"

During that moment, I didn't have a real answer I could articulate, and I couldn't understand why she was so upset. Later, I realized she was tired of seeing her son get hurt. She even told me I could not go. I looked her in the eyes and said, "Mom, no disrespect, but I'm going." I had never been that assertive with my mom before. But I was not going to take no for an answer. I know she was also concerned because I had never driven that far before by myself. But that didn't matter, I had made up my mind, and nothing was going to stop me. In that moment, she knew one way or another, I was going to go. So, she gave in and said, "You can't drive that hooptie of yours all the way to Kentucky! That car might not make it. That's three and a half hours. Here's my keys, drive my car." I told her thank you, packed up my stuff in her car, and drove all the way to Bowling Green, Kentucky.

It was scary driving that far by myself. Thankfully, I just kept making sure I was following the directions and I finally made it before it got dark. That weekend was amazing. It was just him and I. He wanted to show me off like a proud father. So, he took me around to all the women he was dating, about five different women. He would tell them all the things I was doing as if he was really involved. But, I didn't mind. It was just great knowing that he, at least, knew what I was doing and was proud to show me off. I was just glad to be there with him. He had this way of making you feel special while you were in his presence. It was almost magical, how sometimes he could make you feel like you were the only person on the planet when you were with him. He knew how to make you smile and I always felt like a little joyous kid while I was with him. I enjoyed his voice, his smile, his laughter, his way with people, his way with words and how he had a presence that was undeniable no matter the setting or who was there. He was my dad!

That was the weekend I decided two things: First, if this relationship was going to work, I would have to go the extra miles literally and figuratively. Secondly, I would no longer wait on him to come see me, because I was old enough to go see him on my own. It was the weekend I decided to fight for my relationship with my dad!

About six weeks after my visit with my dad I went back to school for football training camp. My junior year in college was statistically my best year in football and track. I averaged 7.4 yards a carry, had 10 touchdowns, and about 800-yard rushing. In track, I barely missed the qualifying time to run in the indoor nationals by 2 tenths of a second. But, it was still an amazing year. I believe it was all because I had a great balance with everything in my life.

I felt like my dad and I had come a mighty long way in our relationship. I believed we had conquered and overcame many difficult barriers. I thought we had graduated to another level in our relationship; however, I learned sometimes the calm comes right before the worst storms. The summer before senior year in college, my dad had moved to

Atlanta. He was getting settled in and we talked about how he had to get out of Kentucky because he needed a change of scenery. He talked about how Atlanta was the great new Mecca. He said it was up and coming and there were always things to do. I shared with him how I wanted to come out there and visit one day.

I also let him know I was waiting on the scholarship money from his job. My senior year, the school built new apartments. So, me, and a few of my football teammates, Desmond, Montel, and Toby decided to room together in this five-bedroom apartment. My plan was to use that scholarship money to pay my remaining balance on the apartment on campus. Usually, it went directly to the school, and they would apply it to my housing account. However, that year, I got a call from the school saying they had not received the payment for the apartment. I told them that my scholarship from GM should be there soon, and it would take care of the balance on the apartment. What is crazy is, it was never late before.

I called my dad again and asked him to check with GM to see if they had sent the check yet. I was only about 2 weeks away from going back to school, and I didn't want my mom and Irie to have to pay out of pocket. My dad said he would get on it immediately to find out what happened. He called me back the next day and said that they were giving the check to him, and he would send it right away. A few days later, he said he sent the scholarship money and said I should be receiving it any day now.

Two, three, four, five days had gone by and no check. I called my dad back and told him the check still hadn't arrived. We were now one week out from me going back to school. He sounded so upset. He told me he would get the tracking number and find out where the check was. My mom, in a very small voice (which if you know my mom, she never has a small voice) said, "Rickey, you know your dad spent that scholarship money." I chuckled and said, "What, no! That's my scholarship money. He wouldn't do something that low. He knows I need that to pay rent for my apartment." Yet, somewhere in the back of my mind I thought, "Could she be right? Was my father capable of doing something that low down? No, we've been doing so well. We've been good! Why would he do something like that?"

Three days had gone by, and my father was still acting like something happened with the post office or FedEx. Finally, I was fed up and asked him straight up, "Dad, did you spend my scholarship money?" He finally confessed, "Rick, man, I'm sorry I spent that money. They must have made a mistake and sent it directly to me. I thought it was for me, so I spent it. Man, I'm sorry!"

I felt like I had been punched in the gut and the wind was knocked out of me. My own father? How could he? Why would he? Who does that? You mean to tell me that here is your son who is trying to do all the right things by going to school, staying out of trouble, playing college sports on scholarship for football and track, and making good grades, and you'd steal his scholarship money? I was crushed, devasted again! I had never been betrayed like that before! It was disappointing to know that the very person you looked up to could bring you lower than anyone else. And to lie to me over and over again was despicable. I had no words for my father. I just hung up on him. I think I was in too much shock to be angry. Surprisingly, I was numb. I kept thinking, "How could he do this to me?"

The level of deception he displayed was almost unforgivable. I had never been deceived like that by anyone, not even a stranger on the street. Even people who lived in the streets had a code. There were certain things they wouldn't do to their own family. It felt like I had been violated and something inside of me was broken. My heart was broken. In a way, my innocence was taken away that day. Innocence in a sense that I believed my dad was capable of disappointing me, but never did I think he could stab me in the back.

What made all this even more distressing was the fact that he made up a whole story, acting as if he was mad too, and even giving me a fake tracking number. The lengths he went to cover up his lies was disgusting. If I keep it real, what hurt most was, I defended him to my mom. I stood up for him, believed in him, and he betrayed my trust. I felt naïve, foolish, and humiliated.

I had to take the walk of shame and tell my mother what happened. It was so embarrassing because she knew the whole time he was lying. And in her consistent fashion of love she said, "Don't worry about it! It's gone be alright. We're gonna get your apartment paid for." My ride-or-die! She was always dependable and always came through. Without dogging my dad out or saying, "I told you so," her and Irie wrote a check and paid the bill. It was never again talked about or mentioned. I suppose the pain was too deep to drudge it up without breaking my heart all over again!

I learned that there was no betrayal like the betrayal from someone you love and trust. The hurt from that betrayal cuts you to your soul and indelibly leaves a scar that never goes away. It's not something that goes away, it is something that you learn to live with. But it is also something that cannot be ignored, it must be dealt with, or it will deal with you. If that trauma is not addressed, it will eat you from the inside out, affecting everything you do.

What was also eating at me was no matter how hurt or angry I was, I didn't think of cutting him off. I often wonder what could make me still want a relationship with a man after he lied and stole my scholarship money? The only thing I can come up with is the grace of God. Forgiveness for me was either a curse or a wonderful gift that I still didn't understand and sometimes didn't want. Although I was sad beyond articulation, some strange, small voice inside of me said, "He's still your dad."

Somehow, I still chose to listen to that still small voice, but it did not make me feel strong, it made me feel weak. I felt powerless, vulnerable, unprotected, and like a punk. How could I let him get away with that? I should have cut him off! Why couldn't I just cut him off? In almost every other area in my life I felt strong, confident, and sure of myself. Until it came to my dad. Then, I felt like a helpless little boy who needed his father. If I was Superman, he would be my kryptonite.

I didn't realize the impact that incident would have on me. I went to training camp a few days later and moved into our new apartment. The first-floor apartment was beautiful and spacious. We had a living room, a full kitchen, an extra bedroom, and two restrooms. We thought we were doing it big. Everybody always wanted to come to our apartment and hangout. But even with the new apartment and everyone wanting to hang out at our place, something inside me was messed up. When my dad deceived me, whatever broke in me did not get fixed because my mom and Irie paid the bill. There are some wounds that money and people cannot heal.

I couldn't focus during training camp. I was always a jokester, but I took it to the extreme. I became a distraction. I started getting into it with coaches, disagreeing with play calling, and became less productive as a running back. Also, my grades began to slip further down. At midterms, I was barely hanging on with C's and D's. The incident with my dad was so detrimental that I was having a hard time trying to recover.

What kept going through my head was how I felt like I didn't matter. The only explanation I could come up with that made sense was that I didn't matter to my father. I was less than nothing. Regular people wouldn't steal a scholarship from a college kid even if they didn't like them. It was one of the foulest things I thought you could do to a person. But deeper than that, I began to feel like if I didn't matter to my dad, maybe I didn't matter at all. And if I didn't matter, then nothing mattered to me. As a result, I lost interest in football. It didn't matter anymore.

Somehow, I can't help but to think that my attitude, along with some key personnel changes to the coaching staff and players, affected the team's morale. It wasn't just me, but other people seemed to not care as well. On top of all of that, we were losing games left and right. The thrill was gone! Many of us couldn't wait for the season to end.

I'm not sure why I did it, but I called my dad and told him my last game was an away game in Kentucky. He said he would come to the game. I almost felt like he agreed to do it out of guilt. But I wasn't going to believe him until I saw him. Yes, I was still angry with him, but it was my last game. It would be his last opportunity to see me play. Maybe there was a piece of me that invited him because I wanted to see if I did matter to him or not. For some part of me, this was a test. If he showed up, I would continue to pursue a relationship with him. If he did not show up, I was done trying to make this work.

It was a game that didn't mean much in terms of winning or losing for our team. It was probably statistically the worst year for our team and me. At that point, we just wanted to get the season over with. There would be no playoffs or trophy hoisted up after that game. It was just a game.

To my surprise, my dad showed up. Maybe deep down inside, it wasn't just a game for me. Because my dad had come, it was special to me. It was especially memorable to me because teammates and coaches who had been an integral part of my life for the past four years, finally got to meet my dad. It seemed almost crazy that I had been in college four years, played two sports, and my dad had never come to a football game or track meet. He never came to visit me, nor had he ever set foot on the campus. Especially since my mom and Irie had been there numerous of times.

You don't realize how much of your life a person has missed until it hits you in the face. In college, one of my best friends, Desmond Fletcher, had never met my dad. That almost seemed impossible. What's even more interesting about that encounter or first introduction, was that Desmond had suffered a concussion in that last game and didn't remember anything during the game or right after. It wouldn't be until years later that he would meet my father again for the first time or at least the time he could remember.

But despite all of that, I was still glad to see my dad's face in the stands. My mom and Irie were staples in the stands. They followed me all around the country as I played football and ran track. I could not have asked for better parents. Seeing my dad in the stands, made everything that much sweeter. All I wanted was for him to see me play and acknowledge my accomplishments. To use an old phrase, even though he was "a day late and a dollar short," at least he got to see me play once.

I learned that sometimes the statement, "better late than never," is true. Your presence can be seen and felt even when you're late. Showing up says that you care. I can say I have the experience of seeing my dad in the stands watching me play football. And even with all he did to deceive me, him showing up gave me a little hope that I did matter to him on some level.

After the football season I went into the track season exhausted. I was drained mentally from all the emotional turmoil with my father and a heavy class load I had to endure to graduate on time. There was also the physical toil on my body from playing three sports in high school and turning around and playing two sports in college. I didn't have much left in the tank. I was ready to complete the season and graduate. In track, I had a few spurts of my former competitive self. However, I ended the season barely doing the minimum to get by. I was just grateful to make it to the end of the season and couldn't wait until graduation.

Graduation day felt like I had just won the biggest game of my life. After all the hard work, late nights studying, books read, papers written, and final exams, I made it. And it was especially gratifying because my family and friends were there, and it was a glorious occasion. I enjoyed all the pomp and circumstance. I loved putting on my cap and gown. I saw the value in the administration and staff being in their robes and regalia. It was something watching everyone's family and friends sitting in the stands celebrating all of us graduates. It meant even more to me knowing what I had overcome to get there. So, when they called my name, joy, gratitude, and thankfulness to God was all I felt. I know other people graduated that day, but to me, it was my day. It was all about me.

But that feeling didn't last too long. As we made it back to my apartment building, so I could get my stuff, I heard what sounded like arguing. I came out of the room, and I was instantly hit with a frightening sound. It was like remembering a nightmare that felt real. But that feeling wasn't from a nightmare, it was from something traumatic in my past. I emerged from the kitchen only to hear my mother and father arguing. Our front patio opened to the main walkway on that side of the campus, and our doors and the patio were wide open. People were walking by pointing and shaking their heads. My parents were in a shouting match right in front of everybody. I don't know what they were arguing about, but I knew this was not the time nor the place for it. Their own spouses were standing there looking confused. They weren't even married anymore, and they still were arguing like cats and dogs.

I stepped in and said, "What are y'all doing? This is supposed to be my day! I can't believe y'all doing this right here and right now!" I could tell at that moment they were slightly embarrassed themselves. They begin to tone it down, but were still saying smart remarks to each other like little kids. Their arguing put a damper on the rest of that moment at my apartment.

I was upset with both of them. I was upset with my mom because she knows better. Why get into a shouting match with my dad? Why put Irie in a position to have to defend her on that day. I was upset with my dad because this was his first time even on campus. He came all the way there for my graduation and found a way to make it about him. It was unnecessary, selfish, and uncalled for. They were two adults who were not even together anymore. Nothing should have allowed them to ruin this day for their son.

I felt like I was deceived because I thought my dad could be this person who cared about others more than himself. Maybe the deception was not his fault, but mine. What if I deceived myself into believing he could be more than what he showed me? If deception is believing something that is false as true, then perhaps I, not my father, told the lie. Could it be that I told myself this story that my dad could be the dad I always dreamed of who was caring, supportive, and attentive to my needs? It got me thinking about how he had never shown me those things. He didn't have certain times when he did that and then times when he acted different. The truth is, he was the same all the time. The lie and deception were not created by him, but by my fantasy of him being more.

I heard an old preacher say, "You can take a pig out of the dirt. Wash the dirt off and put perfume on it. Then, paint its hoofs and put a set of expensive pearls around its neck. But as soon as the pig sees mud, it's going to run right back to the mud regardless of what you did to try to change the pig. At the end of the day, you deceived yourself if you thought a pig would be anything other than a pig." I had tried to dress my dad up by inviting him to be a part of my college experience and more times than not, he messed it up and I ended up with mud on my face. I needed to decide if I was going to keep living out this deception or was I going to stop letting him drag me into the mud with him. Because there is a thin line between you being able to see potential in a person and you deceiving yourself to believe that potential is who they really are. Sometimes you must look at what they are showing you and make the hard decision to believe what you see on the outside instead of what you think you see on the inside.

Who I wanted my dad to be and who he was did not line up. Was the problem with me or with him? I believe the problem rested with me. I needed to accept the truth he was showing me instead of the false narrative I told myself he could be. Perhaps, when I did accept that truth, I could stop being so frustrated every time he showed me who he really was.

REFLECTIONS

Does the person you think your loved one can be line up with who they really are? What if they are not the person you see in them, but the person they keep showing you? What fantasy version of the person you love do you need to give up? What lie have your told yourself about who this person could be do you need to let go?

You may be responsible for the greatest deception in your relationship. The deception you created about who that person is or what they will become based on what you think is best. If you want them to be made in your image, idea, dream, and hope, you may have set yourself up for your greatest disappointment. Only God is wise enough and all-knowing to effectively make someone into the best person they can be.

It may sound like I'm asking you to give up on your dream or the hope that your loved one will change, but I am not. I'm asking you to give up on the idea that they will change into what you want them to be. Your frustration with them is not because of them, your frustration is because of you. Your conflict comes from the difference between who you have fantasized them to be and who they are for real. If you let go of the fantasy, then all you have left is who they are. Then you can begin to set realistic expectations about what they will say, how they act, how they respond, who they are, and ultimately how you will respond to them.

But, how do you change your expectations? It first requires that you deconstruct or throw out the rule that the adult or the older person should be responsible for the relationship. If you are a teenager or perhaps a parent who has witnessed your child experience disappointment from the other parent, this is for you. Just because a person is older in age doesn't mean they are the same age emotionally. That parent may have experienced some emotional trauma as a child. Perhaps their parent was abusive, they were molested, or abandoned as a child. If they do not receive some help to heal that traumatic wound, they may be stuck emotionally at that same age.

My therapist friend, Nathaniel McGuire, calls it "arrested development." According to the dictionary, the term arrested development refers to stopping physical development, emotional development, or mental development before reaching adulthood. This abnormal condition results in someone being stuck in a certain emotional or mental level of development and can be why some adults act like children emotionally or mentally. This means the person or parent you are dealing with may be older than you in age, but emotionally, they could be younger and less mature than you. They could be mature when it comes to business or in their careers, but when it comes to relationships and navigating their feelings, they could be like a child.

When you understand this and accept that your parent, co-parent, partner, friend, or family member could be emotionally immature, you can accept the responsibility of the relationship. What do I mean by accepting responsibility of the relationship? I mean you accept that you will be responsible for initiating the contact and being the more mature person in the relationship that does not allow the relationship to be destroyed by pettiness. You don't allow the other person's childlike behavior, temper tantrums, lack of responsibility, or misunderstandings to get in the way of developing a deeper relationship.

Is this fair? No. It's not about being fair. Life isn't fair. You can't choose who your parents are and what they went through as a child. However, what you can choose is whether or not you want to have the best relationship with them that you possibly can. Doing that may require you to be the bigger person, the more mature, more responsible, and more forgiving person in the relationship. Just like you would be patient with someone younger than you, you must learn to be patient with them because emotionally you are not dealing with the adult, but the child in them.

TWELVE

I was purging myself of the last 23 years of trauma I experienced at his hands

MY PLANS VS. GOD'S PLANS

Why is it so important to follow the instructions? One day, Irie was putting together a new barbeque grill. There were many different components...nuts, bolts, panels, grates, metal pieces, wheels, and all kinds of other items laid out over the garage floor. The scene looked like chaos to me, but for him, it made sense. He stood there in the middle of the garage staring at this big white booklet in his hands. I asked him what he was doing, and he said, "Reading the instructions."

"Why do you need to read the directions when you can see the picture in front of you? Can't you just put it together based on the way it looks in the picture?" I asked.

"No, you must follow the instructions because the picture doesn't show you everything. Some nuts, bolts and screws hold it all together that you can't see from the outside looking at the picture."

It made sense, so I decided to stay and watch him put it together. He followed every step and detail as written in the instructions. And when he was done, it not only looked just like the picture, but the barbeque grill also functioned the way it was designed.

That day stuck with me because it speaks to how important following the instructions can be to success. I saw through demonstration how following the instructions, steps, and the plan can lead to a desired outcome. But what are instructions? According to the dictionary, instruction is detailed information telling how something should be done, operated, or assembled. It is the plans that help you assemble or bring together what is fragmented or in pieces. Good instructions or plans help you to achieve your goals.

But good instructions are birthed out of a good plan. The plan is the brains, the idea that informs the instructions. The plans are strategically created based on what the idea, dream, or future should look like. Some plans can be good because they are well thought out and all the pertinent information needed to make the plan a success is known or accessible. Nevertheless, there is such a thing as a bad plan. Bad plans are usually not well thought out, impulsive, and not built upon facts and relevant information. Many times, bad plans are rooted in feelings and surface information. Therefore, leaving many gaps that cannot be explained or understood.

If following good plans can lead to success, following bad plans can lead to suffering. Unfortunately, I was the architect who constructed many of the bad plans I followed. Some of the plans I constructed left me looking like the perfectly put together picture on the outside, but the inside was falling apart, and nothing seemed to function as it was designed. Eventually, it caused me to question if the difficulty I experienced stemmed from me being a defective product.

There were other times when I questioned how things could be so easy. Some plans I followed were fool proof, everything was almost prefabricated for me. Especially the plans God had created for me, and I trusted him enough to follow. I just had to put in the minimum amount of effort and stay the course. Sometimes all I had to do was show up at the right place at the right time and great things were waiting for me.

The week after I graduated from college, I experienced one of those right time, right place blessings. I went back to my home church, the church I played the organ for in high school. I was visiting because I had not been there in a couple of years. The church I played for in the summer was a good church and they felt like family, but I wanted something different. My parents were still active members of our home church and told me the church had built another sanctuary on the far eastside of the city. I wanted to see some old familiar faces.

When I got there, a friend of mine was still playing the drums and another friend was playing the organ. As soon as my friend on the organ saw me, he asked me to come up and play the keyboard with them. I was glad to come and play with them. We had a great worship and we played well together. I always had fun playing with those guys.

Immediately after service the pastor walked over to the piano and said, "Rick, it's good to see you man. You done with college?"

"Yes, sir! I graduated last week."

"Good! Man, I want to meet with you this week. Are you playing anywhere?" He asked.

"No, not right now."

"Good, I want to meet with you about playing here."

We arranged a date and time, and just like that, I already had a job offer to play the keyboard.

That was not the original plan. In college, Aaron and I talked about moving to Atlanta, but we had not set about date. We were going to write and produce music in the meantime. Truthfully, we weren't in a hurry to leave Indianapolis after graduation. We wanted to hang out a little before getting serious about a job and real life.

The pastor of the church was serious about bringing me on. Instead of him saying what their budget was, he asked me what I wanted to get paid. He didn't know that I went into the meeting ready with a dollar amount in mind. The dollar amount was about 5 times higher than what I was getting paid at the church I played for in the summer, but I felt like I was worth it. My mother always quoted to me the scripture, "You have not, because you ask not." Just like I did with my coach in college, I was not going to be afraid to ask.

I looked the pastor square in the eye and told him my amount and without hesitation he quickly nodded and said, "Ok, great! When can you start?" I was jumping up and down on the inside, but I had to play it cool. I said, "I can start in about 2 weeks. I got a few things to take care of first." Even though all I really had on my schedule was hanging out and visiting people. But right out of college I had a job playing music, making more than I had ever made before. It was a dream come true.

As I walked to the car, I reflected on that moment. I sat there, with the car running, and I realized that I had low balled myself. The amount may have seemed high to me, but if he could answer that quick without giving it another thought, it must mean my amount was lower than his. But it was too late, and I was satisfied with that amount for the time being.

A few months after taking that job, I had a guy reach out to me who I played football and ran track against at a rival high school. He let me know he played saxophone and he had seen me play keyboards somewhere. He was wondering if I could play keyboards with him for a New Year's Eve gig at this club. I told him I had to play at a service that same night, but I could do it if it was early enough. He reassured me that it was early enough that I could play and make it to church on time.

The music he selected was all R&B and a few jazz standards. We rehearsed a few times, and I programmed some drum loops so we could have some rhythm. We gelled together well. Two peas in a pod. We knew where each other was going musically without even looking at each other. He was like my musical brother with a saxophone. We had some crazy chemistry on stage. As a matter of fact, we sounded so good together that we decided to start a band. We grabbed the drummer from my church, who I had been friends with since I was 15 years old, and another buddy of mine who was a bass player. We called ourselves 4Real. I played at church on Sunday and Wednesday and played in clubs and at poetry sets Thursday through Sunday night. On top of all that, Aaron and I started producing demos for a few local artists.

After producing a gospel artist's demo, we decided to go to a gospel music conference to get more knowledge on the business side of production. I was thrilled because the conference was in Atlanta. I loved the city, and I would get a chance to see my dad. I called him a couple weeks before to let him know what day I was coming and how long I would be there. We agreed to catch up and get something to eat when I came into town.

The day after I arrived, I decided to call him and discovered my hotel was only about 15-20 minutes away from his house. He had moved since the last time I was there. I offered to come to his house, but he said the place where we were eating was near my hotel. So, we agreed to meet at a gas station that was not far away.

I arrived early because I was excited to hang out with my dad. I hadn't seen him since graduation a year prior. The time we set to meet came and went. I began to get a little concerned. My first thought was he must have hit some traffic. Then, I began to worry that he might have been in an accident. He said he was only about 15-20 mins away. It was now 30 minutes past the time we set. I called him on his cell phone to check on him but did not get an answer. Then, I called his home number and did not get an answer. I was so confused. What could be taking him so long?

After an hour had past, I went from being concerned to being very upset. I couldn't believe he did it again! I came all the way to Atlanta, and he left me hanging at a gas station waiting on him. I was furious! I drove 8 hours and all he had to drive was 15-20 minutes and he still couldn't show up. It didn't make sense. I had just talked to him 2 hours before. Why would he do this? I waited another 30 minutes and I called him and left a very rude message on his voicemail. I said, "Dad, this is Rickey Jr. First, I pray you are alright, and nothing has happened to you. I hope you were not in an accident. However, if you weren't and you just left me here waiting for you, you don't have to worry about me ever waiting on you again. I never want to talk to you again! I can't believe you did this again! Never again will you do this to me. Have a nice life!"

I hung up and made up my mind that I would never speak to him again. I was fed up. I had hit my breaking point. I couldn't keep doing that. I could no longer keep pursuing a relationship with someone who was running the opposite way. I couldn't keep being a glutton for punishment. This was not just on him; now it was on me because I kept letting him do it. But I was done trying to matter to someone who did not see that I mattered. That day, I decided to stop fighting for my relationship with my dad.

He called me a week later and left a message, saying he was sorry and that he got tied up doing something. I listened to the message but decided I was not going to give him the satisfaction of calling him back. I was sticking to my guns. I was finished with him.

Consequently, I didn't realize it at the time, but that situation hurt me more than I led on. It began to influence my decisions and my behavior. I started making my own plans that were very reckless and risky. I started not caring about how I was treating others and myself. I began dating different women and I found I couldn't get serious with any of them. I was drinking and clubbing even more than before. Every time I played in the club, I had to drink. I was having more and more mornings where I would wake up in bed after a night out and wonder how I drove home. I was not only putting my own life in danger, but I was also endangering other people's lives.

I was living a double life. In church, I was one way, and I was something completely different outside of the church. I pretended to be the good church boy in church, but outside of church, I was the wild, bad boy. But even I couldn't keep those two worlds apart forever.

It all came to a head one Sunday morning. The night before, I played at one club and then went drinking with some friends at another club afterwards. It would have been smart of me to stop drinking around 11 P.M. or midnight; however, I was so reckless, I kept drinking until 2 or 3 A.M. I didn't get home until 4 A.M. Then, I had to turn around and be at church to play at the first service at 8 A.M. I was still drunk as I stumbled into church. I sat down at the organ to play, barely keeping my head up and eyes open.

Once the service started, the minister of music looked at me and called out the name of the song, "Total Praise." I saw his mouth moving and I heard what he said, but it did not make sense. He said it again, "Total Praise." My mind had completely gone blank. Not only did I forget how to play that song, but I also completely forgot how to play. The keys on the organ looked foreign, like I had never seen them before. By that time, there was an awkward pause in the service. Everyone was staring at me, and I just stared at the keys on the organ. Finally, the minister of music walked over to the piano and started playing the song. Halfway through the song I came to myself and remembered how to play.

This was one of the scariest moments in my music career. I always felt like music was kind of my first love. But music was a gift, and I took that gift for granted. It was almost as if God was warning me that he could take it away as easy as he gave it to me. In that moment I realized how out of control I was. My recklessness had gotten the attention of God and now I had to make some changes. That night, I prayed and committed to God that I would not drink the night before I had to play. I wasn't all the way delivered, but I at least started setting some boundaries in my life.

About a year after that incident, I met a woman at church. I used to see her from afar. She would sit on the far side of the sanctuary opposite the musicians. For several weeks, I would just stare at her, but not say anything. One Sunday, she sat a little closer than usual. So, I took it as a sign that I should try to engage her in conversation. I walked up to her and introduced myself and she told me her name. I let her know I had noticed her sitting on the far side for the last several weeks and I thought it might be nice to get to know her. I wanted to do something that I felt would make her feel safe, so I invited her out to come hear my band play later that night. She agreed that she would come.

I saw her walk in and I knew I would have a shot at getting to know her better. After the show, we exchanged numbers. I didn't waste much time. I called her the next day and thanked her for coming out. I began to ask her some questions to get to know her and she shared where she was from and that she had a five-year-old son. She also expressed that she had already made plans to move back to Michigan. She was in the process of buying a house there. It seemed to me that she was unavailable if she was moving back to Michigan, so I didn't really take things seriously.

We talked frequently, but I still had a few other women I was talking to as well. Though, I was not in an exclusive relationship with anyone. I went on a few dates with her and decided it wasn't going anywhere, so I backed off by calling her less and less until I didn't call at all. I didn't really think much about it, until one day, she showed up unannounced at the summer camp I was helping my mentor with. Someone told me that a lady was at the front door for me. I went outside and she was standing there. I admit I was shocked. She was the last person I thought would be visiting me at my job.

It was awkward for me, but I said, "What's up? How are you?" She asked me why I hadn't called her. I kind of got stalker vibes in the beginning, but after she talked more, I realized she just wanted some closure because I left her hanging, as I did many other women before her. She was just the first one to call me out on it. It was a little scary, bold, and surprisingly refreshing. She asked me if we were ending what we started or were we going to continue. I was honest with her and said, that I had wanted to end it, not because of her, but because I knew she would be moving soon, and I wasn't sure if I wanted a long-distance relationship. She said, "I understand, but I'm willing to at least try, if you are?" I then agreed to at least try and see what would happen. Quite frankly, I still didn't think much would come out of it, but I was willing to try because she was bold enough to confront me about my lack of clarity.

Little did I know, I ended up falling hard for her. Which was new for me because I always tried to maintain a sense of control in relationships. I tried to always be the one who "liked the other person less than they liked me." I tried to not let people get too far in, because I was afraid of getting hurt. I would try to keep a level of security around my heart that kept people from getting too close. However, she had some kind of "cheat code" or "hacker's virus" that allowed her to get in closer than anyone had at that time.

Her being so close to me allowed her to have a certain kind of power or hold on me. Some of it was good and some I could not discern yet. In fact, she had so much power over me that she began to have me think differently about some things I had made up my mind years ago about. One thing she influenced me to change was what I thought about my father. She began asking questions about my dad and why I never mentioned him. I shared with her the list of all the foul, hurtful, depressing things he did to me. I also expressed how the last thing he did caused me to cut him off forever. She listened intently and then said, "So it sounds like your dad has some issues. I understand that because my dad has his issues, too. But at the end of the day, he's still your dad. I know you like to think you're perfect, but you're not. You make mistakes just like he does. How would you like it if someone cut you off? I think you should call your dad." I was not happy about that conversation. I immediately shut it down and told her, "Leave it alone!"

Nevertheless, she did not leave it alone. She kept hinting and making subtle remarks about it. Eventually, I became convicted. Not by her, but by my own conscious and my religious beliefs about forgiveness. I began to have an internal debate in my mind about it. One of my favorite, yet, challenging scriptures to read is Matthew 6:14 *"For if you forgive other people when they sin against you, your heavenly Father will also forgive you. But if you do not forgive others their sins, your Father will not forgive your sins"* But, I said to myself, "I forgave that dude a lot of times. That last thing he did was one too many. He reached his limit. I should not have to forgive someone who had hurt me that many times." And I could hear another voice saying, "But remember the conversation Peter had with Jesus in Matthew chapter 18? Peter went to Jesus and asked, '*Lord, how many times shall I forgive my brother or sister who sins against me? Up to seven times?' Jesus answered, 'I tell you, not seven times, but seventy times seven.'"* [6] This is when I wished I hadn't committed all those years ago to reading the Bible. Because the more you know, the more you are held accountable for. I knew I had to forgive him, but I was not convinced I still needed to continue to trust him enough to pursue a relationship.

One day, while my girlfriend was at my house, I told her I finally would agree to call my dad. But I was only doing it on one condition...she had to be there when I called him. She agreed and I grabbed the phone and dialed his number. She was sitting on the right side of me as the phone rang. He answered and was shocked to hear my voice. I hadn't spoken to him in over a year and a half. I didn't waste any time, I rushed in and said, "Dad, I'm sorry for cutting you off and not talking to you. But I was so angry about you leaving me hanging at the gas station in Atlanta. No, I was hurt!" My tears began to flow, and I became so emotional. I didn't stop at the last incident that happened between him and I, I recalled all the events that caused me hurt. I went all the way back to childhood. I had never expressed those things to him before. I was purging myself of the last 23 years of trauma I experienced at his hands.

I had never cried that hard before in my life. I was snorting, my face was hot, I was sweating, and sometimes it was hard to catch my breath. I was having a physical reaction as I was releasing all that pain. My girlfriend left the room and came back with some tissue. She handed it to me and started rubbing my back as I continued for the next 20 minutes. My dad was completely silent the whole time. I wasn't sure how he would react or what he would say, but it was more about me getting it out than what he said. He let me get it all out and when I was done, he said, "Rick, man, I'm so sorry. I never realized I had hurt you like that. I was selfish and inconsiderate. I never meant to hurt you like that. I apologize. I want to make it right and have a better relationship with you now. If you would like to try?" I felt like what he was saying was sincere. I had never said what I said, and he had never said what he said. It didn't sound like he was trying to say what he thought I wanted to hear. His voice sounded like it was full of remorse, regret, and sadness. I decided to let go of the anger and pursue a relationship with my dad again.

I credit my girlfriend at the time, for pushing me to re-establish a relationship with my father. She was relentless in her pursuit to see my father and I reconnected. Had she not gotten into my heart, I don't know if I would have let my father back in. But because she did, she was able to serve as an usher, opening the door to allow my father back into my heart. Later, I realized she was a conduit used by God to reconnect me with my dad. God has funny ways of using people in His plans to push us toward His will to do what we least expect. Ultimately, allowing us the opportunity to take things to the next level in our lives and relationships.

The more I spent time with my girlfriend, the more I wanted to take our relationship to the next level. We had been together for about 7 or 8 months, and I started having thoughts about marriage. Consequently, it was the longest committed relationship I had been in before. I eventually talked with several people about marriage. I spoke with my dad who said he liked her but was hesitant about me getting married at 24 years old. Especially since I would instantly become a stepfather. He warned me of the pitfalls of getting married too young based on his own marriage. He did not discourage me, but he wanted me to make the decision with a clear mind.

I talked with my mom about getting married and she told me to pray about it. I spoke with my grandmother, and she told me she did not think she was the right one for me. She said, "Rickey, it's not that I dislike her, I just dislike her for you. I think you should pray about it." I decided I would take their advice and pray about it.

I prayed for several days and didn't feel like I got an answer. I decided I would put out my fleece like Gideon in the Bible. God sent an angel to Gideon saying to him that God wanted him to lead an army to defeat their enemies, the Midianites. Doubting if the angel had the right person, Gideon asked for a sign.

"36 Gideon said to God, "If you will save Israel by my hand as you have promised— 37 Look, I will place a wool fleece on the threshing

floor. If there is dew only on the fleece and all the ground is dry, then I will know that you will save Israel by my hand, as you said." 38 And that is what happened. Gideon rose early the next day; he squeezed the fleece and wrung out the dew—a bowlful of water. 39 Then Gideon said to God, "Do not be angry with me. Let me make just one more request. Allow me one more test with the fleece, but this time make the fleece dry and let the ground be covered with dew." 40 That night God did so. Only the fleece was dry; all the ground was covered with dew."

So, I did something similar. I said to God, "If you allow me to fast, go without food for three days, and water only, I know she is the one and I should marry. But if I can't make it three days, I will know she is not the one, and I will not marry her." The first day I was just fine. The second day when I woke up, my stomach felt like it was trying to turn inside out. I was physically in pain. I went to work, and I kept trying to hold it together and stay strong. I went all morning and part of the afternoon fighting hard. Then it was like something took over me. I ran and jumped in my truck and went to the closest fast-food place near me, which was Burger King. I ordered the juiciest, loaded whopper I could. I was literally shaking as I went through the drive thru. I must have looked sick to the person at the window because they almost threw the sandwich at me like they didn't want to touch me because I was shaking. I didn't even get out of the line before I bit into that sandwich. I can't lie, it tasted like the greatest sandwich in the world. And after a few minutes I stopped shaking and began to process what had really happened. That was the sign I was looking for. I had my answer, but what was I going to do about it?

My answer was clear, but I was not. I struggled with deciding between what my faith was telling me and what my feelings were saying. Could I be strong enough to put my emotions to the side and walk away from this relationship? Then, I began to think about if I did not move forward with her, how would she feel? I didn't want to hurt her. And there was a piece of me that did not want to let her down. I even asked God why would he let me love her if he didn't want me to marry her? I didn't feel like I received an answer for that question. However, maybe it was not as relevant as the answer I received from the first question about if I should marry her. The truth is, God's plans were different than mine and I grappled with that difference. But in the end only one plan could prevail. And after much thinking, I made my choice.

I proposed to my girlfriend anyway. We made many plans. One plan was for me to move to Michigan with her. She had purchased a house a few months prior and wanted her son to be around her family. I decided it would be easier for me to move there and make the adjustment than for them to move back to Indianapolis. Therefore, I had it all planned to move there right after the wedding. We also planned a big wedding. We had 7 bridesmaids and 7 groomsmen. We had people from all over the country scheduled to come. Many of my high school and college teammates and friends had RSVP'd. We had music, entertainment, and food ready to go. The night before the wedding, we had the rehearsal followed by dinner. The entire time, I was extremely worried. Not because I had the jitters, or nervous butterflies; I was worried because during the entire engagement, leading up to that night before the wedding, the answer I received to my prayer was ringing in my ear. However, I felt like it was too late to go back on my word. I hoped and prayed that perhaps God would be gracious enough to keep us together and bend his plan to my own.

The wedding was in Michigan, and we packed the small church out. Most of my close family and friends were in attendance. The wedding and reception were beautiful. Both sets of my parents were there. We had a blast; it was a day & night to remember. We went on a fantastic honeymoon in Jamaica and returned home to Michigan. Shortly after we got back, reality set in, and the honeymoon was a faint memory. We quickly learned that marriage was much harder than either of us expected.

I had to take a long, hard look in the mirror and admit I was not the man I thought I was. I still had a lot of maturing and growing up to do. We began to have arguments and disagreement after disagreement. I could not seem to find work outside of being a minister of music at a small church that paid less than half of what I was making in Indianapolis. I was so embarrassed because I had a degree and could not find a job. I went on interview after interview, and no one would hire me. I ended up working as a lunch aide for a middle school just to make ends meet. I felt less than a man. And me not providing financially created a further strain on our relationship. Good things had always seemed to fall in my lap up to this point in my life. I always had favor wherever I went. However, it seemed like my favor had run out and I was lost. I had lost my joy and my sense of self. I felt alone and even abandoned by God. I began to lose my sense of purpose and wondered why I was even still alive. I had emotionally and spiritually been drained. I began drinking alcohol every day just to try to cope with what I was going through.

I finally hit rock bottom when I decided I was going to commit suicide one night. I drank as much alcohol as I possibly could to get drunk. I decided I was going to get into a head-on collision on a busy street and kill myself. I got in the car and drove to one of the busiest streets near where we lived. I knew I could go there because traffic was backed up all the time. However, when I got there, the streets were completely empty. I drove for a mile and did not see one single car. I turned off to one of the side roads and parked the car. I cried like a baby. But this time, I was crying out to God.

I asked the Lord why He had left me. And I heard the Lord speak to me as if He was sitting right there in the car saying, "Son, I'm not done with you, yet. You still have purpose. I never left you. I still have a plan for you." That night, I surrendered to God. I told God I would follow Him and do whatever He told me to do. I was tired of trying to do it my way and follow my will. I gave God my word to follow Him from that night on.

The relief that I immediately felt was amazing. It was as if a weight had been lifted off my shoulders. The feeling of depression, despair, and defeat I had was gone. I felt renewed and refocused. I knew then that my next question for God was to find out what He wanted me to do next. But I needed help in taking that journey to discovering where to start.

I called my dad and told him what had been happening and my encounter with God. He listened and gave me some advice to go back to where all of this started. He told me I needed to fast and pray again to get the answer for what I needed to do next. So, I took his advice and started a week-long fast. For seven days straight, I fasted from food and drank water only from 6 A.M. to 8 P.M. I prayed more in those seven days than I had ever prayed in my life.

By the end of the seventh day, I had no clear answer. But I did have something more important than an answer, I had assurance. I had assurance and peace that I was going to be alright. The morning of the eighth day, I received a phone call from the pastor of my home church in Indianapolis. He asked me if I would be willing to come back to Indianapolis to be the minister of music. I told him, "I appreciate the call and the consideration, but I'm going to stay here in Michigan with my wife." He replied, "Ok, let me know if you change your mind." I got off the phone with him and I began to pray again about what was next. It felt as if I had been slapped in the head, and I heard the words, "You got your answer right there." I got up and immediately called him back. I told him I would like to meet about the position.

The next week, I drove to Indianapolis and had a great meeting with him and confirmed that this was what was next for me. I knew the plan was for me to move back to Indianapolis. But my wife decided that was not the plan for her. Consequently, she decided to stay in Michigan. We tried the long-distance marriage for almost a year. It was a strain on both of us spiritually, physically, and emotionally. Eventually, we both realized it was not in the plans for us to remain married to each other. As a result, we both agreed it was time for us to get a divorce.

Getting a divorce was not something I was proud of. Divorce was not a part of my original plan for marriage. Because of my parents' multiple divorces, I wanted to be different, I wanted to have that happily ever after. But I realized, sometimes, things don't always work out the way you plan. However, the plan God has for you is much better than your plan anyway.

I sometimes wonder what would have happened if I had followed God's plan first. Perhaps, because God is all-knowing, He already knew what I was going to do and went ahead of me to make provisions. What I have learned about God is that because He is all-knowing, that means He knows what we will do before we do. As a result, He always has the re-routing feature programmed into the plan for our lives. That re-routing feature is built specifically for disobedience, self-directedness, and other people influenced guidance. Ultimately, the goal is to get us to the destination He has planned.

I told you in the beginning what I learned about watching Irie put together his barbeque grill. I didn't tell you that there was one point he was putting things together that he missed a page because it was folded underneath something else. He missed those steps and realized something wasn't right. He checked the instructions again and discovered the page with the missing steps. He then was able to go back from that place and start again. Sometimes, we can't start all over, but we can start again. And that starting again looks more like a re-route on a navigation system or a GPS (God's Planning System).

REFLECTIONS

Perhaps you are like me, and you have followed your own plan instead of God's plan. You don't have to keep going the same way and doing the same thing when you know it doesn't feel right. You can re-route yourself right now. Sometimes, we must have the courage to admit when we were wrong, and something did not work out. Sometimes, the worst pain is caused not in doing something you shouldn't have, but in continuing to do it even when you realize it is not good for you or other people involved. Today can be your day to re-route to get you back on track to your destiny.

Perhaps, like me, you've questioned if God has abandoned you. You've questioned if you still have a purpose. You may even feel like there's no hope and you've lost your will to fight. I encourage you to seek after God for the answers. Like I did the night I wanted to commit suicide, you can cry out to God for help. God hears every cry and knows every one of our hurts. He hasn't left us. He is standing beside us waiting for us to acknowledge Him. Waiting for us to take His hand and follow His plan. If you have been experiencing suicidal thoughts, or even thoughts of harming yourself or others, please seek professional help. There are hotlines and counselors equipped with the right skills to help you navigate these difficult times. You do not have to be ashamed or embarrassed. Asking for help is a sign of strength not weakness.

How do we know or even follow God's plan? I discovered God's plan starts with surrendering yourself completely to God's will. God's plan is first acknowledging your plans have failed. It is saying yes to God's will and way even before you see the plan. You must admit God's plan is better no matter what it is. No...it is the best plan possible. It is knowing that God always has our best interest at heart. Your journey begins with recognizing God is a good, good father.

God will reveal what He wants you to do next when you surrender. It may require you talking with someone you trust. Seek advice from a spiritual leader or someone you know has a spiritual connection to God. Through conversation and prayer your next steps will be revealed to you.

But, how do you follow God's plan? You follow God's plan by being obedient and doing what you feel led by God to do regardless of how crazy or outside the box it may seem. Often, God's plans do not involve you doing what is easy, but what will challenge you. God' s plans are not to make us comfortable, but complete. Complete meaning fulfilling our purpose and becoming the best versions of ourselves. Sometimes that involves following instructions that we will not understand until we get further along and see how it all fits into the bigger picture.

THIRTEEN

"I did not know who I was without comparison to my dad"

WHO ARE YOU REALLY RUNNING FROM?

Have you ever felt like you were running from something that no matter how fast or far you ran, you could not escape? A story in the Bible that always intrigued me was about Jonah. Jonah got a word from God to go to Nineveh and preach a message that if they did not repent and turn from their wicked ways, God would destroy them. But Jonah did not want to preach that message, because Nineveh was an enemy of Jonah's people. Therefore, Jonah did not want them to be saved. So, he ran.

Jonah ran and got on a boat heading in the opposite direction of Nineveh. It seemed like he had gotten away from God and his assignment, until a fierce storm hit the sea and began to destroy his boat. The men on the boat inquired about who had made their God angry with them. Jonah spoke up and told the men the storm was his fault, because he was trying to run away from God. Jonah's solution to save everyone else on the boat, was for them to throw him overboard. The men finally agreed and threw Jonah overboard and the storm ceased.

I often wondered what about Jonah's assignment frightened him so much that he would try to run away? What was he so afraid of that it would cause him to run in the opposite direction from what he was being drawn, called, and pulled toward? But even more importantly, was Jonah running from God or something else?

I knew what it felt like to run in the opposite direction of where I felt drawn and called. After being back in Indianapolis a little over a year, it was very sobering to sit with the idea that I had gotten a divorce. I judged my father so harshly for years for not holding together his marriage to my mom; now I was divorced like him. The more I ran away from being like my dad, the more I ended up being like him. As a result, in some cases trying so hard to not be like my dad almost caused me to run away from a great opportunity, take drastic measures to prove I wasn't a failure, and nearly prompt me to walk away from what I felt called to do. Only to later realize maybe I was not running away from being like my dad, but I was running away from something else.

At church, things were running smoothly, and I enjoyed being a minister of music. I had several people directing different choirs, but I spent more time with one particular choir director, Robyn. She was kind, sweet, and gentle hearted. She had a genuine spirit of help. I watched her for months and saw how she gracefully interacted with others. She never complained no matter what was asked of her. She was faithful and had a heart for God and ministry. I saw how she was always ready to step up to encourage, assist, and go above and beyond for anyone she met. I enjoyed seeing how she was never trying to get anything from anyone, but always trying to give. Everyone seemed to love Robyn.

But she was no push over. I observed her assert herself and set boundaries about what she would or would not do or allow to be done to her. Especially when it came to men. Some guys tried to date her, but she was not settling for just anything.

I also observed how she was with her daughter. They were like two peas in a pod. She seemed to be loving, nurturing, attentive, supportive, but also had a stern hand. She didn't allow her daughter, Brittany, to get away with anything just because she was an only child. Robyn was a strong single mother. She was amazing, not only with her own daughter but also with other children. So many of the youth and teenagers at church would hang around her, calling her "Ms. Robyn." And on top of all those wonderful things, we got along well.

She seemed too good to be true. Not that I thought she was perfect, but she was close to perfection as anyone could be. And if that wasn't enough, she was physically one of the most beautiful women I had ever met. From head to toe she was all that! She was just as beautiful on the inside as she was on the outside. I wasn't just attracted to her, I admired her from afar for months.

Robyn also came from a good family. Her mom was an educator who was full of life, well cultured, and into the arts. Her dad was someone everybody at church respected and admired. He was an upstanding man in the community who helped many troubled youth and adults who were struggling with reintegrating back into society after incarcerations. He just seemed to be an overall good guy who I highly respected. Therefore, it was strange and ironic that I got a call from him one day. He asked if I would sing at a surprise birthday party he was giving for Robyn. I gladly agreed. I also thought it would be a great chance to try to get to know Robyn a little more.

The more I thought about it, I realized I needed to take advantage of the birthday moment. So, I finally built up the courage to ask her if she would go to lunch with me. She agreed and we met at an Italian restaurant. It was instant love at first lunch. We were only scheduled to meet for lunch for an hour on her break. However, we looked up two hours later and we were the only couple left in the restaurant. I had never felt a connection like that with anyone. In that moment, it was as if we were not just the only two people in the restaurant, but we were the only two people on the planet. I opened up and shared things with her that I had not shared with anyone else. We had a soul connection. We both knew we had experienced something special. And you would think I would run headfirst into a relationship with someone I felt such a special connection with, but I found myself almost running in the opposite direction.

We started dating and I felt the need to let her know she should not get too serious with me because I could, at any moment, decide I don't want to date. I shared with her how I was still dealing with the grief of my divorce and was not sure if I wanted to commit myself to a long-term relationship, yet. The more time we spent together, the closer we became, and the more I found myself putting up my guard and doing things to her that kept her at a distance. I was inconsistent and wishy washy at best. One day I would be very affectionate and the next standoffish. I could tell at times that she was frustrated because she would ask me why I felt the need to repeatedly tell her I wasn't sure about being in a long-term relationship. However, she was consistent and patient regardless of my mood.

But why was I acting like this? If Robyn was such a great person, why was I going to such great lengths to push her away at times? After many weeks of asking myself that question, I discovered I was afraid of having another failed marriage. Because somewhere in the back of my mind, I felt like I was the reason my previous marriage failed. I blamed myself for not being more of the man I should have been. I wrestled with the idea that I could have done more to keep the marriage together. I also hated the fact that in my previous marriage, I saw in myself, glimpses of the monster I saw in my dad all those years ago. When I became angry, I did not physically abuse my ex-wife, but I would verbally say things that hurt her. I would bring up things that I knew would hurt her to her core in a heated argument. I may not have physically caused her harm, but emotionally, I inflicted many wounds that left her with scars. This part of me was scary. I wasn't sure if I could control myself when I got angry. Perhaps, deep down inside, I was pushing Robyn away from that part of me that I knew could hurt someone I loved. But if I was going to continue to pursue this relationship with Robyn, I needed to get some help.

Ironically, my dad was the person I spoke to about this. If anyone knew about that monster inside of me, it was him. I confessed to him that I could be verbally abusive when I got angry and asked his advice on how to gain some control over my anger. He gave me some life changing advice. He suggested that I practice not speaking when I am angry. If possible, I should ask Robyn if we could continue the conversation tomorrow or the next day when I felt myself getting angry. This would allow me time to think about what I wanted to say and to come up with a more constructive and effective way of communicating that message. I decided to have a conversation with Robyn about my dad's advice and let her know I would be applying his advice the next time I felt myself getting angry. Although she liked to deal with conflict immediately, she agreed to allow me the space to gather my thoughts. It was an adjustment, but I needed not to say things I could not take back and keep from hurting her.

Now, this did not mean I couldn't tell Robyn the truth. Sometimes, the truth hurts because it cuts deep to perform surgery on our soul to remove infections caused by lies, false ideologies, and beliefs that do not line up with who we were created to be. However, harmful words cut deep to cause the infection the truth is tasked with extracting. I decided that when it was necessary to speak the truth to Robyn, that I would do it with empathy as someone who was frequently in need of that same truth. Because we were both in the same boat at the end of the day, needing someone to see our blind spots. This changed everything for me. Instead of running away from Robyn, I started running toward her. I let her into my heart because I felt like I had more control over the monster inside of me.

After dating for over 15 months, I knew it was time for me to ask God if she was the right one to marry. I, again, set out my fleece. If I could fast for three days with just water to drink, I would know she was the one for me. I made it through the first day with ease. The second day, I was worried the whole day. But strangely enough, I was not hungry. I made it through the second day much easier than I thought. But to my amazement, I felt like I was full all day on the third day. The next morning, I was grinning from ear to ear. I had made it three days fasting with only water to drink. I knew then, she was the one. I went that day to purchase her ring.

A month later, I talked with Robyn's daughter, Brittany, and her parents about marrying Robyn. They all agreed and were ecstatic. Brittany even said, "Thank you for asking me. It means a lot that you care about my opinion. My mom is so happy with you. I'm so glad for both of you!" I also spoke to my mom about marrying Robyn and she was happier than I was. She told me she was waiting on me to say something because she knew it was going to happen.

When I told my dad, he was happy, but he asked me a question, he said, "What are you going to do different in this marriage that you didn't do in the last one?"

I immediately answered, "Listen to my heart. Listen to that small, still voice inside of me telling me I don't have to prove I'm a man or the head, but just be Rickey. When I am angry, I will take time to think before I speak. Let go of the chip on my shoulder and know this marriage is about me, her, God and not anyone else."

He replied, "Ok, I think you're ready!"

A couple of weeks later, I planned a surprise engagement dinner at the restaurant where we had our first lunch date. I invited her parents, my parents, my sister, Racheal, and her children. They met at the restaurant a little early. I brought Robyn; she thought we were just going to dinner for a celebration for someone in the family. We ordered our food, then I got down on one knee and shared with her how she had changed my life and brought healing to places that were broken, and how I was ready to spend the rest of my life with her.

I asked, "Robyn, will you marry me?"

Thank God, she said, "Yes, I will marry you." I was the happiest man on the planet! I was marrying the woman of my dreams!

A few months before the wedding Brittany, who played volleyball, had a national tournament in Atlanta. I thought it would be a great time for my dad and his wife, Georgia, to meet Robyn and Brittany. After the tournament was over, we stayed with my dad for two days. My dad barbequed and we had a good time. My dad pulled me to the side and said, "Son, you got a good one! Keep her." It felt good to get his affirmation of what I already knew.

The wedding day came, and it was more beautiful than we had planned. There were over six hundred people at the wedding. Everyone who meant something to us was there. All of my siblings were there, as well as, all of our parents. It was truly a day to remember. I even wrote a song and sang it to Robyn as she walked down the aisle. There wasn't a dry eye in the room, including me. That day, I married my best friend and the love of my life.

Within a year, I would also learn new meanings of love. I was a new husband and a new father to one of the world's greatest young ladies, Brittany. I took a page out of Irie's stepdad book. I was consistent when she needed me and ready to advise whenever she asked. From day one, we had a phenomenal relationship.

I would also learn what it meant to love someone the first time you meet. About three months after the wedding, we discovered Robyn was pregnant. I was overjoyed at the thought of us being parents. But I was a little nervous about what kind of father I would be because of the father my dad was to me. I wanted to prove I could be a better dad. Therefore, I had my mind made up that I was not going to just be a good dad, but the best dad ever.

Brittany had just gone off to college in New York on a full ride for volleyball. She hadn't been there two months before she had to come back for the birth of her sister. The big day finally came, and Robyn and I welcomed our first child together, Aaliyah. I instantly fell in love with her. And in her own fashion, she came into the world following the beat of her own drum. She did not open her eyes until the third day after she was born. I knew we had a great leader on our hands.

I learned that sometimes you can take wanting to be the best to the extreme, forcing you to try to live up to unrealistic expectations. I wanted to be so different from my father that I strived for "the best" instead of "my best." I was so determined to be a great dad that I bit off more than I could chew. After a couple of months of maternity leave, Robyn had to go back to work. But daycare was a concern. We didn't know at the time who we could trust. When Robyn had Brittany, she had her Aunt Delores watch her like she watched Robyn. However, Aunt Delores had passed away.

Now we were stuck with making a difficult decision of who would care for Aaliyah. Without really doing any research, I enthusiastically, accepted the challenge to keep Aaliyah during the day. My job was flexible. I only had one meeting per week and my choir and band rehearsals were in the evening. I had a plan of how I could make it work. Robyn reluctantly agreed to let me keep Aaliyah at home. I had no clue that I had no clue what I was doing.

I thought I could get Aaliyah to conform to my schedule, but I was sadly mistaken. I was trying to take care of her and when she was sleep, clean the house and work on music. I didn't realize how hard it was to do all those things while not getting sleep at night because she got up every three hours. I was trying to prove I could be strong, and I even made it four months. But my tipping point happened when, one day, I was getting Aaliyah ready to go with me to a meeting. I put her in her car seat, then put the car seat on the couch. When I turned around to go get something, I heard a thump, and then, crying. I realized I had put her in the car seat, but I had not strapped her in. I ran in the living room, picked her up and check her all over. Thankfully, she was fine. But, I wasn't. I was exhausted. I finally admitted that I couldn't handle taking care of Aaliyah during the day and working in the evenings.

I immediately called Robyn and told her, "We need to find a daycare this week. I can't do this anymore! I'm too tired!"

"It's all good. I have already been looking and I think I found a place," she laughed.

We visited that place a couple of days later, and the next week, Aaliyah was in daycare.

I realized that I was trying so hard to prove I was a better father to my children than my dad was, that I went overboard. I was running away from being a failure as a father. As a matter of fact, the more I reflected on that time, the more I realized I became him in some twisted way. I over committed and underperformed. I was so drained that I could not be present with Aaliyah even when I was physically there. I barely had any energy to attempt to play with her. I was physically there, but emotionally absent. I tried so hard to not be like my dad, but I became an alternate version of him.

The reality began to set in that I was not trying to be super dad for Aaliyah, I was doing all of this for me. My actions were selfish at heart. I was trying to protect her from being hurt and disappointed like I was as a child. Therefore, I became overprotective, overbearing, and overcompensating as a parent. When we are overprotective and overbearing, we protect the people we love from outside threats, but ultimately, we become the inside threat that hurts them the most. We smother them, stifle their growth and creativity, and keep them from experiencing the very things that allow them to become the people they were born to be. If we try to keep our loved ones from hurt, we hurt them by keeping them from being shaped into whom they were destined to be. I realized the hurt I experienced from my dad shaped me into a compassionate, loving, considerate person. Without that pain, perhaps I would not have developed such empathy for those who are lost, abandoned, and hurting.

It took me a while to finally get it, I didn't have to be super dad, I just needed to be dad. I didn't have anything to prove to anyone. My value as a father was not determined by how much I was doing for her, but who I was being with her.

I was also trying to find my identity when it came to ministry. A few months after Aaliyah was born, I began struggling with what I felt called to do in ministry. For a few years, I saw myself as a musician, singer, worship leader, and minister of music. However, I started feeling restless, maybe even anxious about what I should be doing next. I had this feeling that I should be doing something different. I couldn't put my finger on it, but I knew what I was doing was not the only thing I should be focused on anymore.

I spoke to my friend, Rolando, about it, and he suggested I go back to school and get my master's, and eventually, my doctorate. He had just been accepted into law school in Louisiana, and was leaving in a few months. That was sad for me, because he was a good friend. But I was happy for him for having the courage to change what he was doing to follow his dreams and calling. If I'm honest, his courage was contagious, and I found myself being courageous enough to search for what was next for me.

Music was satisfying, but it wasn't fulfilling something greater in me. I began to look at master's programs for music. I thought maybe I needed to go back to writing, producing, and maybe even learn to score music. After some research, I inquired about the University of Indianapolis' music program. I had reached out to the chair of the department and was waiting for a response. But something happened in between me waiting for a response. I received another response from God about what I should be doing next. God had another plan.

My wife loved planning grocery shopping trips. I hated going to multiple stores just to save $1. Most of the time I would stay home, and she wouldn't invite me because I was a little bit of a grouch when I went. Shopping just always seemed to make me sleepy. But on this particular day, she invited me to go. We walked into Walmart near our house and a gentleman from our church was sitting on a bench near the entrance. He perked up when he saw me and said he wanted to talk to me. At that point, Robyn smiled at me and said, "Hello Mr. Boykins. Rickey, see you later. I'm going to shop." She was on a mission to get the grocery shopping completed and I didn't mind the distraction.

Although I was a little surprised that he even stopped me. When I led worship, he always sat in the second row in the front of the church, and it looked like he was making mean faces at me. I thought he didn't like me. I later discovered that he was not making mean faces, most of the time he was crying, but I was too far away to see his tears. But as he began to talk, I quickly realized how wrong I was. He knew so much about me and shared how he followed me since I started playing at the church when I was 15. He shared how we had music in common and how he was a band conductor in the army. I was amazed at how much we had in common. I was so glad I stopped to talk to him.

Suddenly, he asked, "What are you supposed to be doing right now?"

I told him I was getting ready to apply to the University of Indianapolis for a master's program in music.

"That sounds good, but that's not what you're supposed to be doing. You have a greater calling on your life."

As soon as he said it, I knew exactly what it was. But I wasn't going to say it out loud. So, I answered, "I don't know."

"You're supposed to be preaching, aren't you?"

I just put my head down. I tried to dismiss what he said. "

I'm getting ready to go to music school and start back writing and producing."

Then, he said something to me that pierced my soul. He said, "Son, God has all the time in the world, you don't!"

I was reminded of what I told God in the car that night I was saved from committing suicide. I told God I would say yes, to whatever He wanted me to do. I knew in that moment I needed to surrender not to my will, but God's will for me.

I went home that night understanding why I had been so restless in ministry. I decided I would pray for the next week to seek guidance on how to proceed forward with accepting my call to preach again. After that week, I spoke with Robyn about how I believed God was calling me to preach. I could tell by her face that she was scared to death about what that may mean for us as a family and her as a wife. We had just recently found out that she was pregnant again. I don't believe she ever doubted that I would preach, but maybe she didn't know it would happen that soon. After the quick look of shock wore off, she said, "Ok, babe! Whatever God is telling you to do, we gone do it. I got your back!" To hear her say those words were like music to my ears. Just to know I had a wife who had my back no matter what, made me feel stronger and more powerful. When Superman was feeling weak, he would fly toward the sun and be strengthened. I was grateful that God gave me a mini sun in my wife to help strengthen me when I felt unsure, weak, and vulnerable.

I reached out to my dad and told him what happened. He suggested that I go to my pastor and share my calling to preach with him. He said, "He'll be able to guide you on what their process is for ministers." I reached out to my pastor, and we met for dinner. I shared with him what was going on and he said he already knew. He was just waiting on me to say something. It was such a relief to be able to tell him and for him to have already sensed my calling as well. I was more relieved because of an incident between him and me, a couple of years prior, where I felt like he dismissed something I shared with him. I shared with him about a dream I had. It felt so real. He was upset, no, furious with me about something that I couldn't identify in the dream. But it was obvious in the dream it was severe enough that he publicly humiliated me and went off on me in front of the whole church. I was so disturbed by the dream that I went to him a week later and shared it with him. He just laughed and said, "Maybe you ate something wrong the night before. I'm not mad or upset with you. That was just a bad dream." I know he didn't think it meant anything, but I knew there was more to it. Because I would have a dream just like it at least two times a year after that.

But he did not dismiss what I had to say this time, and I felt validated. I asked him what the next steps were, and he told me to sign up for a class he was teaching called "Sermon Preparation" at the church's Bible Institute. It was a great class. I learned so much about how to prepare for a sermon, to research, the different styles of preaching, and different sermon types. The final assignment was helpful in that we had to write a sermon. Consequently, that sermon I wrote in the class would be the sermon I would preach for my first sermon.

The pastor gave me a date to preach my first sermon a few weeks later. To say I was nervous was putting it mildly. The same pulpit I stood in every week to lead worship would now be the same pulpit I would preach from. You would think it would be the same, yet, the same platform with a different assignment makes the platform feel and look different. The platform doesn't make the assignment, the assignment makes the platform. The way I looked at it, this was an assignment that had the weight of people's soul attached. I had to take it seriously and approach it with fervor, prayer, and respect.

Robyn and my mom helped me invite all my family and friends to come to that service where I would preach. We also invited everyone to come over to our house afterwards. Robyn was extraordinary at planning parties and events. My Aunt Tammy and Aunt Rita came with all my little cousins from Marion. Mom's parents came, and some of my high school and college friends came as well.

I was super excited that my dad came. His preaching was the most influential on my life. When I was young, I hung onto every word, infliction, movement, syncopation, and phrase he spoke. He was my Michael Jordan of preaching. I was always amazed at how I could see him in the pulpit one way, but see him outside of the pulpit another. For whatever reason, I always respected what my dad did in ministry. And even when I did not like what he was doing outside of the pulpit, I would never take away from him what he did in the pulpit. There were certain areas of his life in which he struggled, but preaching was never one of them. When he preached, you would leave convicted, enlightened, laughing, encouraged, and hopeful about getting closer to God again. He just had an anointing for preaching. So, to have him in the audience was an honor.

I preached what I believed God had given me to preach that night. I was nervous, but I was confident in what I had studied and put together. I knew the sermon inside and out. But more importantly, I had already lived the sermon and it was in my heart. I knew what it felt like to be alone and have God rescue you from the brink of death and destruction. I knew what it felt like to suddenly have hope for tomorrow. I knew what it felt like to find out that your life was worth living because the future of your life was in the hands of God.

Afterwards, I knew this was what I was meant to be. It wasn't something I was just meant to do, but *be*, as a person. Someone who encourages, uplifts, convicts, inspires, motivates, challenges, brings hope, gives good news, and draws them closer to God with my words and how I live my life. That night, there was no doubt in my mind what I was supposed to do next.

Later, I understood why I ran so long from preaching. At first, I thought I was just running from being a preacher like my dad. I even thought I was running away from surrendering to God. And in a way, I was running away from what God was calling me to do. However, it was much deeper than that. I wasn't just running away because I did not want to surrender to God, I was running away because I was fearful of disappointing everyone. I felt like accepting the call to preach was very honorable and it automatically put you up on a pedestal. My fear was that people would start looking at me as a model and I would let them down. I still felt a piece of me was unpredictable, and I did not fully understand yet.

Underneath the surface, I always dealt with this fear I would mess up, fail, or disappoint everyone. As a result, that anxiety would sometimes cause me to not chase after what I wanted or take advantage of opportunities. If I didn't feel like I could be almost perfect at it, I would run from the moment or the challenge; often leaving me with regrets. For example, one time I met this famous producer in the gospel industry and asked him if he would mentor me. To my surprise, he invited me to a studio session to watch. After the studio session, he invited me to his house in Nashville. I went and he introduced me to some amazing people and artists. I went home fearful that I was out of my league. Therefore, I never called him again. To this day, I still have regrets because he was opening the door for me to do what I loved, and I ran the opposite direction. My fear caused me to have what my dad called, "paralysis of analysis." I was paralyzed because I was thinking too much about if I failed. And unfortunately, for years, I felt the same thing about preaching.

What helped change my mind was a quote I heard someone say. It is said that Martin Luther, the one who nailed his ninety-five theses to the wall of the Catholic church to start the Protestant Reformation, once said, "The best sermon you will ever preach is the one you live." Something about the quote spoke to me to reassure me that I could not fail at the act of preaching because preaching was not an act, it was how you lived your life. I wanted to be different in the sense that my best and greatest sermon would be the one people get to watch and hear about because of the way I lived my life. Not that I would strive for perfection, but obedience. The bible says David was as man after God's own heart. David was by no means perfect, but he was humble and obedient to God. My desire was to be someone God could depend on inside and outside the pulpit.

A few months after preaching my first sermon, I decided to go to seminary. My pastor had expressed the importance of education as ministers. But I also wanted to gain the knowledge and the experience that would help build my faith and confidence. Besides, I loved learning, and it seemed like a good fit. Amusingly, the new youth pastor at the church was in his first semester at Christian Theological Seminary on the west side of town. I applied and was accepted.

As excited as Robyn and I were about me going to seminary we had some concerns. We had a 9-month-old baby at home and about five months away from having a new baby. But, I would soon find out that if you make room for God, He will make sure you have room for what you care about. When you are doing what God called you to do, He will make sure you take care of those who call on you. I couldn't wait to tell my dad. He was just as excited as I was. He said, "Rick, you're doing things different than I did. I never had the time and discipline to go to seminary. I'm so proud of you. You're going to have your Master of Divinity Degree."

The semester flew by relatively quick. I was learning many new concepts, theologies, and meeting great people. The end of the semester came with a whole new set of blessings and obstacles. Our youngest daughter was due the same day as my biggest final. It was a 20-page paper in my Intro to Theology class. The final was over all 10 theological styles and authors we had studied. I had been working on it for two weeks. The night before it was due, I did not go to sleep. Once I got to the hospital, I knew there would be no time to write and finish the paper. So, I made the sacrifice and stayed up all night. We were scheduled to be at the hospital at 6 A.M. We had agreed to leave the house at 5:20 A.M. At 5:10 A.M, I was finishing the last paragraph. I saw the time and knew I had to hurry. I could see Robyn pacing the floor. She said, with an irritated voice, "Babe, are you ready!?" I kept saying, "I'm almost done. Give me one second." Even when she was mad and irritated, she was still patient and loving. I finally finished the paper and pressed send. It was finished!

We finally made it to the hospital and Robyn gave birth to our third daughter, Melodey. I noticed quickly that her demeanor was already different from Aaliyah's. Melodey's eyes were wide open from birth and curiously observing everything around her. As I held her in my arms, I wondered who she would grow up to be and would she be compared to her sisters or not. I prayed Melodey would one day discover her identity not based on a comparison to her sisters, but based on the path she decided to pursue. And I was just grateful that I would get to be there to guide her along the way.

In that moment, I had a revelation. I realized, perhaps, that I was running away from Robyn, from failing as a father, and preaching because I was afraid of who I would be in all those roles. I had spent so much of my then, 30 years of life, identifying myself based on not being like my dad, that I did not know who I was without comparing to him. I had measured what kind of man I was based on the man I believed my father was not. I wasn't running from being a husband, father, minister, or even from following God, I was running away from finding me.

For so long, I hid behind the trauma I experienced at my father's hand. Eventually, the pain became my excuse to not do the work to discover who I really was without the pain. I was afraid of learning that I might be the one who doesn't measure up or the inconsistent one. I was running from me. I was scared to find out what kind of man I really was. Could I be a man who was faithful, honest, kind, caring, strong, wise, and full of integrity? I needed to know.

But if I was ever going to find out who I was, I had to let go of my emotional crutch or the idea that my pain is an excuse to not be accountable or live beneath my potential. I had to take the time to find out, or better yet, become the man I wanted to be. A man who took full responsibility for my actions and did not blame my father for what I was doing or not doing. And the only way I could do that was by running toward things that were scary and trying to understand them instead of running from them. In this way, I believe I became a blessing to Robyn, my daughters, friends, family, and those I ministered to. I was able to help others when I started running toward the people and things I felt called to.

This reminds me of Jonah. After Jonah was thrown overboard after running from God, a large fish swallowed him. He stayed in the fish for three days. When the fish finally released him, he ran toward the city of Nineveh and preached the word the Lord gave him. The people believed his message, repented, and all of them were saved. The people of Nineveh were blessed because Jonah decided to stop running away from his assignment or calling, and ran toward it with conviction and confidence. I believe we, like Jonah, become a great blessing to others when we become people who run toward the unknown to discover who we are being called to be in that season. The journey to discover who you are may, at times, feel like you have been thrown overboard, swallowed up by life, and spit out. But who you become afterwards will make the time of uncertainty worth all you had to endure.

REFLECTIONS

Identify who you have been comparing yourself to. Have you been like me and comparing yourself to who a person was not being to you? Do you find yourself measuring the type of person you are based on what they did or did not do? If so, perhaps it's time to stop using them as a crutch because you have not determined what type of a person you desire to be. If you measure who you are based on who they were not, you may still be setting the bar too low for yourself.

Make a list of things you have been running away from. Write down the benefits you believe you have received from running away. Then, identify and write down what running away from those things have most likely kept you from. What opportunities do you think you have missed out on because you have been running away? Take notes on what steps you think are necessary for you to run toward that thing. Who do you need to talk to? What do you need to change? Decide who you want to be and write it down. If you took away all your excuses, what would you do or who would you become?

Don't get to the end of your life and regret that you did not live your life to the fullest. Live your life with no regrets. It is better to have run toward an opportunity and it didn't work out, than run away from an opportunity and you never know what could have, should have, or would have happened. We get one life, don't waste it living in fear of things that are not real.

FOURTEEN

"I was willing to risk failing to move forward."

STAYING IN THE STRUGGLE MAY SAVE YOU

Have you ever asked, "Why is this person making this relationship so difficult?" Sometimes the people we love can make things complicated. It can be frustrating to know that you are making compromises and concessions and they still don't want to meet you halfway. It can cause you to wonder if what you are offering them in the form of a relationship, is worth the struggle. However, if you wait long enough and put in the work, you might just see that the struggle has more purpose than you think.

When I heard the stories about the heroic efforts of the firefighters on 9-11, my admiration for them was taken to another level. One story that fascinated me was about Captain Jay Jonas. He and his men rushed into the 2nd tower of the World Trade Center. They were looking for survivors. While everyone else was running down the stairs to save themselves, he and his crew were running up the stairs to save others.

The firefighters found one lady who needed help but had to stop looking for more survivors because the first tower started to fall. As they ran down the stairwell, the lady kept stopping and breaking down crying because she was so scared. Eventually, she stopped on the fourth floor and decided she was not going down any more steps. As they were trying to calm her down to get her moving again, that's when it happened. The whole building began to collapse. They could hear all one hundred floors collapsing on top of each other and eventually all around them. As the collapsing floors got closer, they wondered if they would survive. I wondered if they were thinking, "Are we going to die? If this lady had not been so difficult and stubborn, we could have made it out before the building collapsed."

I have never been a firefighter, but I have experienced people being difficult and stubborn in relationships. I have felt like I was trapped in the relationship because the other person did not want to do what was necessary to move forward, thinking if they would just listen to me, things would be so much easier. Only to, at some point, wonder if I should have walked away from them a long time ago, hoping that the relationship had not cost me too much of my time, energy, and resources. And yet, no matter how much I want to put all the responsibility on the other person, I feared that I had some part to play in things being difficult. But my question remained, "Could there be any meaningful purpose in staying in a difficult relationship?"

Throughout seminary, students talked about what was next for them. Some aspired to be youth pastors and chaplains to serve in their local hospitals. But others wanted to become a senior pastor of a church. Many of the students were willing to relocate to take a pastorate position. Some students started putting in applications at churches with vacant pastorate positions. A select few were already pastoring. Whenever friends in seminary would ask me if I put in any applications anywhere or what I was going to do afterward, I would give them a vague answer like, "I'll see what God has for me." That was just a spiritual cop-out. The truth was, I didn't know. I hadn't made up my mind on what direction to go.

I was comfortable being a minister of music. It was easy for me, and I was compensated well. But I knew in the back of my mind that being a minister of music was no longer the position I was destined to hold. I suppose subconsciously, I knew what I was being called toward. But why couldn't I accept that calling? Why couldn't I accept that I was called to pastor? What was stopping me? Perhaps God was in a difficult relationship with me. Maybe I was the one who was complicating things by not listening to his directions.

I think what was stopping me was behind me. My past kept finding ways to try to stop, hinder, block, and stand in the way of my future. I knew that pastoring was for me, but what I watched my family go through when my father was pastoring seemed too horrific to overcome. I had put so much energy and effort into my family that I saw pastoring as a threat to what I had built. But why did I see it as a threat?

The more I reflected on my fear of pastoring, I realized it came from me feeling like my dad put ministry before us as his family. I didn't want my wife, nor my daughters to ever know the feeling of rejection in that way. That feeling of rejection led to me feeling less than and always feeling like I had to compete for my father's love and attention. I wanted my wife and daughters to know that they never had to compete or fight for my attention. They would always be a top priority for me.

But the deeper I dived into what happened with my father, the more I realized it wasn't church or ministry that took my dad away, it was him. His desires to fulfill whatever he was chasing after. I don't even think it was just the fortune, fame, or females, I think it was something much deeper. He had a void that he was trying to fill with everything but the right thing. I knew I didn't have to be afraid of doing the same thing, because instead of running away from God and my family to fill the void in my life, I was running toward them.

One day, while running some errands, I got a call about one of our choir members having knee surgery. I decided to go and check on her. We talked and laughed for a little bit and then almost out of nowhere she said, "So, when are you starting your church?" My head went back like someone just swung a punch at me. I was so dumbfounded by the question. I looked at her as if she was speaking another language. Sure, I had thought about pastoring, but not starting a church. I had seen my dad start at least 4 different churches in 4 different locations and they all ended with being shut down. I remember how hard it was with him starting and our lights being disconnected because he had to pay the lights at the church. I saw him do everything by himself, from sweeping the floors to preaching in the pulpit. I just couldn't see myself doing that to my family or myself.

Once I regained my composure, I responded, "Uh, no. I don't know anything about starting a church. I'm not starting a church. You know you something else." I started laughing. Then, she replied, "Ok, just let me know when you do because I'm coming!" I laughed it off again and changed the subject. I stayed a bit longer, and prayed with her before I left.

During the walk down the hospital hallway and on the elevator, I couldn't get that question out of my mind. *"When are you starting your church?"* I didn't make it back to my car before I had to stop right in front of the hospital and pray. "Lord, is this what you want for me?" I asked. "Is this why I have not felt led to put in any applications to churches with vacant pastorate positions? Do you want me to start a church? Can I just go to an existing church? I saw my dad start a church and it was so hard!" I stood there crying out to God. It seemed like just when I got over one fear, I had to deal with another.

In that moment, it was as if I was having a conversation with God. I heard Him loud and clear say, "I will leave that decision up to you. You can decide whether to go to an existing church or start a church." I began to think about several friends of mine who went to existing churches, and they talked about all the drama that was going on behind the scenes. How there were things happening that he or she could not see while interviewing and talking to members. They expressed how, on the outside, it looked good with the salary, resources, and ministry opportunities, but the spiritual foundations of the churches were cracked and unstable. I then thought that if I started a church, I could start fresh and build something quality from the ground up where the foundation would be firm and solid. In that instance, I decided that I would start a church. Instead of running away from it, I decided to run toward what I feared. I knew it would be hard, but the difference was, I was willingly running toward it. It was my choice, and I was willing to risk failing to move forward.

I finally made it back to my car and called my wife. I told her what had just happened and how I believed God was calling us to start a church. She gave a silent pause and then said with a cracked voice, "Ok, I got you babe. I guess we're starting a church." We discussed how we were going to go on a 40 day fast praying about us, the church, the people God would send, who to speak to, and how to start the church the right way. For those 40 days, I gave up watching TV (which was a major sacrifice for me), sweets, some meats, and I committed to praying every morning and evening for an hour each. Then, on Wednesdays, I fasted from food and only drank water from 6 A.M. to 6 P.M. I desperately wanted to hear from God. I knew God answered my prayers when I fasted and prayed before, so I believed He would do it again.

At the end of that 40 day fast, I heard the Lord loud and clear. I was leading worship as I did every Sunday. In the middle of me singing, I heard a voice say, "It's time to leave!" I was so stunned, that the rest of that service was a blur. After service was over, I was still sitting in my seat as if I was glued to it. I had to have had a glossy look over my eyes because I almost didn't notice a woman waving me to come to her. I walked down from the stage and said hello. I had met her once at a birthday dinner for someone in the office. We sat next to each other and had a great conversation. She looked at me and said, "I don't know why God told me to come over here. I just need to say, God told me to tell you, 'It is well!' I hope you know what that means." As those words, "it is well" came out of her mouth, a calmness and a peace washed over me, and I knew I was going to be alright. I didn't know what the future would hold, but I knew who held my future in that moment. I told her thank you and I knew then that I had to get to work preparing myself to get a team together and start the church.

A couple of weeks later, I was on my way to support a friend of mine who had just left Indianapolis and went back to his hometown in Ohio to start a church. I was excited for him because he was embarking on a journey that I was getting ready to begin. We had similar stories in terms of us both being music directors at a church. We both felt the call to go further in ministry. A few years after both of us accepted the call to preach, we felt led to go even further.

Driving to support him in his first service was scary and exhilarating. I was nervous for him as if it was me. In a way, perhaps, I did feel very invested. We shared many of our dreams, aspirations, fears, and concerns regarding him leaving what seemed like security, to walk into the unknown. However, we both had reached the point where we would rather be uncomfortable in a place of the unknown than be comfortable in a place where we knew our season had ended.

One of the people I was dreading talking to was my dad. My dad, for years, seemed to have resented his experience with starting churches. While I was in seminary, he took every opportunity to let me know that I needed to find an existing church to pastor. And for a while, I thought the same thing. However, I was clear that going to an existing church was not going to be the path for me. I could never seem to find the perfect time to tell him. So, I decided I would just tell him the next time I spoke with him.

When my dad called, we had just gotten on highway 24 toward Toledo, Ohio. He asked how I was doing, and I told him where I was going. Then, I just blurted it out, "Dad, I feel like God is leading me to start a church!" His response shocked me. Truthfully, I was not sure what he might say. However, what he said stunned me. He said, "You're making the biggest mistake of your life. Why would you start a church when you have a degree? You can go to an existing church instead of working so hard to start your own. I think you're making a mistake. Didn't you see what happened to me? Maybe you need to pray more about this." I did not expect that...not from him.

I was crushed! I felt like a powerless little kid. "Why can't you just be happy for me?" I asked "I thought you would be proud of me. Why does everything have to be so difficult with you?" He said, "I just don't want you to make the same mistakes I made. Why don't you pray about it? Make sure this is what you're supposed to do." For me, this wasn't a moment to continue to pray. I had prayed for months, and this was the answer that kept coming to me. I didn't have to put out a fleece like times before. Gideon was uncertain, insecure and was not used to hearing from God. This wasn't my first rodeo. I had spent time praying about making major decisions in my life before. I knew when I felt certain about what I should do. That doesn't mean that I could control the outcome, variables, or the results of my decisions, but I knew I was sure about my decisions.

Did I realize that he was concerned and wanted to look out for me? Yes, I knew that intellectually, but emotionally, I wanted to hear something that sounded less condemning and more celebratory. There would be plenty of time for him to voice his concerns later. I was looking for something that I looked for my whole life with him. It wasn't just about this incident; it was about my desire to have my father's approval. Especially in big moments when I had made life-altering decisions. I just wanted to hear my dad say, "I'm proud of you, son! You're going to do well. You got this! Let me know I how can help!" But no matter what my dad did or did not say, I was running toward what I felt strongly about. I was going to start our church.

My wife and I started assembling our team like the Avengers. We got a group of nine people to be the core of the launch team. What was amazing was that every person we spoke to told us they were waiting on us and that God had already spoken to them about starting the church. There was confirmation at every turn.

After meeting with the launch team for two months, I decided it was time for me to resign as Minister of Music. I set up a meeting with the pastor and had my resignation letter in hand. I sat down and told him everything that was going on and how I felt led to start a church and I was giving him my two weeks' notice. I expected him to be a little blindsided because we hadn't had a one-on-one meeting in over a year. And that last year, we weren't always on the same page. I admit I was prepared for some pushback and maybe some critical feedback. But certainly not to the degree he would give.

"Where do you think you're getting the members from? I hope you don't think you're going to get them from here. You really could have been something. I had plans for you. Now no one will ever know who you are," he responded.

Those words cut deep. I knew he was upset, but I didn't realize how hurt he would be. He had been my pastor since I was 15 years old. I understood he wanted me to apply for an existing church and perhaps take the path he took and start at a small church for the first couple of years, get the experience, and then go to a larger church. But that was his path and not mine. I was hurt more than angry. I looked up to him, but I understood he was sad and didn't know how to express it. Consequently, my dream eight years before about him being angry with me came true.

Around the same time all of this was happening, I was still in my last semester of seminary. I was doing one of the last required parts of my Master of Divinity degree. It was called Clinical Pastoral Education (CPE) and was a supervised program for chaplaincy at Methodist Hospital. This is where we learned how to provide spiritual care to patients and hospital staff.

While there, I met several powerful and unforgettable people. One of them was William Taylor. He was a staff chaplain at the hospital. He was tall, and favored the old school actor, Billy Dee Williams. But his presence was even larger than his appearance. When he walked in the room, people immediately gave notice. When he spoke, people stopped to listen. I could even tell some of the managers who were over him were intimidated by him because he was so confident and profound. I sat in meetings with him, observing how he moved and engaged with others. I was blown away. I had never seen anyone like him before. I needed to know what he had and how I could get it.

I saw William walking in the hall one day and he stopped me and said, "What's up young brother? I see you out here doing your thing. Keep it up!" I told him thank you and then asked him, "Man how did you get to be like this? What do you have and how can I get it?" He chuckled, clearly being caught off guard he asked, "What do you mean?" I told him how I observed his presence, confidence, and the respect he commanded from others. He told me about a program he had been a part of called Landmark Forum. He talked about how he was like that because he learned to put the past in its proper place and that was behind him. Therefore, affording him the opportunity to see people and things as they were and not as he interpreted them as being. He told me to check out their website and tell him what I thought. I told him I would and then we went our separate ways.

That night, I googled Landmark Forum, and it was a 3-day leadership seminar in Chicago. It seemed very interesting to me. And besides, I was already sold because I saw the results in William. We were already meeting with our launch team and preparing to start having prayer vigils and bible study. My wife was the only one working at the time. We had some money saved because we weren't sure what would happen with the church. However, because I was so convinced that this was a good thing, I took a chunk of that money and invested it in myself so I could participate in that program.

It was an all-day Friday, Saturday, and Sunday seminar coming back on Tuesday for a celebration. This was hands down the best leadership seminar I had ever been to, if you could call it that. It was hard to describe. It was not just how to be a leader of people; it was more like how to be the leader of yourself. And one of those ways to be a leader of yourself was to clear your pathway of hurt you experienced and the hurt you inflicted on others as a result of your hurt. Because that hurt becomes the skewed lenses in which you see the world and your future. Clearing our path of that hurt would allow us to see people for who they are and see that anything was possible in our future. Clearing that pathway freed me to go after my dreams with a clear conscience.

I received many revelations that weekend. But one of the most profound was exposing the impact my relationship with my dad had on all my other relationships. I was so painfully made aware of my interpretation of why my father would sometimes disappoint me and not show up. I believed that my father wouldn't show up because I was not worth his time. Consequently, I also believed that if I was not worth my father's time, I was not worth anyone else's time either.

This revelation would explain why I was so guarded when it came to relationships. In romantic relationships, I always felt like I had to either break up with them first or get them to break up with me. Either way, I needed to feel like I was in control. Therefore, I sabotaged relationships with females that were good to me and for me. (I want to take this time to say to anyone I dated that I may have hurt, I am sorry for the pain I caused you. I pray that pain has not kept you from freely loving others.) If I found the slightest thing wrong, I would leave them. But I wouldn't just leave them, I had a twisted way of making things so uncomfortable and so horrible, that they would eventually break up with me. All because I felt like it was only a matter of time before they realized I wasn't worth their time.

At that seminar, I realized how this was playing out in my current marriage. I found myself constantly nagging about things my wife was not doing. Yet, I knew nagging was not drawing her closer, but pushing her away. I realized I was pushing her away to prepare myself for if she ever wanted to leave me, then I wouldn't be too attached. It's almost as if I was preparing myself for her to leave me even though I was the one forcing her to do it. My misinterpretations of my dad not keeping his promise was costing me my marriage and I didn't even know it.

I remember calling my wife and apologizing profusely. After I explained my revelation to her, she understood. That night, I made a promise to her that I would no longer push her away in fear of her leaving me. I also promised God that I would stop complaining about what she was not doing and focus on what I needed to do. I told God I would be the husband he called me to be regardless of what she was or was not doing. My responsibility as a husband had no bearing on what kind of wife she was being. I recognized God would hold me responsible for the husband I was being and not for what kind of wife she was or was not being.

That night changed my marriage. It wasn't a change that could be seen from the outside. The difference was a change on the inside. For months, I focused on being a better man and being the best husband I could be. I was not perfect, but I kept giving it all I had. But it looked like she was not changing at all. However, I kept being a good husband. And almost eight to nine months later, I saw the change in her. All the things I had been praying about her changing, she was doing. I think my consistency showed her she could trust that my change was permanent. But I also believe God wanted me to focus on myself while He was focusing on her. When you work on changing you, God will change the things and people around you.

But this interpretation, "If I wasn't worth my father's time, then I wasn't worth anyone's time, " grew into an anger that I had come to live with. I had to conclude that I had not forgiven my father for the things he had or hadn't done. I used to think I forgave easily. I used to think I was blessed to let things go, forgive, and move on. I thought somehow, I had mastered forgiveness because I kept pursuing a relationship with my dad even after he hurt me time and time again. However, Landmark opened my eyes to the truth. Not mentioning a hurt and acting as if it did not happen is not the same as forgiveness. I was just doing the same thing he was doing to me. He would hurt me by not showing up and then I would stop calling him for a while which was my way of trying to hurt him back. Then I would call out of the blue and not mention what happened.

Yes, I still spoke to my dad from time to time, and we could still laugh and joke, but I hadn't truly forgiven him. If I was honest with myself, I was holding his mistakes, lies, and broken promises over his head as ransom or a manipulation tool. I was not good at forgiveness; I was good at compartmentalizing.

Forgiveness is giving a person a pardon or saying that person no longer must suffer consequences for their offensive actions. Compartmentalizing is a defense mechanism where you suppress thoughts and emotions. I hadn't removed expectations of my father suffering consequences, because I felt like my presence and pursuing a relationship was his consequence. My constant pursuit of the relationship served as a continual reminder to him that he messed up. I had a twisted subconscious way of punishing my father for all the hurt he caused me. I hadn't forgiven my father; I just learned my presence was his worst nightmare. The fact he couldn't get away from me was the punishment I was trying to inflict on him. I was like the monster in the scary movie that you can't get away from no matter how fast you run. I was a bad dream he couldn't wake up or escape from.

Whenever my dad would do something or say something I didn't like, I had to stop talking to him for a while or I would say hurtful things to him. I felt like him talking to me was a privilege. I felt like I was doing him a favor by still talking to him. Especially since most of my siblings didn't speak to him at all. I thought he should feel blessed to talk to me after all he'd done.

I was ashamed of myself. Here I was being self-righteous like I had not made any mistakes. I was holding things over his head that I wouldn't want anyone holding over my head. I thought I was a better man because I let him talk to me and because I still communicated with him. However, I was not being genuine, I was not a better man, I was acting like a little boy who wanted to get back at his dad by trying to make his dad feel guilty for what he had done.

I finally understood that I had traded in my victim clothes for prison guard clothes. I was keeping my dad in an emotional prison because of what he had done. And I didn't plan on letting him out until his time served had caused him to feel enough guilt and shame that would equal my pain and disappointment. There, I had the epiphany that you are still in prison, whether you are wearing prison clothes or guard clothes. The emotional prison I built for my dad trapped me in also. I saw a quote once that said, "Unforgiveness is like a prison that you put someone in. The only problem is you have to stay in there with them to keep them there."

This emotional prison had taken its toll on me. I always felt like I was one situation, one disagreement, one problem away from snapping. Holding on to unforgiveness did not make me feel powerful, it made me feel pathetic. The prison was hurting me more than him. Because now, I had not only become my father's prison guard, I had also become the one who was keeping us apart. It finally registered, my dad and I were both difficult to be in relationship with.

In some twisted way, I had become him. I was doing to him what he had done to me. My communication with my dad gave him a false sense of hope that we could connect. However, I knew I would fail to show up and connect on any deeper level than the surface. Oh, how the tables had turned. The victim had become the perpetrator. Unfortunately, my father was not my only victim. I had left a whole trail of people who thought my communication with them was a promise of connecting with me.

Like my father, I had a way with words. People gravitated to what I said. I knew how to treat people as if they were the only person in the world that mattered. I learned to listen to their hearts' dreams, desires, and pains. However, I knew I could not deliver on connecting my heart to theirs. I had become good at promising people my heart, but all they got were empty words. Sometimes the very thing you try your hardest not to become, you transform into it and sometimes even worse.

While at Landmark, the facilitator challenged us to call whoever we had hurt and ask them to forgive us. Not just an empty apology, but one that expressed how we now understand the trauma, hurt, disappointment, and impact that our actions or inaction caused them. I made my list and started making phone calls. I had so many phone calls to make. I was up all-night apologizing to people I had hurt. I started with my wife, mother, Irie, Racheal, best friend, ex-girlfriends, ex-wife, daughters, former pastor, and many others. I had never felt so vulnerable, guilty, embarrassed, and authentic in my life. This was the start of a new me. The me who could be open and truthful to the people I loved.

Do not get me wrong, apologizing was extremely exhausting. But it was the good kind of exhaustion, like after a good hard work out. I knew this hard work was going to pay off. It was a purge if you will. I was shedding so much weight. I felt lighter with each call. Like I could go and take off running in any direction and run for days. After I had finished my calls, I thought I was done. I thought I had talked to everyone I needed to apologize to. I crossed out all the names on my list. I went to sleep satisfied, knowing I had done the right thing. I was finally free from the weight of carrying the hurt I caused others. Little did I know I did not exhaust the complete list of people I hurt.

After some self-reflection during the next day's session, I was crying my heart out. I realized I left off my list one more person. I had gotten a revelation about him being the source of the pain I caused others, but not thought about how I needed to apologize to him for the pain I caused him. As soon as I went on my break that Saturday evening, I called my dad and apologized for holding on to all the pain, hurt, and disappointment I suffered. I asked him to forgive me for harboring unforgiveness in my heart and for holding everything he did and did not do over his head. I will never forget his response. He said," Rick, I forgive you. From now on, I'm going to be the father you need me to be."

At first, the thought that I needed to apologize to him was repulsive to me. He should be apologizing to me, right? However, I realized that whenever you begin to use your status as a victim to gain power over someone else, you are no longer a victim, but you become a perpetrator. And all perpetrators have victims whom they have knowingly or unknowingly hurt or harmed. No one is innocent when unforgiveness becomes the path you choose to travel.

As a result, when I traveled home, I also reached out to my former pastor and apologized for not allowing him an opportunity to be a part of my journey to starting a church. I just assumed he would disagree with me, but I at least owed him the right to refuse to be apart, instead of just assuming. He apologized to me for what he said and how he said it. We both realized we had made mistakes and were willing to move past them. I wished him well and he did the same for me.

When I left that seminar, I was ready to run forward. That weekend, I discovered my "why" for living. I found I stood for the greatness of others. Ever since I was a little boy, I cared about other people and wanted them to win, do well, and become the best versions of themselves. I was running toward pastoring because I had a heart to help other people even if that meant facing my fears. In a way, my heart to save other people also allowed me to be saved from my own past.

The difficult relationship with my dad may have caused me heartache and some pain. However, I realized that pain had purpose. The pain led me to seek out help. Which in turn, forced me to confront my own demons, deceptions, and lies that hurt others. Ultimately, compelling me to restore broken relationships and keeping me from destroying others. Remaining in a struggling relationship with my dad opened my eyes to my purpose of standing for other people's greatness. Sometimes the most difficult people in our lives can serve as unsung heroes in saving our lives.

Captain Jay Jonas knew what it was like to be saved because he had a heart to save someone else. During 9-11, that woman was determined not to go down another floor in that stairwell. After the building had collapsed on them, they realized that they were still alive by the grace of God. All the floors above them and below them were destroyed. The floor where the woman was being difficult and stubbornly refused to leave, was the only floor that remained standing. They were saved because they took the time to save someone else. They were saved because they stayed and struggled with someone who was complicated, hard to understand, and headstrong. Sometimes staying in a relationship with someone who is difficult may help you as much as them.

REFLECTIONS

Is there a relationship or relationships you are in where you would label that person as difficult? I know they have their issues, but you have no control over when or if those will change. Perhaps changing them is not your responsibility. The one thing you do have control over is your part in producing stress and unnecessary struggle in the relationship. Sometimes, when we are in a relationship with someone considered difficult, we can think we are there to help them. However, sometimes we are in their lives so they can help us grow.

Name someone who you are in relationship with that you have labeled difficult. Name what you think is difficult about them. Now name what you think others would say makes you difficult to be in relationship with. Take the 21-day challenge:

1.) Change those things in you that make you a difficult person to be in a relationship with.

2.) Do not tell the other person what you are doing.

3.) Do not complain about what the other person does or does not do.

Do you have a trail of hurt people from your past? Do you have people you know you have wronged? To clear your path going forward, you must go back and forgive and ask for forgiveness. Forgiveness allows you to see your future clearly without the past being in the way. The pain we have experienced becomes a lens in which we view the current world and current relationships. Some of us are seeing through the lens of betrayal, deceit, abandonment, rejection, and other emotional trauma. Each of those lenses skew or distort what we see and hear and can cause us to hurt others. Which is why asking for forgiveness provides a way to clear your conscience. Whether we realize it or not, the hurt we cause others, hurts us. The harm we cause others has a way of eating us up from the inside out. When we inflict pain on others, we lose a piece of our compassion for others. With some help from a counselor or trusted advisor we can discover the origin of the emotional injury and how to navigate healing. When we focus on getting things right with others, God has a way of healing us from the inside out. Yes, it will be challenging, but it will pay off in the end.

FIFTEEN

"Trust your instincts not your insecurities"

JUST WHEN WE STARTED SOMETHING SPECIAL

Have you ever had a hard time starting something? We often have a hard time starting something new that we know will be difficult and perhaps involve a long commitment. Such things as working out, a new diet, meditating, or quitting something like a bad habit are always difficult to find the motivation to get started. We are waiting on something that inspires us or some epiphany that is so great that we spring into action. However, I heard someone say, "Motivation does not usually come before you get started, but after you have started something." We should not let the lack of motivation stop us from initiating something new. The initiation itself will eventually produce the motivation needed to continue.

I have learned that forgiveness and reconciliation are a journey that we must start, not because we are motivated, but because it is necessary. It is a necessary journey filled with ups, downs, plot twists, antagonists, and unexpected antithesis; not to mention its share of ghosts, skeletons, unspoken grief, and misunderstandings. Unfortunately, my father and I were not exempt from all those things catching us by surprise and almost negating everything we had said and built.

My dad and I had started out doing great. We talked several days a week, every week. He was there, walking me through the complex process of starting the church. I kept him informed and updated on what was going on daily. I was so grateful that he wanted to be a part of the process. I thought this was the start of something really special.

We launched Sunday worship services and things were growing and moving fast for our church. Four months after we started the church, we planned a Pastor Installation service. I had asked my father to come and preach for the morning service of my installation. He came that morning and heard me give the new members class orientation. He listened so intently with this nod of what I thought was his approval. I felt like a million bucks because my dad was at my church and was listening to me speak. I felt like we had come full circle. It was truly an honor to have him there.

That morning service, he preached, and it was amazing. People gave their lives to Christ. People were excited and encouraged by the word he had given. On top of that, he was the first guest preacher to preach at our church. So many milestones were achieved that day. It was a perfect day, and I couldn't have written or dreamed it up any better.

The next day, I was thrown off when all hell broke loose. My dad called to ask why there wasn't more about him in the new member's packet. More specifically, why weren't there more positive things about him. Then, he asked why I had not invited him to our house. I was confused. The packet was not about him; it was about me and how the church came to be. And my dad had never come to our house before. Every time I had invited him, he insisted on staying in a hotel. I was so confused about where all of this was coming from. After a while, I got upset because he was upset about what I felt was nothing. He started shouting and I started shouting. Before I knew it, he said he was not going to talk to me anymore. And I said, "Fine, that's on you! I ain't got time for this!" I couldn't understand how he would start an argument after an almost perfect day.

I thought he was tripping and maybe was just having a bad day. I figured I would give him a few days to cool off. However, he still would not return my calls when I started calling. Why was he so upset? I had not done anything wrong. The more I went over the situation and the new member's packet, the more I realized he was not upset with me, he was upset with himself. The new member's packet was a reminder that he was not present in my life in so many key moments. But I still believed that he just needed time to cool off. After all, we were in a good place before this debacle.

Furthermore, several months ago, he had promised he would attend my graduation from Seminary, where I was receiving my Master of Divinity (MDiv). I just knew he would get over it by then. It was a month away. I was sure he would come to his senses in a couple of weeks.

Up to this point, he had attended all my graduations. He came to my high school and undergrad graduation. I knew he wouldn't miss this one. He was happier about the MDiv than I was. But after that conversation, I did not hear from him. Subsequently, he missed my graduation. It was like he dropped off the face of the earth. How could he miss a big moment like this? Was he that upset? It seemed like a bad dream because I couldn't understand what would make him that mad at me.

One night, I had a dream. I dreamed I was at a church with my former pastor. He and I had some heated discussions. Then, we began to have a deeper conversation where we apologized to each other. We were reaching out to hug each other when something strange happened. I knew I was hugging my former pastor, but something seemed different about his back. Something seemed familiar, but I could not pinpoint who or what it was.

It was not my former pastor that I was hugging. It was someone else who was awfully familiar. I remember crying in the dream. It was as if I had finally found what I had been searching for my whole life. When I pulled away to see who it was that I was hugging, it was my father. He was smiling at me and saying he was proud of me.

I woke up the following day and decided to call him every week until he answered. But I did not just say this to myself, I made that promise to God that I would call him until he answered. Once or twice every week, I would call and leave a message. *"Hey, Dad, it's Rickey Jr. Just thinking about you. Hope all is well. Give me a call when you get a chance. I love you."*

May, June, July, August, September, October, the first week of November, still no answer. Seven months had gone by, and there was still no answer or call back–total silence. However, I would still leave a message every week. *"Hey, Dad, how are you? This is Rickey Jr. Just thinking about you. Hope all is well. I love you. Give me a call when you get a chance."* The phone rang but no answer. The first week of November went by, no answer. The second week, no answer. I told myself I was done. I'm not going to call him anymore. I've done my part. He doesn't want to have a relationship with me that's on him. But as soon as I came to myself, I felt something inside reminding me of my promise to God that I would call him until he answered. The third week went by and still no answer. The fourth week, I called him and by this time, I think it's pointless, but I'm doing it out of habit and because I said I would. It was literally on the last ring; I know this because I got used to counting how many rings it took before his voicemail would come on. Out of nowhere I heard, "Hello." I was shocked. I almost didn't say anything because I couldn't believe he answered. I muddled out, "Hey, Dad!"

What he said next would take away any joy or celebration that I had about finally hearing him answer. He said "Hey, Rick. What's going on? I knew you would need me. I had a dream, and in the dream, you were a little boy again and you were telling me you needed me."

I immediately felt like I was on fire! My blood was boiling. I did not even know I could get angry that quick. The audacity of him saying something like that after not answering my calls for all those months. It took everything in me and what I didn't have, to restrain from cursing him all the way out. I know it was nothing but the Holy Spirit that kept my mouth closed. I just don't think I'm that strong. What I wanted to say would not come out. However, what I did not want to say somehow flew out of my mouth, "Dad, you're right. I do need you." Little did I know, this statement would be true in more ways than I could ever begin to explain.

The truth of the matter was, we needed each other. We both were conduits that God chose to use to bring healing to each other. We both had open wounds that left us vulnerable and subject to living subpar lives as men, husbands, fathers, ministers, pastors, and as followers of Christ. God orchestrated it so that I would be his healing salve and he would be mine, so a generational curse of fathers not connecting to their children would end here!

The enemy did not want to see us emotionally well, so he did everything he could to keep us apart. My dad eventually told me that he listened to every voicemail I sent. My perseverance is what gave him the courage to answer. He later admitted he was wrong for getting that upset over something that was not my fault. He realized the new member's packet reminded him how he failed his children. He didn't know how to express or articulate that, so he tried to push me away by being upset. But he couldn't escape from God because God had been convicting him through his dreams. So even though he wasn't answering my calls, I was still on his mind.

Too often, we think we must force people to do the right thing. If we are consistent enough and let God work on them, sometimes they eventually come around with a little bit of God's nudging. We slowly began to talk once a week to rebuild our relationship. But something inside of me said we needed to do more.

After a few weeks of us building some consistency in our communication, I suggested that if we are going to reconcile fully, we need to come together, face-to-face, and talk. No distractions, no other people, no other family, just him and I. So, I suggested we meet somewhere between Indianapolis and Atlanta. We decided on Nashville, Tennessee.

I knew there was a possibility he would try to skip out or make up an excuse not to come. Therefore, I was prepared. And just as I suspected, he called three days before we were to meet.

"Rick, man I think I got a gout flare-up. Man, I think my knee is swollen. I'm not going to be able to come," he said

He must have forgotten how persistent I could be.

"Well Dad, if you don't come, I'll just come to Atlanta."

With hesitation he said, "Let me see what I feel like in a couple of days."

He called me back the next day and said, "Man, you don't have to come all the way here. I'll meet you in Nashville."

What happened that weekend was nothing short of a miracle. Three whole days alone, just me and my dad. I decided to listen and understand instead of talking to be understood. Stephen Covey says, "If you want to be understood, you must first take the time to understand."

After we checked into the hotel, we decided to get something to eat. He was a big fan of Waffle House. It was not my favorite place, but I just wanted to spend time with him. As I sat there at the table, listening to and learning about him, it felt like I was also learning about myself. There were so many things I did not know about myself that I learned by listening and watching him, such as, wearing my feelings on my face and my sleeve because our hearts were so big. When your heart is big, feelings can't be hidden, it shows up physically, as well as, emotionally.

When you don't know your parents, there is so much you do not know about yourself. The stories he told me were my own. The pain he had was my own. The temptations he experienced were my own. The fear he had was my own. We were more alike than I ever could have imagined. It was as if I finally got the opportunity to meet my real dad. The real him that did not come with commentaries from others or stories I made up because I didn't have all the information. I no longer had to fill in the blanks, he was filling them in for me.

I finally understood why he did some of the things he did. I understood why he reacted the way he did to my siblings and me. I'm not saying it made me feel better about what happened, but I, at least, could say I understood. But one of the greatest things I discovered was that my dad did not think I was not worth his time. He did not think I was not valuable enough for his time. He said something that blew me away. He wouldn't show up because he felt like we didn't need him.

He said, "Rick, the reason I wouldn't come around or talk is because I felt like y'all didn't need me. Your mom had gotten remarried and y'all were doing so well in life. I felt like y'all didn't need me. The more successful y'all became, the more I felt like y'all did it without me. So, I felt like there wasn't a reason for me to be there for y'all. I would only mess it up. I had made so many mistakes with y'all. I thought I would never get another chance to get it right. I fell into a state of depression. I wanted to end my life. I had a gun in my hand and decided to call a hotline. I could no longer deal with what I had done to your mother and to y'all. I had to start seeing a therapist. She is the one who helped me to finally answer my phone and talk to you.

I was telling the therapist that you kept calling. I couldn't understand why you would want to talk to me. I had messed up again. You were doing so well with your own family and church and degrees. I asked my therapist, 'Why does he keep calling me?' She said, 'It's not the grown man who keeps calling you, it's the little boy in him who still wants his father.' And it was then that I realized, I'm still his dad. Regardless of what I did or did not do, I'm still your dad. There is still something I can give you and be to you."

I was at a loss for words. My dad was so transparent and vulnerable. I saw him bare his soul to me. And I realized the very things I thought would bring my father around was the very thing that was pushing him away. I thought me doing well in sports, getting my education, and my success in ministry would bring my father around, but all it did was push him away. My success became a reminder that he was not there for us and for him, a sign that we didn't need him. Sometimes the misinterpretation of our plans can push a person further away rather than drawing them closer.

I didn't realize how far we were away from each other. I had no idea my dad dealt with depression. But at the same time, what my dad shared explained how much we were alike, because I had dealt with depression and suicidal thoughts. There was something encouraging about knowing my dad may have had a hard external shell, but the inside was sensitive and caring. My dad opening up to me confirmed that he had a heart and cared about me. I was so grateful that he reached out for help during the lowest point in his life. Him calling that hotline saved his life. And the help he received from his therapist saved our relationship.

The truth is, I asked myself the same question my dad asked his therapist. Why did I keep calling my dad when he was rejecting me? In me, the grown man wanted to let go, be done with him, cut him off, and move on. However, the little boy in me, who used to touch my dad's hand on the pew, the one who admired and wanted to be like his dad, still wanted his father. This time I was grateful I allowed the little boy in me to lead and not the grown man. Because of that little boy in me, I got a chance to reconnect with my dad again.

He told me how he didn't think we wanted him around. He was convinced that he had messed up too many times for us to forgive him. He felt like our life would be better without him. But I told him that he is still our dad no matter what. I pressed a little deeper and asked why he felt like that. He said it was because we had Irie in our lives. He felt like because we had our stepdad, that was the reason we were doing so well. He felt like if we were doing that well in life without him, then we did not need him.

I reassured my father that Irie had a place in our life and had taught us things that were important to us being who we are. But the foundation we had, came from our dad. He placed in us the drive, the will, the spiritual fervor, the heart to help others in need, and the desire to please God. There was always room for our dad. I told him there were things Irie could not teach us because the two of them had two different life experiences. I had the best of both worlds because I had a dad in Irie who taught me about practical life experiences, but my biological dad taught me about spirituality and ministry. It did not have to be either/or; there was room for both in my life.

On the second and third nights, we talked about dreams. We were both dreamers. Our dreams were often warnings, symbols, or something about the future or what would happen. He shared with me dreams he had never told anyone else. He told me two of his dreams he never understood. One was of him carrying large fruits. And the other was him going to the bank with a million-dollar check. But the check didn't have his name on it. When he got to the teller, he quickly wrote his name on it. The teller looked at him and said, "Why did you do that? I know who you are. You didn't have to write your name on it."

I did not understand or have an interpretation of the second dream. However, as soon as he shared the first dream something came to me. I told him the fruit represented his children. We are the fruit of his loins. I shared that the dream was that his fruit would be great and big. He said, "You know what, I never thought about it like that. You are so right." He was grinning from ear to ear. We were in the zone, on one page for the first time in our lives. We were just moving through from one subject to the next seamlessly.

Somehow, we started talking about sports and he told me about him being on the wrestling team in high school. I knew he was on the team, and was undefeated at some point, but that was the extent of my knowledge. He shared that he was undefeated, but he quit because he was disappointed that none of his family would attend his matches. He thought being good at wrestling would get his family's attention and they would show up to watch him. But his family still didn't come. This sounded all too familiar. I was doing the same thing to him. I was trying to get his attention through sports. I thought sports was a way to get his approval. It all made sense. He did not show up at most of my sporting events because that was what he experienced. Unfortunately, he repeated what his family did to him. The importance of showing up for other people was hard because people did not show up for him. Therefore, him coming to watch me wrestle that one time in high school and play football once in college was more than what he had received. He had shown up more for me than his parents had for him. What an unfortunate, awful generational curse.

That weekend, I realized my dad was not the sum of his mistakes...he was so much more. He was not a monster; he was a man who had a little boy in him who was traumatized and scared just like me. I had suspended him in time in this picture of what I thought he was based on what he did. I did not realize that he was so young when everything happened between him and my mom (he was just in his twenties and early thirties). Even in that, he was so much more than those rough moments.

I received my revelation that weekend that my dad was a good man who had made some bad decisions. The fact that he came this far and was in my life the way he was had miracle written all over it. I had to free him from this prison bondage that I had put him in based on his decisions as a younger man. How could I judge him? I had made my own mistakes in my twenties and early thirties. I had my own demons and skeletons in the closet. I had suspended him in time. It was as if I had pressed pause and he was stuck on a screen in mid-motion. Even though time had gone on, I still saw him as the man I knew as a child. But that was not fair. I realized I needed to press play and allow him to show up as he was in the present. When I did, he became much more real to me, and I was able to learn from him. But more importantly, we could touch each other, and both left different.

We both walked away from that weekend having new perspectives about each other and how valuable our relationship was. We both had a greater respect for each other as men. We broke down some great walls that had kept us apart all those years. Now we could see each other for who we were instead of who we thought each other was. That weekend was the start of something special.

A few weeks after our trip my dad started complaining about a pain in his stomach. He told me he was riding his motorcycle one day and his vision became blurry. He went in for some testing and the results said he was developing diabetes. He started taking some medication for diabetes, but he knew something else was going on. I suggested he go for more testing. If he was taking the medication and was still in pain, it had to be something else. He had more extensive tests done, and they called him and said the doctor wanted to see him in person to give him the results.

"Dad, I would like to go with you when you go to see the doctor."

"Ok, Rick, I would like for you to come."

A few minutes later, he called me back and said, "No, let me and my wife, Georgia, go to this one. We need to find out what is going on first."

At first, I just kept saying, "Are you sure?" And he kept replying in a shaky, unsure tone, "Yes, I'm sure."

As I sat and thought about it more, something didn't sit right with me. So, I talked to my wife and then called my sister, Racheal. They both advised me that I needed to be more assertive. After all, we had started something special, and I was not going to allow his fear to stop me from being there for him in a time he needed me most. Consequently, I called him back and explained how he and his wife were not in this by themselves. He was my dad, and I wanted to be there with him when he received whatever the news may be. He finally gave in and said, "Yes, Rick, I want you to come. And I'm actually glad you are coming."

When we got in the room with the doctor, he showed us the X-ray picture of the black area on his pancreas. The doctor said, "I'm sorry to tell you this, but you have stage 3 pancreatic cancer. It is one of the most aggressive cancers there is. Most people do not live past a year at your stage."

We asked the doctor if surgery was an option to remove it.

"Honestly, at this point it is not. Because of where the cancer is located. There is a major artery next to where the cancer is. We don't want to risk having surgery and hitting that artery because you would die. Perhaps we can do chemotherapy and try to shrink the cancer and then hopefully, surgery would be an option."

In front of my dad, I was strong. I encouraged him and sat in silence with him. However, on the inside, I was praying to God. I had just gotten my dad back. I pleaded with the Lord not to take him away. It seems like every time we took a few steps forward, we would take three or four back. And now, cancer. We had just started something special. Why cancer? Why now?

I wasn't ready to lose him. I wasn't ready to live without him. I hadn't received everything I needed. I still had questions. I still had a hole in me that was not completely filled. A wound not fully healed. I prayed, "Lord, you can't take him right now. He's too young. I thought there would be more time! This is not the right time! God, I still need him!" I drove home that weekend thinking about how short life can be. How quickly things can change. We believe, or at least, act as if we have all the time in the world, but we don't.

REFLECTIONS

We never know when something will come along and threaten to end something good that we just started. Don't waste time waiting on the motivation to start something special with the people you love. Don't waste your energy fighting with people you love. Don't waste opportunities to connect with your family and friends because of something petty. Don't waste moments you will never get back because you choose to hold on to your anger about things that won't matter in the end.

Tomorrow is not promised, do what you need to do today. Fix whatever relationships you need to fix today. Don't be responsible for creating your regret. Don't miss out on some of the best moments of your life because you can't let go of a few brief moments of pain that happened earlier in your life. Don't let your pain and disappointment ruin your chance at starting something special.

I know you may be looking or waiting for the right motivation before you spring into action on what you are thinking about right now or who you are thinking about. However, the motivation has already been given. The fact that you are thinking about that person is the motivation. It is the inspiration, the tug, the nudge, the sign you need. Trust your instincts not your insecurities. Trust your faith rather than your fear. This may be the moment you can't get back. You will look back on the time and either be grateful you acted or regretful that you didn't.

In fact, stop what you are doing now and make that phone call, text, write that email, go to that person's house, or even go to their job if you have to and get it right, right now! Not only is life too short, but this is too important to your soul and their soul to leave this up to chance or "one day." The only moment we have promised to us is right now. Start something special right now!

SIXTEEN

"I had to adjust my expectations to maximize my relationship with my dad"

MY DAD BECAME MY CONFIDANT AND COUNSELOR

Have you ever underestimated someone? Perhaps you thought they could only do so much, and you found out that they could do much more. One day, I played basketball with my nephew Dominique at the gym. I was picking my team when a new guy walked in. He was scrawny, medium height, and did not look like he could play basketball. He approached me and asked to be on my team. I looked him up and down and hesitated. He must have noticed because he quickly said, "Man, if you pick me, you won't regret it. Nobody in this gym plays harder than I do. Please, man, pick me up." Because of that speech, I picked him. I still didn't know if he could play or help the team.

We started playing and immediately, he was getting rebounds, jumping over everybody, stealing the ball, and shooting three-pointers. I was floored by his performance. I didn't expect that. He was better than I could have ever hoped for. We benefitted from everything he brought. What he gave was more than we expected.

That day, I learned to not judge a book by its cover. I also discovered that sometimes the fantasy we create about what we think we want is not always better than the real thing. Sometimes the real thing doesn't always show up in the package we want, but the gift inside is far more valuable than the package it comes in. We just have to decide to look past the package and the delivery to receive the gift.

I wish I could tell you that the package my dad came in was nice, neat, and consistent, but it wasn't. After we met in Nashville, I wish I could tell you that we lived happily ever after. I wish I could tell you that we never had any more issues, and everything was perfect from then on, but that would be a lie. I learned reconciliation is not an event, it is eventually. Reconciliation doesn't happen because you had one good conversation or memorable moment. Reconciliation happens because you continue to put in the time and effort required to reconnect and create a new relationship.

The relationship with my father seemed to be going well all things being considered. My family knew my father had cancer, and that time was limited. We were hoping and praying for a miraculous healing, but we knew death was possible. My dad and I talked almost every day, but I knew he was a little out of it. And rightfully so, he was still trying to process the diagnosis of cancer.

The last year had gone by quickly. My first Pastor and Wife Anniversary was coming up. The church was still growing, and my daughters were getting bigger and bigger. Despite my father not feeling well, he told me he was not going to miss our first Pastor and Wife Anniversary. I was so excited and anxious to show him the new building we were leasing. I knew he would be impressed.

I told him he could either stay with us or we could get him a hotel. He didn't want to inconvenience us. He would rather stay in a hotel. Everything was set. The day he was to arrive, I called and called and couldn't get a hold of him. I thought *no, this is all too familiar.* He didn't answer.

The day of the anniversary came. I remember, I couldn't smile like I usually did because my dad didn't show up again. I was disappointed. My wife kept trying to cheer me up. I couldn't get out of the rut. I felt so bad because our church members were so happy for us, but I couldn't enjoy it because all I wanted was my dad to be there so he could see what God had done through us.

But this time was different. I wasn't angry, I was sad and concerned. I realized my dad didn't show up because he was sicker than he had led on to be. But he was also depressed. All the signs were there when we would talk on the phone. He sometimes seemed like he was not engaged in the conversation, distracted, and forgot things he normally stayed on top of. Him not showing up that time was different than the other times. I knew he was having a hard time dealing with his fear of dying.

I called him the next day to check on him. He apologized for not coming. He said he just didn't have the energy. Between the chemo and medication, he didn't feel like himself. I began to share how I had noticed that he seemed deeply depressed. He then shared how all he could think about was how it was over. He was going to die soon. He told me he stopped leaving the house, and even took his motorcycle back to the Harley Davidson dealership because he knew he would never be able to ride again. It finally registered to me that he was in worse shape than I had initially thought. This was much deeper than I could have imagined. I prayed with him and told him I would continue to pray with him about his depression. I also encouraged him to seek some counseling.

This situation was heartbreaking for me. I could only imagine what was going through his mind. I didn't know what to do or how to comfort him and make him feel better. The only thing I knew how to do was stay consistent, continue to pray, call him, and commit to seeing him every other month. I realized then that this would take much more work than I ever anticipated. Fairy tale endings are not real. If I wanted to be there for my dad, it would take everything I had to prove it.

A couple of months later, my dad started feeling much better. He was seeing a counselor and he started getting back to himself. I knew it would be a process, but I could start to see he was gaining a little hope. We would continue to talk daily, and I would share things that I was experiencing as a leader. One day, I called him and discussed a decision that I had made in ministry. I thought he would be excited about it with me. Instead, he began to critique and give all these cons to the decision. I was so frustrated that I said, "Why can't you just be happy for me? Why do you always have to be so negative?" Out of frustration, he replied, "Rick, I can't be who you want me to be. If you want me to be your dad, I have to be me. You have a fantasy in your mind of what kind of father you want me to be, but I'm not that person. This is who I am. Take it or leave it. I want to share the little bit of wisdom and knowledge I have, but I can't be someone else."

Those words stung, but they were true. I had been trying to get my father to be this fairytale dad I always wanted or imagined he would be. However, I asked God for my dad and that's exactly what I got. I had to decide to accept who he was and receive what he could give me or keep being disappointed because I expected more than he could give. Yes, there were some things about him I did not care for, but if I could learn to put that to the side, the good far outweighed the bad. The person who needed to change was not him, but me. I had to adjust my expectations to maximize my relationship with my dad. He had so much to give, and I had been wasting my time focusing on the few things he could not. One of the greatest gifts he had to give was great counsel and advice. I had to learn to listen to his heart behind his response. Because whether I understood it or not, his counsel always came from him wanting the best for me.

I did not know it at the time, but I would need his counsel sooner than I thought. My brother, Ryan, was going through his own sickness with drugs and mental health. He had gotten married, and they had a daughter, Heava-Scyia. One night, he got into a fight with his wife and the police were called. When the police arrived, they arrested his wife because she had a warrant out for her arrest. My brother told the police that he couldn't care for his daughter by himself, and someone needed to come get her. The police notified child services and they took Scyia to foster care.

When my mother heard about it, she immediately went there to get her out. Scyia stayed with her and Irie for several months. Then, she reached out to me about keeping Scyia in my care. My mom expressed how they were older, and it was harder for her to keep up with her. I discussed it with Robyn, and she told me it was up to me. She would support whatever decision I made.

Then, I called my dad and told him what was going on. I thought he should know about Ryan and what was going on with Scyia. He began to share his experience in the foster care system with me. When he was a little kid, he told me his father went to work and his mother would bring different men over to the house. The bedroom door to her room would not completely close and he saw her sleeping with these men. She was also involved with the man across the street.

Consequently, one day, the man across the street got so jealous that he came over and stabbed my grandmother in the head seven times with a screwdriver. She was rushed to the hospital and was in a coma for months before she regained consciousness. As a result, my father and his six siblings were taken into the foster care system.

He pointed out that it was in the foster care system where he was molested, beaten, forced to be with adult women, and even put in a dog cage. He begged me not to allow Scyia to return to the foster care system. He said, "Rick, whatever you do, get her out of that system!" After hearing his story, there was no way I could allow Scyia to stay in the system.

My wife and I decided to have Scyia move in with us. We also became licensed foster care parents. But, that was not enough. We wanted to get her completely out of that system. We knew the only way to do that was to adopt her. Therefore, after a lengthy process, my brother and his wife gave up their parental rights. They both courageously accepted that they were not in any position to take care of Scyia. I say "courageously" because I know both were afraid to let her go, but they knew she had a better chance in life with us than if she stayed with them, especially, while they were still on drugs.

It was difficult to navigate the complexities of adopting Scyia and processing that she was no longer our niece, but our daughter. It was hard for her to make the transition as well. Even though we referred to Scyia as our daughter, she still called us Aunt and Uncle. My dad was the one who suggested that I give her the option of calling me Uncle Rickey or dad. When I gave her that option, she chose to call me dad. I think part of it was, she did not want to be different than our other daughters. Particularly, while at school with Aaliyah and Melodey. But regardless of what the reason was, I was proud to be called her dad. It was my honor and my joy to be her dad as well. And just like that, my love expanded to include Scyia, just like it did with our other daughters.

I was so grateful for my father's counsel and him being vulnerable and transparent in sharing his own unimaginably traumatic experience. That experience also began to shed light on why my dad had certain unhealthy coping mechanisms. It also explained why he was so closed off emotionally for years and why it was so hard for him to receive love. Love, for him, had always been transactional. Meaning, I give you something and you give me something in return. In other words, he did not believe he deserved the love of others if he did not do something, first, to earn it. I believe this is why he distanced himself from his family whenever he made a mistake, because he didn't feel like he deserved our love. Which explains why he struggled with understanding he didn't have to do anything as a father to earn our love, he already had it. We never required him to do anything, all we ever wanted was just him.

When my dad showed up just the way he was, he always had encouraging words or advice. That encouraging word or advice made you feel like you could do anything. One day during a random conversation about ministry, he asked me if I had thought about going back to school to get my doctorate. I chuckled at first and told him that it sounds like it would be a lot of work. I wasn't sure if I could or wanted to do all that work with classes, reading, researching, and writing a dissertation. But he said, "Rick, I think you could do it. Just look into it when you get a chance." After that conversation, I said ok, but never really thought much about it.

A few months later, as I was leading worship at Christian Theological Seminary, the chapel director, Brenda Freije, pulled me to the side and asked, "Did you know they are starting a new doctoral program here? They have several new concentrations. One of them is for leadership. I think you should apply." I looked at her and laughed. Me, I thought, a doctor? My dad had just advised me about getting my doctorate. I thought I couldn't go to college at one point in time. And now I had a master's degree and was talking about possibly applying for a doctorate. However, my question was could I juggle the responsibilities as a husband, father, pastor, singer, and student?

I started looking at the requirements for the doctoral program. On the surface it seemed manageable. The degree was designed for a student to go at their own pace. There were only a few required courses and the rest of the courses you could choose yourself. It started looking more appealing to me. I thought, maybe I could do this. I should at least try.

My dad, who did not go to college, received an honorary doctorate from a seminary. He said he received it for his work in the community. He was proud of that honorary doctorate and put Dr. Rickey A. McCray Sr., on everything he did. He was the first Dr. Rickey McCray in the family.

I told my wife about the doctoral program. She excitedly responded, "Do it! Yes, you got this babe!" Then, I told my dad about it, and he was ecstatic! He said, "Rick, you gotta do this man! You gotta put in the application. You can do this! I believe in you!" He then said something I would never forget. "Now, there is going to be a real Dr. Rickey McCray in the family. You are going to earn this doctorate." It was a proud moment for me. That is what I needed to step out of my comfort zone and be courageous. My dad always gave great counsel and advice.

The application process for the doctoral program took a little while for me to complete. I had to get several references and a letter from our church and complete all the writing requirements. The questions in the writing portion of the application forced me to be intentional and future focused. I had to think about where I wanted to be in five to ten years. Those questions made me look in the mirror and ask myself, "Why do you want a doctorate? What do you think having a doctorate will accomplish for you? Are you doing this for you or for others?" When I added it all up, I concluded, this is for me! I knew other people would be proud of me, but them being proud of me was a byproduct, not the reason. After having several people proof my work, I hit send!

A month later I received a letter from the doctorate program in the mail. I was nervous as all get out! I was sweating bullets. I grabbed a letter opener and slowly and carefully slid it across the top of the envelope so as not to rip the sides. I even peeked inside to see if I could see some key words that would indicate if I got accepted or not. I pulled the letter out and slowly unfolded the paper. All I could read was the first few sentences. It said, "Hello, Rickey A McCray Jr. We are pleased to announce you have been accepted into the DMin program at Christian Theological Seminary." I screamed at the top of my lungs!! I just kept saying, "Thank you, Jesus! Thank you, Jesus! Thank you, Jesus!!"

I ran to my phone and called five people; my wife, mother, father, big sister, and Irie. Being accepted into the program was huge for me. I never thought I could go to college and now I was going to one day be a doctor.

Only God could do something like that!! Everyone was so happy for me. My dad told me, "From now on, I'm calling you Dr. Rickey McCray." There is nothing more gratifying than knowing the people you love are proud of you.

I always had support from my mother. She was the one telling me I could do anything! When I married my wife, Robyn, I gained a best friend and confidant. My sister, Racheal, was my ride-or-die. She was going to be with me to the wheels fell off. I had other friends and family who were right there cheering me on. My dad was the missing piece to the puzzle. I had always had all these other important pieces in my life, but my dad helped complete my circle of support I needed for the next leg of the journey! With my "Amen" corner intact, I felt like I could do anything. I knew I was ready to take on whatever challenges I would face getting this doctorate.

But there were still some other things that I needed to face. Something I had been trying to ignore and put off. One of them was the fear and anxiety I felt whenever I went back to my old church. It wasn't anything anyone did or what they said, it was the fact I did not feel validated because of how I left. Validated meaning legit or affirmed by the church leadership. However, that would change after a scripture and one phone conversation.

One day, I was reading the Bible and came across the scripture Jeremiah 3:15. *"And I will give you pastors according to mine heart, which shall feed you with knowledge and understanding."* (KJV) I realized that pastors are called by God and not by people. Therefore, I did not need anyone's permission but God's. That was my first revelation. My second came when my dad called me out of the blue as I was going to my former church for a funeral. He said, "Rick, I was just up praying, and the Lord told me to reach out to you and tell you that no one can make you feel inferior unless you give them permission. Stop giving them permission." Immediately, I knew what that meant, and I took back the power that I had given to people who did not understand my calling to pastor. I had come to myself, and it was as if I remembered who I was. That day, my confidence was restored. I walked into the church with my head held high. I no longer felt like I had anything to prove.

That day, I gained some understanding that my experience was never about what anyone else had done, it was about me learning to believe in myself. I had to learn to see myself the way that God had seen me. I had to see myself as a pastor, preacher, and leader. That conversation with my dad was him counseling me to open my eyes and help me believe I was who God saw me as.

My newfound confidence spilled over into a greater vision for our church. I started seeing our church as building and property owners. We had been leasing a building for three and a half years. I had been in prayer about us having our own. I had heard about some church buildings that were for sale. I went and looked at one that I thought would fit us. The sanctuary was not that large, but the rest of the building was considerably large. I liked the layout and scheduled for our leaders to take a walk-through. I heard the murmurs and the whispers of "can we afford this?" or "Pastor this is really big isn't it?" I said, "Yes, but we can grow into it." I had big visions for utilizing the other space in the building. I had a vision of a shelter, food pantry, leasing space to other churches, and a school. However, I left that viewing with the leaders discouraged because they couldn't see it, too.

A few days later I was talking with my dad about something at church and he said, "Man, I forgot to tell you about my dream I had the other day. You were getting ready for church, and I was with you. But there were some leaders from your church at the house with us. You were already dressed, but they were still getting ready. You became anxious because they weren't ready, and you decided to leave them. Then, you walked into this building that looked good on the outside, but behind the walls and cabinets were termites and holes in the wall. Then I woke up."

He went on to explain that he thought it was a warning. He told me, "Man, you are ready, but the people are not ready, yet. And you are trying to walk into something that is not what it seems on the outside. The outside looks good, but the inside is rotted."

Immediately, I knew the dream was about the building my leaders and I had just visited. What was crazy, is there was no way of him knowing about the building or the leader's reactions because I had not told him about it yet. I took his counsel and advice, and I did not pursue that building. I talked to my leaders about getting us in a place to be ready to purchase a building. It gave us a chance to get on one accord.

After the leaders and I got on the same page, we began a fundraising campaign to purchase a building. It was highly successful. People gave and were excited about purchasing our own building. One day, while walking in the building we were leasing, I heard God say, *'Purchase the building you are in.'* Honestly, I had never really thought about it, but it did make sense. The building we were leasing had four units in it. We were leasing out two units and the other two units had tenants. Which meant, their rent would pay for the mortgage and part of the utilities. It was a great business plan. I spoke with the leadership, and they were on board. I reached out to the owner, and he agreed to sell the building to us.

That day, I started walking around the building praying. I promised God I would walk until we purchased the building. I imagined it might be a couple of months. However, a couple of months turned into six months. And when we finally closed on the building, I decided to keep walking and praying. I realized that I needed a deeper prayer life to have wisdom and discernment as not just a pastor, but as a building owner and landlord. I knew that this next level would require greater leadership from me. But, I was also confident that we had capable people on our leadership team, and I had a dad who was also a great advisor, even though I was unsure how much longer he would be with us.

My dad had stepped up and became his own kind of father to me. He continued to give me raw, critical, and sometimes abrasive advice. However, it was always truthful, honest, and helpful. When I learned how to change the way I heard and received the message, I was always better for it. But more importantly, I had to learn to trust my father. I had to trust that his words came from a genuine place of love and concern for me in his heart. When I trusted him, I made better decisions.

I'm glad I made the decision to choose to accept my dad for who he was over the fantasy I had created. Yes, the fantasy dad I created in my mind gave me what I wanted, but the real dad gave me what I needed. If I'm honest, what I wanted was for him to stroke my ego, but what I needed was for someone to hold me accountable. And it is in giving me what I needed that I matured, grew up, and learned what accountability and responsibility really looked like.

REFLECTIONS

Who have you been upset and frustrated with because you have expected more than they could give? Who have you been wanting to stroke your ego, and make you feel good, instead of keeping you accountable and having convictions about what you are doing? Don't miss out on all you could receive from them because you're obsessed over what you can't. They are more valuable to you if they are being themselves than if they are being who you want them to be. In other words, don't limit their value in your life based on what you think you want from them, but rather what they have to give you.

Take some time and reflect on who that person is in your life and identify what they have to offer. Perhaps it's advice, encouragement, truth, accountability, redirecting, a critical thinker, a strategist, a realist, a problem solver, a presence, honest feedback, a person who asks questions, or someone who just listens. Whatever they have to offer, it will be helpful for you on your journey to becoming all you were created to be.

SEVENTEEN

"He stood on those beliefs even in the face of the worst news"

HE'S MORE THAN JUST MY DAD

I always wondered what people meant when they said, "You're only human?" The phrase always seemed to be in a negative context where someone made a mistake or failed at something. I grew to believe that phrase was synonymous with being weak and vulnerable. I saw it as an excuse to justify poor behavior or performance. Therefore, being human to me meant you were less than you had the potential of being.

However, the older I got, the more that phrase began to take on a new meaning. I realized that what it meant to be human was much more complicated. Being human meant we were weak in some areas of our lives, but we could also be strong in others.

We could be vulnerable in one area and guarded in another.

We could be a follower when uncertain, but a great leader when familiar with other areas.

We could be rude in one instance and the kindest person in another.

We can be filled with doubt about one thing, but full of faith regarding something else.

We could be all things at different times and sometimes simultaneously.

Being human did not mean we were restricted to being who we had always been. We have many layers to us. We have our personalities and what others could see from short encounters, but more layers expressed, beliefs, fears, joys, and deepest desires. Those deeper layers were usually something that not everyone got the opportunity to experience. However, if we spend enough time with certain people, we will see their humanity always exceeds our expectations.

After almost a year of chemotherapy with my father, we expected the cancer to reduce in size considerably. Through further X-Rays, the oncologist determined that the cancer had indeed decreased. However, the doctor also expressed how he had hoped the chemo would have decreased the mass even more to avoid surgery altogether. Nevertheless, now surgery was going to be the best option.

Surgery was set and it would be a difficult recovery. The doctor said they would take some veins from his legs to reroute them somewhere else. My dad would have to learn to walk again and take medication for the rest of his life. But the surgery could prolong his life. My dad agreed with the surgeon.

On the day of the surgery, Racheal, my dad's wife, Georgia, my dad's brother, Uncle Tony, and myself met the doctor in the consultation room. The doctor explained the procedure and how long it would take. He said we were looking at around 6-8 hours of surgery. We prayed with dad, and they took him back. He was in good spirits as always, but I knew he was scared.

After about an hour, the doctor came out and wanted to speak to us. He said, "I'm so sorry. We went in to look at everything before we started the surgery, and we noticed the cancer had metastasized. It has spread to his other organs. There is nothing we can do surgically. He should be awake in about an hour, and you can see him."

I asked, "What does this mean? If the cancer has now spread, what is his course of action?"

The doctor very bluntly said, "I'm sorry. It is now only a matter of time before your dad dies of this cancer. It has spread too much. It will continue to spread throughout his body. He may have six months to a year left to live. We will continue his chemo treatments. Which should hopefully buy us some time. But I can't guarantee how much. I'm so sorry."

I immediately called my wife, barely being able to speak. I was in a fog and only remember her saying, "Pick me up at the airport. I'm on my way." I was devastated. How could this be? The chemo had been going so well. The doctor said the cancer on his pancreas was shrinking. He was having surgery to prolong his life. And now they were giving him six months to a year to live. Reality had set in. This was no longer a question of *if,* but *when* my father would die.

Waiting on my dad to regain consciousness felt like the longest hour of my life. We were waiting on him to awake from the anesthesia. I was in foreign territory. I had never been here before, not knowing what to do, think, or say. I just walked around the hospital flooded with memories of all the times we've had. I wandered all over that hospital feeling like I was having an out-of-body experience. I knew I was physically walking, but I was out of it. I kept thinking, is this a dream? Was this really happening? After I worked so hard to get him back, was I really about to lose my dad?

The anesthesia wore off and my dad was awake. We were right there in the room by his side. He immediately asked if the surgery went well. We had to tell him what the doctor said. You could see the disappointment in his eyes. He was shocked. He just knew the cancer was going to be taken out. But what he did next showed his faith and strength. He said, "Y'all, it's gone be alright. I told y'all, I'm gone live until I die. This doesn't change anything for me. I'm gone keep living until I die."

Who we are and what we believe is what always emerges out of the most difficult times of our lives. My dad modeled this every day. It doesn't mean he was not afraid, but that he decided to be led by his beliefs rather than his fears. He stood on those beliefs even in the face of the worst news. Most people would have crumbled and changed their tune. However, one thing about my dad, his faith was not just something he proclaimed, it was something he practiced. The surgery did not go as planned, but my dad still believed God had a plan. This was another layer

I never knew my dad had. Although I was in new territory, at least I knew the territory would be navigated by faith.

In the end, I am glad the doctor suggested the surgery. If the doctor had not suggested the surgery, the surgeon would not have spotted the cancer in other places. If we had not found out about the cancer metastasizing, perhaps we would not have had time to prepare for what was now inevitable.

That same night, reinforcements came. My dad's favorite uncle, Uncle Tommy, and his wife, Aunt Beverly, drove from Memphis to Atlanta to be with us. Uncle Tommy was a mentor to my dad and a pastor in Memphis. They were extremely close.

I also picked up Robyn from the airport. Racheal's husband, Kevin, drove to Atlanta. All of us and my dad met in my Uncle Tommy's hotel room, where Uncle Tommy encouraged us all. He kept repeating to my dad what my dad said in the hospital, "Nephew, you gon' live until you die!" At first, it just sounded funny. We were all kind of chuckling. But the more I thought about it, the more profound it became. He was really encouraging my dad to live his best life, do all he wanted and could do, until he could not. If my dad was going to die, there was no reason for him to live like he was already dead. Especially if he was still alive and had strength in his body. My dad was not going to sit around and wallow and be depressed, he was going to do everything he wanted to do and then some. My dad kept repeating after my uncle with the mantra, "I'm gon' live until I die!"

We all decided to meet at Denny's for breakfast the following day before everyone headed home. My dad, Georgia, Uncle Tommy, Aunt Beverly, Uncle Tony, Rachel, her husband Kevin, my wife, and me. We crowded into this small Denny's to fellowship and encourage dad. I would discover that my dad and I still had some layers of emotional conflict to work out.

The service at Denny's was not the greatest. The place was filled to the brim, with people waiting inside and out. Our server had our table and several others. Usually, with a large group like ours, they would have someone help. However, they looked short-staffed. I knew we would be in for some bad service.

We waited for a long time to order and even longer for our food to come out. Some of the orders were mixed up or not correct at all. Eventually, the server got the orders right. During breakfast, everyone expressed heartfelt words of hope and affection. My father was very touched by all the genuine love and concern. The moment was beautiful. I believe it was just what he needed. We all shared how we would be with him every step of the way. We promised him that he would not be alone.

After all the touching words, the check came. I was going to pay for everyone's meal. However, my dad insisted that he pay. He was always generous like that. I finally conceded with one condition...that I would take care of the tip, and he agreed. I did what I normally do, and gave a big tip. My dad was upset that I had given the waitress a big tip. He felt like she didn't deserve a big tip because the service was horrible. I shared with him how I felt they were understaffed, which is why the service was bad. He began to get loud and tell me I didn't know what I was talking about and how unwise I was. How I was perpetuating bad habits of the waitress by rewarding her for bad work. I tried to calmly explain to him that I was just trying to do something different by blessing her, knowing it wasn't all her fault. But no matter what I said, he came back at me.

I didn't realize at that point, we were getting louder and more intense. Instead of me letting it go, I had a comeback for everything he said. We were now yelling at each other. My wife very slowly reached under the table and gently squeezed my hand. I quickly became aware of how embarrassing this was to my family. I was ashamed of myself. How? Why? What had happened? How did I let this get out of hand so quickly? Why did I need to argue and justify myself and my actions? This was inappropriate considering where we were and the news we had just received the day before.

I realized that I was still very confrontational with my father. I was trying to be assertive with him by getting into heated arguments because of my need to prove I was strong and independent. Winning at all costs was my strength and my weakness. Never wanting to be wrong or more importantly, always wanting to prove I was right, was my Achilles heel. And now I had embarrassed myself in front of my family and a restaurant full of strangers.

I felt so bad. Arguing with a man who had just been told he had a death sentence. I completely let things get out of hand. I took things farther than they ever should have gone. What kind of a person was I? Was I still that angry that I would stoop down to arguing with a man who was just given the worst news of his life? I knew then that I still had some aggression and pain still pent up inside. I needed to get rid of it. It had been a long time since my anger had reared its ugly head, but it was still there despite all the growing and developing I had done.

There was something else lurking beneath the anger. Perhaps even the source of the anger that day. I believe fear got the best of me. The fear of losing my father. I wasn't angry at him as much as I was angry because I felt powerless to help him. I was angry about losing him. I also believe he was not angry with me, he was afraid of dying. Fear got the best of us that day, but I would not allow fear to succeed at destroying what my father and I had built.

The next day, I called and apologized to my dad. I shared how inappropriate and out of line I was and expressed how I feared losing him. He told me he understood and was scared, too. But he reassured me, "Rick, we gone get through this together!" I also called my Uncle Tommy and apologized to him and my aunt. I shared with them how I was disrespectful, and there was no excuse. I should have been more discerning and aware of the emotional tension in the air. Besides, this was not the time to prove how strong I was, but how supportive I could be. Uncle Tommy forgave me and told me my dad would need me to get through the remaining time he had to live. He expressed how he sensed my dad was terrified and it would take us all coming together to walk with him in this season. He concluded with, "Nephew, your dad is gonna live until he dies."

My dad was not kidding about him living until he died. He called me up one weekend and said he was ready to get back on the motorcycle. He just needed to find another one he wanted to buy. I told him I would come there the following weekend and help him look for one. I also told my dad I secretly wanted a motorcycle, too.

The next weekend came, and I was on my way to Atlanta to look for motorcycles with my dad. While driving, I began to reminisce on my journey of wanting a motorcycle. It all started on my 30th birthday. I told my wife I had wanted a scooter ever since I was about 8 or 9 years old when a kid from my neighborhood got one. I'll never forget, it was black and purple. He was popular and especially with the neighborhood girls.

Everybody thought he was so cool. I remember asking him if I could ride it. He seemed to go so fast on it. He always said he would let me ride, but never did. I knew one day I wanted to get a moped or electric scooter.

I did have that scooter once. After my two weeks stay with my dad when I was 15 years old, I came home to a surprise. My mom had bought my brothers and I a motor scooter. It was a dream come true. And it was everything I always fantasized it would be. I remember getting on it and feeling free! The wind was in my face, I could go anywhere! I could go fast or slow.

And on top of that I loved how the other kids looked at me when I went flying by. It was one of the greatest feelings in the world. But, then, someone stole it and stole my dream of riding with it.

All this desire for riding was buried until my 30th birthday. I started feeling that urge again to be free. I told my wife I would buy a motorized scooter for my birthday. She laughed at me. She thought I was joking. Then, when she realized I was serious, she begged me, "Please don't get a scooter. You gon' look like you got a DUI or something. You know the only grown men who ride scooters are those who have lost their licenses."

We both laughed hysterically. She was right. She also, suggested, "Why don't you just get a motorcycle?" I don't ever remember thinking about a motorcycle. I told her, "Ok, I guess that would be a grown man scooter!" So, I quietly thought about it and put my motorized scooter dream on hold again.

It would be four years later before I considered it again. One day, before my dad got sick, he called me excited. He told me he bought a motorcycle. He said, he had always wanted one. He sent me a picture of this pearl white Harley Davidson. It was beautiful! I asked him how it felt. His answer was a familiar one. He said, "I never felt so free in my life. I wish I had bought one years ago." That's what I felt like all those years ago. I had so many questions.

I asked if it was hard to learn. He said he took a class. I was now intrigued and excited for him. I had never heard him sound like that. He sounded like a little kid in a toy store. He absolutely loved riding. It was his outlet, his stress reliever. But more than that, it brought him joy!

After finding out about the cancer diagnosis, my dad did what I thought was the unthinkable when he sold his motorcycle. I couldn't believe it. How could he sell something that gave him so much joy? When I spoke to him about it, he said he was in a bad space, thinking that he wasn't going to live, so there was no reason to keep the motorcycle. It was then that I recognized how devastating the diagnosis was to my dad.

As I stopped reminiscing, I only had a few more hours left of driving to reach Atlanta. I finally reached my dad's house and as soon as I got settled, we left the house. On the way to the motorcycle dealer, my dad told me he had a vision from God that he would live and not die. And that he had changed his outlook on life. He said, "I have been diagnosed with cancer, but I don't have cancer. Because as soon as I admit I have cancer, it means cancer has me. Rick, I'm going to live until I die." And after making that declaration he said, "Let's go look at some motorcycles."

Every time I would go to Atlanta for the next several months, we would look at motorcycles. We went to different motorcycle shops where we would sit on motorcycles and take pictures of ourselves on them. We talked about our dream of riding together. It was our "thing." The thing that he and I shared that we didn't share with anyone else.

I loved going to the motorcycle shops with him. Some of it was because of my dream of maybe riding myself one day. The other reason is that my dad and I got a chance to spend time together and share a fascination and love for riding. I learned so much from my dad while going to motorcycle shops. I learned that it's important to find common ground with others. Finding common ground draws you closer in relationships.

I will never forget the day he called me and told me that he had found a motorcycle online that he wanted to buy. He sent me pictures of it and asked me what I thought. I looked at the pictures and told him that he should go for it. And so, he bought the motorcycle. I remember the smile on his face when he began to ride his motorcycle again. It was almost as if riding a motorcycle allowed him to escape from cancer's pain, worry, stress, and reality. When he was riding, time stood still and he was not dying, but living.

What's amazing is that my dad taught me so many life lessons through motorcycles. Like how time is important. If you want to do something, do it now. Tomorrow is not promised. Look deep within yourself to see if the excuse you have for not doing it, will measure up in the end if you miss the opportunity to be or do something you love. Or spend time with a loved one even though you could make up an excuse or valid reason for putting it off.

My dad also taught me how important it was to balance work and play. He taught me how important it was to have something in your life that causes you to feel free! Finding that thing that causes you to feel free gives you something to look forward to after the hard work and sacrifices you've made for God and others. My dad was like an onion. I discovered so many new, deep, profound, and courageous layers to who he was as a man and human being.

In 2016, I finally got the courage to take the motorcycle class. When I told my dad, I was taking the class he sent me a helmet, gloves, boots, and a jacket. He was super supportive. He kept saying, "I can't wait for us to ride together!"

After I completed my class, I called my buddy, Bob, and asked if he would let me ride his bike to get some practice and he agreed. I went over to his house, got on the motorcycle, and took off pretty well. His bike was much bigger than the ones we trained on, but I felt like I could handle it. Until I tried to turn around in the middle of the street. I felt the bike tipping over and I hurried up and jumped off the bike before the bike hit the ground. I was in such shock, I lifted the motorcycle up with one hand, and lifted up the seat, which had broken off, with the other. I just stood there in the middle of the street. The only thing that was hurt was my pride. I was completely embarrassed.

Bob came running down the street asking what happened.

"I don't know."

He grabbed the motorcycle, put the seat back on and told me to meet him at his house. When we got back to his house, he said, "Let's go over to this school so you can practice."

I was still startled and didn't want to get back on. Bob looked me in the eyes and said, "You have to get back on the horse now, or you'll never ride again."

I agreed, and it was the best decision ever. I rode around that parking lot for hours getting the hang of riding a bigger bike.

I called my dad afterward and told him what happened. "It's all good," he said. "Everybody falls at some point. When you get here, I'll let you ride my bike, and you'll get some more experience."

The next week, I went to Atlanta to visit my dad. He told me to get on the back of his motorcycle because he was going to take me to a large parking lot so I could practice riding. I had never been on the back of a motorcycle. It was a very strange and scary feeling to put your life in someone else's hands. Specifically, on a motorcycle where you have nothing around you to protect you if you get into an accident. Even more than that, my dad was sick and, still, he was able to find the strength to hold me and the motorcycle up. I wondered how he was doing it. Perhaps, he had some experience riding others.

We finally got to the Walmart parking lot. My big moment had arrived. I had practiced on Bob's bike, and now I was going to ride my dad's bike, which was even bigger than Bob's. I was nervous because I didn't want to drop my dad's bike. I got on and started out going really slow. I worked on turning and stopping. It started feeling good to me. But my confidence booster came when my dad said, "Rick, you got this! You're a natural!" I felt like I could do anything when he encouraged me. I started speeding up, making sharp turns, quick stops, bobbing and weaving through parking spots and obstacles. I was ready.

Then, he said, the unthinkable. "Why don't you go out on the street and then the highway?" I was petrified! Highway?! Then he said to me, "You got this." There's something about when your father says you can do something. It's an instant confidence booster. So, I went on the street a few times and then jumped on the highway! It was amazing! Being on the open road was heavenly. It was like a little piece of heaven on earth. It was freeing, peaceful, relaxing, energizing, and I felt connected to everything around me. This was even better than my motor scooter experience. I was born for this!!

When I got back to the parking lot, my dad rode us back to his house. When we pulled up, I had to ask, "Dad, you seemed real comfortable riding me on the back, have you ridden passengers before?" He replied, "No, you were the first person I rode on the back. I figured I wouldn't tell you, so you wouldn't get nervous. I knew I wasn't gonna let you fall." Again, I was dumbfounded by my dad's ability to keep surprising me. There were so many layers to him that reminded me of myself. That is exactly something I would say and do. I heard people call it, "Fake it to you make it."

What was more amazing to me was his words, *"I knew I wasn't gonna let you fall."* I heard those words as more than just pertaining to the motorcycle, but life in general. I had an eye-opening moment in that instance. The thing I had prayed for, and hoped for my whole life, I was now living. I was living my dream. I had a great relationship with my dad. I had all the things I wanted from him: attentiveness, support, care, interest, and dependability. That was the moment I realized God had already answered my prayers about my dad.

I believe it was because of those answered prayers that I did not go out and immediately get my own motorcycle. My dad asked me when I was going to buy my own so that we could ride together. I kept putting it off. I want to say that I kept stalling because my wife and I were intentional about paying off debt so we could become debt-free. It just wasn't in the financial plans to purchase a motorcycle. But as I reflect on that time, I wonder if it was something deeper.

Maybe the real reason I kept putting it off is because, on some level, it was my excuse to keep driving to Atlanta every month. Because I did not have a motorcycle, going to Atlanta was my only opportunity to ride and to see my dad. Perhaps, somewhere in the back of my mind, me purchasing my own motorcycle meant I wouldn't have to drive to Atlanta as much. The truth is, I needed my time with my dad more than I needed my time on the motorcycle. The motorcycle was just the bridge that brought us closer.

The more my dad and I hung out, the closer we became. One day, I was in Atlanta, and my dad and I stopped to get some smoothies. We sat down on a bench outside and talked for a couple of hours. He said something that kind of blew my mind.

"Rick, you may not believe this, but I have been a way better father to you than my father was to me."

I was a little in shock over this statement. I immediately went back in my mind and quickly ran through all the disappointments and struggles we had. If he was talking about the last year and a half, I could see that. However, if he was talking about before then, I found it hard to believe his father was worse. Or that my dad would have beat out someone else for the "Father of the Year award." But, I kept that to myself, because I wanted to hear his case for being a better father to me than his father was to him.

He dropped a bombshell with his opening statement. "I never had a long deep conversation with my dad like I have with you. I wasn't even sure of what his real name was. Everyone called him LC, but was that his first name, a nickname, or initials? He never sat me down and talked with me. He never shared anything about his experiences. He had a severe stuttering problem, and he did not talk much. I learned two things from him, how to work hard and he taught me how to play the guitar."

I was instantly convicted! I realized I was judging him for not being something he had never seen before. There was so much more to my dad's story than I realized. I understood for the first time, my father had done the best that he could. He had improved on fatherhood for the next generation. He couldn't give me what I was asking for because he didn't know how to give it. He just knew to give more than his father did.

My dad shared how he and his siblings grew up in extreme poverty. And how sometimes they only had enough to share a piece of chicken. How he had to wear the same underwear for days at a time. I could see why his sending child support was a badge of honor. He supported us financially and it was something his father never did for him. Also, my dad didn't mind sharing his past experiences with me. The good and the bad. He was not shy about sharing his mistakes and about how I should avoid the same pitfalls. My dad gave some of the best advice in the world. I began to break it all down, he was right, he was a much better father to me than his father ever was to him.

This was a staggering revelation. I even began to be grateful for my experiences with my father. For the first time, I think I really appreciated my father and who he was as a person. It finally hit me; my father was a hurting son like I was. He longed for and needed his father, too. That day, I saw him as more than just my dad, he was a human being. He was just like me.

REFLECTIONS

Perhaps you were like me, and you have been judging someone based on the limited knowledge you had about them. Remember, people are always more than what we can see and have experienced. If you take the time to pull back the layers, I believe you will discover you are more alike than you would like to give them credit. There is a saying that goes, "Hurt people, hurt people," and I totally agree. But I also understand that hurt people are so much more than their hurt. But it takes you being able to take the time to see the greater layers of them that they are trying to show you.

Don't deprive that person of their right to be human. Don't take away their God-given right to be more than what you can see on the outside. Don't rob yourself of the chance to see you in them and them in you. There is always more than meets the eye when it comes to us humans!

EIGHTEEN

"Do you want to be right or in relationship?"

THE GIFT OF THE PRESENT

Why is it so hard to be in the present? What does it take to master the moments we have now? One year for Christmas, my mother gave my siblings and I a book on CD. I was about 22 years old, and I was expecting to get some money or something thoughtful. However, I was confused when I received this audible book on a CD. I was even more baffled by the title. "The Present" by Spencer Johnson. Despite my apprehension, I decided I would put it in my car to listen to when I was bored.

To my surprise, the book was amazing. It was about a young boy's journey into adulthood. The little boy meets an old man who tries to tell him about this mysterious gift the old man calls the present. The old man describes it as the best gift you can ever receive. The boy didn't understand what the old man was trying to explain to him about this gift of the present. It was not until the boy grew into a young man disillusioned with work that he comes back to the old man seeking answers. The young man then goes on a relentless pursuit to find this mysterious magical gift that holds the key to him being happy and successful. Yet, while the young man was on this journey, the gift seemed too elusive, and he wanted to quit his search. He wondered if the old man tricked him or if he was just wasting his time looking for something that could not be found.

Halfway through the book I realized what the gift of the present was. I realized the old man was talking about the gift of right now. The author wanted us to know being aware of the here and now and not being in the future or stuck in the past was a gift. In athletics, coaches tell you to have a short memory. They say you must forget the last play because the current play is the only play that matters. To be able to take advantage of what was happening in the moment was a gift. Too many people miss seeing the good things presented to them in the present moment because they are looking behind or ahead. The only way you can make the most out of what has happened or impact what will happen, is to see the opportunities in the now. To benefit from the gift of the present, experience true happiness and peace, you must learn to stop and be in the moment.

There are moments when I felt like I had stopped and was present and aware of everything going on around me and I experienced that happiness and peace. But there were other moments where I was stuck hanging out in the past or the future and missed opportunities or caused more stress on myself and others. Mastering the gift of the present was hard because it seemed easy to recognize in some moments, and harder to hold on to in others.

As a father to four lovely daughters, I was always coming and going. I did most of the school drop off and pickups for our three youngest daughters. After a couple of weeks of driving them back and forth to school, I realized this was a gift. The time I had with them in the car was the perfect opportunity to make meaningful memories. I introduced our morning routine. We recited daily affirmations, scriptures, had conversations, I encouraged them, and prayed over them. I tried to take full advantage of our 15-minute rides together.

I had a set schedule. We would arrive at the school, and I would walk them inside, talk with other parents, and head outside for my morning conference call. That call was with my dad. We talked almost every day. He was an early morning riser because he used to get up so early when he worked. His body never let him sleep late.

We would talk about any and everything. Our conversations could be deep and serious or light and laughing. We talked about sports, ministry, politics, or whatever was happening with my daughters. We never had an agenda; it was just about us.

Before long, I looked forward to our morning calls. Sometimes calling him even when I did not want anything or was just bored. I knew he was available most of the time unless he was at a doctor's appointment, chemo, or taking a nap. He became my go-to person. We talked more in a month than we did in the five years before we reconnected.

He was becoming more than just my dad; he was becoming one of my best friends. We spent so much time talking that we thought and said the same thing from time to time. One day while we were talking, he said something to me I never imagined he would say. He said, "Rick, you're more than just my son, you're my best friend!" That blew my mind! Yes, I had thought the same thing, but he said it aloud. Wow! I never imagined we would be at this place in our relationship. I just wanted to have some resemblance of a father, son relationship. I never in a million years thought it would grow into a friendship. This was better than what I had hoped and prayed for.

After being completely taken off guard, I answered, "Yes, Dad! Me too!" Who would have known that taking time to be present when visiting my dad and having morning calls would lead to me getting my father back, and gaining a new best friend? Being in the moment with my dad on our morning calls allowed us to get to know each other beyond the titles of father and son, to a title of friend.

Friendships can be a beautiful blessing that enhances your life. A great friend can help support you through difficult times, be a shoulder to cry on, or encourage you to live up to your potential. However, the closer you become and the more time you spend together gives you more opportunities to see each other at some of your greatest and worst moments. Usually, the worst moments are because you are either stuck in the past or unavailable because you're focused on the future. For friendships to stand the test of time, you must endorse the practices of forgiveness and reconciliation.

Forgiveness and reconciliation are not for the faint of heart or people looking for a quick fix. It takes hard work, and it must become a way of life. Forgiveness is a lifestyle that you wear daily. And it will be tested to see if you really subscribe to this way of living or if you only sport it when it seems convenient.

I have this habit of praying before I call people. I pray and ask God if I should call them right now or not. It is my way of being aware of the present moment. I believe timing is everything. It can be the right or wrong time. You can call someone and be a blessing at the right time, or a bother at the wrong time. Before I called my dad, I prayed about if this was a good time. I felt like the Holy Spirit was saying "No, don't call him." But I ignored the warning and called anyway. He answered and I asked him what he was doing. He said he had just finished taking chemo. I should have taken that as my sign that this was not a good time, but because I was so focused on the future and fearful of not spending enough time with him, I pushed on anyway. I asked him if he wanted me to call him back, but he said no.

The conversation quickly went left after I shared with him about a dream involving my wife. My father said things that sent me from 1-100 in seconds. We both said some hurtful things to each other. The call ended with him telling me not to call him again and my response was, "Don't worry, I won't."

A few hours later, still fuming from the call with my father. I walked into my office at the church when the Holy Spirit said, "You need to apologize. You should not have called him right after his chemo treatment. Do you want to be right or in relationship?"

I struggled with this and had that lump in my throat. The one you feel when it's hard to swallow your pride. My pride and ego were fighting tooth and nail to stand their ground. But I knew the ground I was standing on was quicksand! My anger was not from his words but what his words triggered. There was no real merit or reward, I wasn't in the present, I was stuck in the past reliving old trauma and pain. So, I surrendered to the present. It didn't feel good. I had to put my pride, ego, and feelings of being wronged to the side so I could do what was right. Sometimes doing the right thing doesn't always feel good in that moment, but regardless of how it feels, it is still the right thing to do.

The real sign of strength, power, and maturity is being able to be obedient to God even though your emotions and feelings may contradict what God is saying. I have found that things work out better when I'm obedient to God's voice. Especially when I listen to that part within me that is always calling me to be a better man. Being a better man or woman is not about being comfortable but being courageous enough to correct something when you are wrong.

We have been tricked into believing freedom is doing what we want and feel when we want and feel like. However, we can become slaves to our wills and desires because they are usually based on the fear of something in the past or future. When we allow the fear of something that is not currently happening to control us, it can be detrimental to ourselves and others. The temporary feeling of fear can cause us to lash out or seek revenge. Unfortunately, the consequences usually last much longer.

I knew I had to call him, but I kept thinking, "He is the parent. He should be calling me to get it right." It's interesting how quickly I time-traveled to the past and reverted to the title of "father and son" when things got difficult. Was it because the title of "father and son" allowed me to blame my father for what went wrong; inevitably, holding my dad responsible for making the situation right by apologizing first? Regardless of how I felt, I broke down, called him, and apologized after I got over myself. Even though I felt like I was constantly apologizing and trying to make things right, I knew being the more emotionally mature person in the relationship dropped the responsibility in my lap. I also realized that just because someone is the parent or older, doesn't make them the more mature person.

That day, I decided to be a better man rather than be bitter, angry, scared, or try to prove a point. I didn't need to prove I deserved my dad's love, prove he was wrong for not being there, or wrong for hurting and disappointing me. I chose that day to be a better man and in doing so, I chose to take back what was lost. I took back my joy, peace, happiness, self-esteem, and more importantly, my life. I realized it may not have been the right time to call him, but it was the right time for me to decide to be a better man.

A couple of weeks after the phone call incident, I still felt like a new man. I felt like I was taking control of my life, being present with my family, friends, church, and everything was going well. I felt like what was happening was not happening to me, but for me. It was all working together for my good. One of my favorite scriptures is Romans 8:28(NIV).

"For we know that all things work together for the good of those who love the Lord and are called according to his purpose." No matter what I faced, it was somehow working out for my good.

I experienced some of that good on July 22, 2016, which was my 37th birthday. Our daughters had a special final performance for their summer camp. It involved dancing, singing, skits, and awards. I was glad to be able to make it. It had been a long summer with dad being sick and me constantly traveling to Atlanta. I was looking forward to my little ladies doing their thing on the stage. They always loved performing and I loved watching them perform.

My wife and I arrived separately and subsequently were seated apart from one another due to the size of the crowd. Strangely enough, I kept seeing this guy from the side who looked familiar. I thought, *"Who is that guy and where do I know him from?"* He kind of looked like my dad from the side. But I knew it wasn't my dad, I spoke to him earlier in the day and he was in Atlanta. *"I must be tripping. But wow, this must really be his doppelganger. This dude looks just like my dad. Same hair and some of the same features,"* I thought.

When the show was over the guy stood up and turned toward me. It was my dad! I was so shocked and excited at the same time. I was like a little kid again! I ran over to him and gave him a huge hug. I said, "Dad, what are you doing here? How did you get here? I didn't know you were coming!"

"I wanted to surprise you for your birthday! Well, it was really Robyn's idea. She flew me in today. I was on my way to the airport when I was talking to you earlier."

"Man, you kept that a secret! I had no clue!"

This was truly one of the happiest days of my life. Being surprised by my dad on my 37th birthday. That night, my wife had another surprise. I took my dad out for a late lunch and when we arrived at the house, cars were everywhere. She had also planned a surprise birthday party! She invited many of my friends, family, and church members. I was floored! This was the most amazing birthday ever!

It was also the first time my dad had been to our new house and the first time he ever stayed with us. He stayed with us for four days. It was amazing. My daughters got a chance to spend some time with him. They asked him questions about himself, and he got a chance to play some games with them. He also took me shopping and bought me clothes. I don't remember him ever taking me shopping as a kid. But I remember that weekend, I was a kid again.

The fact that my dad took the time get on an airplane and fly to come to be present with me, even while he was sick, was the greatest sacrifice and show of love he could ever demonstrate. It felt like we were getting a chance for a do-over. I was ten years old all over again. I finally got a chance to have my dad at my birthday party! It was truly a joyous occasion!

When you are a child, your parent's job or responsibility is to provide, protect, pour into you, and help you grow and develop into a responsible adult. But I realize, as parents, that a sense of responsibility for your child does not go away just because that child becomes an adult. Time does not stop a parent from being concerned or wanting the best for their child. Covering your child is a lifelong honor. And my dad was taking his role very seriously. Even though he was sick, he was still attentive and seeing things in me that I could not see.

About two months after my surprise birthday party, I was in a weird season. I definitely was not in the present. I was emotionally everywhere. I found myself being distant from everyone and very irritable. That was not like me. I was usually the happy, energetic, entertaining person, but I felt like a Debbie Downer for a few weeks. I couldn't seem to pull myself out of my rut.

This emotional rollercoaster all started with me being upset with my wife, our children, and our church. Every time somebody around me bought something new, material wise, I was upset. If my wife bought something or even if she bought my daughters something, I would get upset. When the church bought something new or gave money to someone, I was bothered. The proverbial straw that broke the camel's back was when I had a flat on the side of the road. I changed the tire and was riding on the spare for three months. My wife kept asking, "Why are you still riding on that spare tire? Why don't you go get another tire?" I would reply, "I'm good. I don't need anything." But on the inside, I was thinking, "Don't you see the length I am willing to go through to make sure you and the girls have what you want and need? Can't you see the sacrifices I'm making so you can look good?"

I was sharing with my dad about what my wife had said. He told me, "Why don't you just get a new car?" This question made me even more angry. I didn't say anything. I just made up an excuse to quickly get off the phone. However, I couldn't understand why I got so upset. He just suggested I get a new car. He didn't say anything wrong, but I couldn't articulate why I got so angry with him for asking that question. It was as if something that had been buried deep within me was pushing its way into my stomach and now, I had that lump in my throat again. What was the source of my anger with my dad and my family?

My dad called me a few days later and said he had a dream. In the dream, he said he was holding this little gold box and he couldn't understand why I was so upset with him about the gold box.

"Rick, I think the dream means you are still holding on to something from the past that you are still angry with me about."

I immediately responded, "No, I don't know what you're talking about. I'm good. I got all that out." But then I took a moment to think about it. I knew exactly what it was, as well as, when it started.

When I was about seven years old, I wanted to get a new pair of shoes. My mom told me that we couldn't afford a new pair of shoes at that time. However, my dad walked around in new suits, alligator, and crocodile boots. I thought, *"I have to make sacrifices, so he looks good?"* And when my parents divorced for the last time, I felt like I had to be the one to make the sacrifices for the family. I decided I would go without so that my sisters and brothers wouldn't have to. I was determined to be the opposite of my father. Which led to a misinterpretation of love for family as meaning I would always have to take care of myself last or many times, not at all. In my mind, my decision would make things financially better for the family, but I didn't anticipate it would also make me bitter.

As a teenager, I would work, cut grass, and do whatever to make my own money to buy stuff. Even when my mom could afford it, I wouldn't ask for the shoes or clothes I really wanted, I would ask for something cheaper. I even developed anxiety and guilt around doing nice things for myself. I could buy and do nice things for others, but I always hesitated and took a long time to decide when it came to myself. Often, if I did something nice for myself, I felt so guilty afterward that I would return it to the store or not use it. I never wanted people to think I was selfish. Ultimately, because I never wanted to think I was like my dad.

I was living out of the past. I was stuck in a philosophy of love created by my seven-year-old self. And that philosophy of the past guided how I acted in my marriage, parenting, and pastoring. I felt like I had been making sacrifices for all those around me and no one noticed or cared. I was making sacrifices for everyone else to get what they wanted, while I suffered silently not receiving what I wanted for fear of "what if they might need something?" I even took a lesser salary at church, not just because I wanted to be a blessing to the church, but because I was afraid something would happen, and the church would not have what it needed financially to meet the need.

When I took a deeper look, my mindset was manipulation at its purest level. It was quid pro quo. I do something for you and in turn, you give me something like praise or adoration, which made my connection with people very transactional versus relational. Because when you are in a relationship, the other person does not have to give you back what you gave to them.

I was trying to force people into loyalty by being nice and giving to them. I was manipulating people to control them. Because I felt like if I could control them, then in the end, I wouldn't get hurt or disappointed by them. My giving was selfish at its core. I was not giving just to help, but to keep me from being hurt. No matter how I tried to go about it, I ended up being selfish like what I was trying to avoid. In the end, I was more selfish than my father. I was deceitful and had no right judging him for being selfish.

My dad said, "Wow! I never knew you felt like that. You're right. Back then, I was selfish. I was so busy trying to look like a preacher and do what I saw other preachers do, that I didn't realize what that was doing to y'all. But you can change all of that now. You don't have to hold on to that. Let this go. It is causing you to be angry with me, your wife, your children, and your church."

In that moment, it all made sense to me. That is why I rode around for three months on a spare tire. I wanted my wife to notice my sacrifices for the family. I thought it would buy her loyalty to me. I thought she would notice and give me a big proverbial pat on the back. However, she never asked or required me to make those sacrifices. She was never the one holding me back. She only wanted the best for me.

When I finally went in to get a new tire, the salesman said, "Did you know your tire is under warranty? Because the hole is on the side, we will give you a brand-new tire for free." I was riding around embarrassed, looking pitiful, and wanting someone to feel sorry for me in vain, because I had a new tire waiting for me.

There are seasons where we spend time wondering if anyone sees the good that we are doing. However, God sees it all. We already have a warranty, and it is called a promise given in Luke 6:38 (NIV). *"Give and it will be given back to you..."* You don't have to walk around trying to make people see your sacrifices for them. God has noticed everything you have done, and he is judging your heart, and the reason behind your giving. You don't have to buy someone's loyalty you already have God's.

A few days later, my dad called me.

"Rick, I want you to write down ten things you want to do for yourself. Ten things you want. This is your opportunity to be selfish. You've sacrificed for everyone else, now it's your turn to get something."

At first, I was still a little hesitant. However, later that day I made my list. It took me a couple months to save up and get everything, but I did. And to my surprise, it felt great!! I felt lighter. I felt less angry. I was no longer angry when my wife or children bought something new. It was a relief. Who would have known taking the time to take care of me, would help me to be a better husband, father, and pastor.

I had to learn that giving to others was not about what I could get out of it, but what others could get through me in the moment. More than that, I had to learn how to give without expecting anything in return, understanding that the greatest reward was being a conduit to give. This is why I love that scripture in Acts 20:35 that says, *"In everything I did, I showed you that by this kind of hard work we must help the weak, remembering the words the Lord Jesus himself said: 'It is more blessed to give than to receive.'"* The true blessing in life is experienced when we give not worrying about how people took advantage of us in the past or fearing the people we just gave to will not appreciate us, but being present to the fact we get to be a blessing to someone right now.

Determine your self-worth based on how big of a heart you have to give and not on what people give in return. As my father used to say, "Your blessings are not predicated on other people's response, but your obedience." See giving as an honor that God entrusted you to be his conduit or vessel to bless someone else. Which ultimately means I can let people off the hook. I can let my loved ones off the hook for what I've given, love that I've shown, and the sacrifices I have made. I could let my dad off the hook for the sacrifices and the love that I had shown to him. I no longer had to hold a debt over his head that he could not repay. I could love him without expecting something from him. Because the ultimate honor was, I was just a vessel for God to get his love through me to my dad, people I love, and the world.

I also learned that forgiveness and reconciliation have many different stages. And if you want to reach your ultimate goal of healing, you cannot skip these stages. You cannot be healed unless you go through the healing process. This process takes time, patience, honesty with yourself, and others, as well as, reflection, and the willingness to change your perspective, your heart, and your opinions. It also requires you to uncover the pain and trauma that you have deep inside, commit to being a better person, and rely on God for your strength. Remember, this is not just for the relationship, but for you. Moreover, the process will all be worth it when you are healed.

My dad was a champion for enduring the worst pain because he knew whatever sacrifice he was making was worth the discomfort. I could tell the cancer was taking its toll on him. Occasionally, I would see him moving slower and wincing a little bit. But despite suffering through pain, he tried to make sure he would be there to help others, specifically, as he had turned over a new leaf and was a new man. Cancer and a new perspective helped my dad to see the benefits of showing up for other people in their time of need.

One day, while I was out with Robyn, I got a phone call that no one ever wants to get. My brother, Rueben, called me to tell me there was an accident and that his wife was in the hospital dying. He was distraught. She had a son, and they had a little girl together. I rushed to the hospital to be by his side. The doctors came and let the family know that she no longer had brain activity and to begin making arrangements for her funeral. I watched my brother lose his anchor and his rock that day.

She was so young, with her life and career ahead of her. It seemed like it was not her time, and especially not the right time for my brother to be a single father to a five-year-old. My heart hurt for him and the family. I knew her son and little daughter would now have to grow up without their mother. I was so sad. My heart was so heavy. All I could do was be there for my brother.

As soon as I left the hospital, I called my dad to update him on what was going on. He felt my brother's emotional pain. Even though he was in his own pain, he did not hesitate to say he was going to come to the funeral. He wanted to be there in support of his son who had just lost his wife. He said he could not imagine going through something like that. He knew my brother would need all hands-on deck for this.

My dad told me he was driving up the night before the funeral. The morning of the funeral, he was standing next to my brother. He had made it. He traveled over nine hours in pain to be there for my brother in his most difficult moment. I was glad he was there. I know it meant a lot to my brother and the family to see him.

After the funeral, we decided to go over to Racheal and her husband Kevin's house. Racheal had reminded us that the next day was my dad's birthday. So, we planned a surprise birthday party for him. We got cake, ice cream, and some candles. We wanted to surprise him with a small birthday party because dad was turning 58 years old.

As me, Robyn, my daughters, Racheal's family, Reuben and his daughter, and Kevin's family sat around the table talking to my dad, Racheal slowly crept up with the cake. We pulled out the cake with the candles that had his age on it and yelled, "Surprise!" We sang "Happy Birthday" to him in harmony. Well, we had to sing it twice. The first time was just a hot mess. I reminded everyone we were recording, and I told them, "We are a family of singers. We cannot record a happy birthday song singing flat and without energy!" We all just laughed! So, the second time we did it, it was the bomb! We sang that thang!

My dad was smiling from ear to ear. He did not know what to do after the song. We had to tell him to blow out his candles and make a wish. He said his wish out loud. He said, "I wish to live to see 59." We all yelled, "Dad, you're not supposed to say your wish out loud." We all laughed. He then told us, he had never in his 58 years had a birthday party. This was his first birthday party! For a second, we were all speechless! Then Racheal said, "Wow! Dad, we got a chance to throw you your first birthday party!" After that, everybody hugged, and we put on some music and started singing and dancing. It was beautiful seeing him enjoy himself. From the look on his face, you could tell that he was having the time of his life. I think we all recognized that this birthday could be his last.

After he told us it was his first birthday party, we were just as excited as he was that we had thrown him the party. We just thought it would be something nice, but we had no clue that it would be significant in more ways than one. That night, we got a chance to see my dad become a kid again. That night, for a brief moment, we were so in touch with the present that we forgot about the pain of losing my brother's wife, cancer, and past disappointments. That night will always be a magical moment where we experienced the gift of the present for me. That was the night my dad really found out how special he was to us.

Too often, we wait until people are dead before we give them their flowers. We fill up churches with people, have programs full of people who speak kind words, and surround the casket with flowers. There is nothing wrong with those things, however, the person in the casket cannot enjoy any of them. If you want to show someone how special they were in life, do it while they are still alive. Do it while they still have the energy to enjoy it. Do it while there is still time.

If we learned anything from the birthday party, it was to cherish today while we still have it. We all saw my father's health decline, and we knew what was coming. We just wanted to maximize the time we had remaining.

Racheal always came up with ideas to get people together. It was kind of her gift. One day after dad's birthday, she called me and said, "We should all go to Dad's for Thanksgiving! It would be so fun to get all of us as siblings and our families to go to Atlanta and spend Thanksgiving with him." Of course, she left out the details of me convincing my dad and my stepmom, Georgia, to agree to this plan. Surprisingly, they both said yes. We talked with our other siblings, Reuben, Ryan, and Ricketa, and they all agreed to go. However, at the last-minute Ryan was not able to make it.

We all met in Atlanta the day before Thanksgiving. We mapped out where everyone was sleeping because my dad had never had this many people in his house. My wife and I, and three of our daughters, Racheal, her husband Kevin and one of their children, Ricketa, her husband, and their two children, Reuben and his daughter. It was like a good old-fashioned sleepover. We crowded in small bedrooms, and kids slept on the floor with inflatable mattresses. We had so much fun staying up all night talking.

The following day was Thanksgiving and my sisters, and my wife cooked breakfast for everyone. It was the bomb. For dinner, each of us prepared our own signature dish. It smelled so good! We could not wait to eat. My dad kept walking by the kitchen saying, "Oh yeah! This gone be some good eating!" He was filled with joy to have his kids and grandkids in the same house.

Uncle Tony and his girlfriend came over. It felt like we were in a scene from the movie "Soul Food." As the smell of good food was in the air, so was the aroma of love and family. This was truly a family reunion. Finally, the big moment we had all been waiting for had arrived; it was eating time. We all gathered around the kitchen island and held hands. We decided to have everyone say what they are thankful for. When it got to my dad, he shared how thankful he was to have his children with him for Thanksgiving. How this was the first time we had all been together for Thanksgiving. He shared how much he loved us all. Then he prayed, and we ended the prayer with an "Amen" that resembled a football team coming out of a huddle, saying "Break!" It was eating time.

We all ate until we were rearing back in our chairs holding our stomachs. Then, we sat around watching football and movies for a few hours. But after our food digested a little, we started a ping pong tournament. My dad had a ping pong table in his garage. He was really good at it. Him and I played a lot when I came to visit him. He would beat me most of the time, but I would get lucky every once in a while. We would laugh and talk crazy to each other about who was going to win. That day, neither one of us won. My sister's husband beat us both! And we had a big laugh about it!

After the tournament, I pulled out my dad's motorcycle. I took everyone, who was willing, for a ride. What's real crazy is, I had never ridden with someone on the back before that day. If that was not bad enough, I also had only been riding for about 4 months. I did not share that info with everyone else though. The only person who knew was my dad. Everyone was either terrified, excited, or both! But I reassured everyone that I was not going to let them fall. I guess "the apple doesn't fall far from the tree."

I saw my dad sitting on the front porch a few hours later. I put the motorcycle up and went to sit next to him. I asked him if he had enjoyed his time with everyone. He replied by saying that it was the best Thanksgiving he'd ever had. To see all his children and grandchildren, except for my brother Ryan, and Ryan's son, was amazing. A dream come true.

As I sat there talking to him, I became present to my dad's physical appearance. I noticed he looked a little more tired than usual. There were bags under his eyes. He looked like he had lost some more weight. As I stared into his face, I could discern he looked a little older. He appeared to be frailer than a month ago. His hair had thinned out some more. The chemo was starting to take its toll on his body. He seemed a little weaker this visit.

I asked him how he was feeling. He said, "Rick, you don't know this, but I'm always in pain. The cancer causes me to always be in pain. I take some medication to keep it manageable, but the pain is always there. I just choose not to bring attention to it. I decided I'm gone live until I die. There's no use always mentioning my pain. I want to live, not keep telling people how much I am hurting." I was stunned! I knew he was in some pain, sometimes. But I didn't realize it was all the time. When I saw him playing ping pong he seemed to be moving well. I've seen him on the motorcycle riding. I know he's driven 9 hours to Indianapolis, he has done everything that he was doing before cancer. And the whole time, he was in pain and not complaining. It was one of the most inspiring things I had ever witnessed.

He was showing me how to go through sickness. Anybody can be joyful, cheerful, happy, encouraging, uplifting, and continue to have fun while healthy. However, it is much harder to do those things when your body is sick, and chemo is making you weaker and weaker. It is hard to be yourself when you are in constant pain. Pain usually has a way of bending you to its will and causing people to transform into the worst versions of themselves. However, my dad was somehow able to transcend the typical behavioral modifications of pain. Instead of allowing pain to control his emotions he allowed joy to have full command of his actions, words, and deeds.

This type of joy does not emanate from what is happening, but it is a choice to experience appreciation and satisfaction based on what you believe. My dad believed he was going to be healed. He believed he was going to live and not die. My dad believed he was going to beat cancer. The old saints at church used to say, "This joy I have, the world didn't give it and the world can't take it away!" My dad's joy, not even cancer or chemo, could take it away.

My dad's belief system was his pain management. What he believed about God being present with him was his foundation for everything he did. His faith did not stop the pain, it just gave the pain purpose. My dad's faith was rooted in God's precious gift of the present. I believe my dad could endure the pain he constantly felt because he focused on what was happening right now, in the moment. For him, his time with us was more powerful than the pain he felt in his body. I gained a newfound respect for my father and his character. You don't really know who you are at your core until you go through something very difficult. I believe that is when the real you will come to the surface. The real person in my dad was emerging as a true hero in my life.

That night, we all went to the mall for Black Friday. I shared with the family all about Dad being more tired and how he was always in pain. I also shared how I noticed he was getting weaker. We all agreed to make sure we were present and checked on him and visited as much as we could. I think we all intrinsically knew this could be the last time we would have Thanksgiving with him.

REFLECTIONS

In the book, "The Present," the young man who desperately searched for the gift of the present in the end finally found it. It was in him the whole time. He just had to stop long enough to see it. I know life is busy and we are conditioned to associate busyness with productivity. However, sometimes the many activities we partake in cause us to miss what is right in front of us. The most important things in our life are the moments we create in the present.

What moments will you create today? Who will you stop everything for to create a memory today? What family member will you show how special they are to you today? What friend will you give your attention to demonstrate how important they are to you today? Don't let work, agendas, guilt from the past, or fear of the future to stop you from making this moment magical for you and someone else today.

Plan the trip, the lunch, the dinner, the event, the holiday, the memorial, the gathering, or just a walk in the park. Shut everything else down. Work, the house, the other people in your life will get along without you for a little while. Go stand still long enough with someone to experience the magical gift of the present.

NINETEEN

"He remained faithful and kept growing as a person through it all"

WHEN YOU'VE DONE ALL YOU CAN

What does it mean when a person says they've done all they can do? One of my favorite songs is "Stand" by Donnie McClurkin. This song helped me understand that there comes a point when you've taken all the actions you possibly can. You can go no further. You've exhausted all your options, reached the end of your resources, given all you could, and are possibly at the end of your strength. At that point, there is nothing left for you to do.

When you are at the end of what you can do and what you know, you get the chance to experience something greater. That is the place where you experience the supernatural. That is the place where you experience revelations that surpass your understanding. The place where the meaning of life goes beyond this life into the next. That is the place where you come to the realization that what you learned from your loved ones can live on in perpetuity in other ways.

Because we were spending so much time up and down the highway, Racheal and I had become best friends. We had been visiting my dad almost every two weeks. After Thanksgiving, we saw how he began to decline even more. He started losing weight and sleeping more. But he was still strong, and his mind was still quick. He even rode the motorcycle from time to time. But I could see the signs of the end. I had this urge to do all I could do to capture our moments together. But I didn't know what that looked like.

I was randomly scrolling through YouTube and came across an interesting story about someone's last will and testament. As a part of this person's will, they put a small tape recorder in a safety deposit box with personal messages for their family. This video gave me an idea. I didn't want my dad's words or his voice to go to the grave with him. He was always giving out great advice or having dreams. I wanted him to be able to record them. So, I went to Target and bought him a digital voice recorder.

Racheal and I couldn't wait to give it to him. I knew he would be happy. It took so much for me not to give the surprise away when we talked on the phone that week. But I waited until the next time I went to visit him. I had it all wrapped up in a gift box. I said, "Dad, we got a gift for you." He was looking at us with that curious smile and his head turned to the side. He said, "What is it?" I handed it to him and told him to open it. When he tore open the package, he saw it and his eyes immediately got big. He said, "Naw Rick! This is nice! I can't wait to use it!"

I explained how he could use it to share any words he had for us or other family members. I told him to record himself telling those dreams he had been having. Also, anything he felt like he needed to say he could record it and we would have it forever. He was ecstatic and could not wait to learn how to use it. We took a little time so I could show him how to use it. He quickly picked up on it and he was off recording.

The following day, we were eating breakfast and he said, "Rick, I want to thank you again, man, for that recorder. I'm going to record everything. This was the greatest gift you could ever have given me. This is better than a million dollars! One day, you will be walking in a park and taking this recorder with you, and I will still be talking to you and sharing with you long after I'm gone. Rick, with this, you'll always have me with you."

I knew even after he died, I would still need to hear an encouraging word or two from my dad. It reminded me of Superman. In his fortress of solitude, he had his father's holographic program that guided him. Even though his father was dead, his words and wisdom remained alive. I could see myself one day sitting at a park bench with no one around and I pull out my dad's old voice recorder and begin to listen to him speak. I can imagine his words will still be as powerful and uplifting in that moment as it was in the past. I am sure his voice will still make me smile, laugh, and cry even long after he is gone.

The following day, we were getting ready to get some breakfast when my dad brought up this old story out of nowhere. He said, "Rick, remember that time I took you and your brothers fishing and you got up on that branch?" We all started laughing. We all knew I was a curious kid who always got into something. Which, in turn, caused my parents always to have to get me out of it.

He started re-telling the story.

"I wanted to take you and your brothers fishing as a time for us to bond. As soon as we got to the river, a branch was kind of hanging over the water. I immediately looked at you and said, 'Rickey, don't get on that branch!' You quickly said, 'Yes sir.' We went a few feet over and started putting the bait on the fishing hook. While I was focused on putting the bait on the fishing hook, I heard the twins say, 'Awwww! Daddy! Look at Rickey Jr on that branch.' I looked over at you and you had climbed that branch and was right over the water. As soon as our eyes met, the branch broke, and you were in the water."

My sister and I was in tears laughing!!

I said, "Yes, I remember that. I was so scared when I fell in because I couldn't swim. You had to jump in and save me."

Then he said, with a very serious, somber voice, "What I never told you was, I was more afraid than you."

I chuckled and asked, "Why were you more afraid than me?"

"Because I didn't know how to swim, either. I jumped in knowing I couldn't swim, but me saving you was more important. I had to do all I could to save you. I couldn't let you drown, even if that meant me losing my own life."

My tears of laughter turned into tears of joy. I asked him, "Why did you do it? Why would you risk your own life to save me?"

He looked at me and said, "Because you're my son and I love you!"

All I remembered about that day was falling into the water, getting yelled at, and getting in trouble. I realized in that moment that I was not the only person in that story. My dad had a different perspective. One in which he risked his life by doing everything he could to save me. It made me wonder, where else had I only seen one side of the story? Where else had I been self-centered, focusing on what happened to me and not on everyone else in the story? My dad did all he could do by jumping in and saving my life, and miraculously, he survived. He jumped in, not knowing what was going to happen, and he not only saved me, but he got to experience a miracle by him not drowning. There is always more to the story.

I also concluded my dad was a good guy, and being a father was scary for him. Like many of us parents, he was jumping into fatherhood, not knowing how to swim. Not having any training, good role models, or blueprints. He just jumped in and did the best he could. And some days, he was drowning, and other days, managing to transform himself into a lifeguard to save me from drowning. How could I fault a man who, at least, had the courage to jump in and give it all he had? At the end of the day, I realized, I owed my dad my life.

That day, I realized I needed to jump all in as well. My dad had mentioned a few times about him and I riding motorcycles together. We talked about going on a short trip together. I decided to purchase my own bike so we could ride together. I knew it wouldn't be long before he didn't have the strength to ride. I told one of my best friends on the planet, Keith, that I was going to purchase a motorcycle to ride with my dad, and he told me that whatever I came up with in cash, he would loan me the remaining balance, so I didn't have to use my credit. He knew how serious we were about being debt-free. So, I took him up on his offer. I found a bike, told him what I had, and he wired me the rest. It is wonderful to have great friends and to see what can happen when you trust God.

I texted my dad a pic of my new bike. He was so happy for me. I was excited to get to ride with my dad finally. We planned for me to come to Atlanta two weeks later. I had to first complete my final course for my doctorate. It was a week-intensive class, meaning it was 8 hours a day for five days. The following week, I would put my bike on a trailer, trail it to Atlanta, and then ride with my dad.

I was on a lunch break during the third day of my final course when I got a call from my dad. I could tell by his voice something was wrong. He didn't quite seem himself. I asked him what was going on. And what he told me next was like a punch in the gut. He said, "Rick, the doctors said they've done all they can do. They put me on hospice today." My heart sank! It felt like my heart fell to the bottom of my feet. My mind flooded with thoughts. I knew somewhere in the back of my mind that this day would come, but it seemed like it came too quickly. I thought I would have a little more time. We were planning on riding motorcycles the following week. Oh, no! I waited too late. Why didn't I get a bike a few months before? What was I thinking? Now we'll never get the chance to ride side by side.

I thought I would be ready when this day came, but I wasn't prepared. It hurt emotionally, but my body went numb. Then, my mind went blank. I was walking around in a daze. I guess I was in shock. I don't even remember the rest of that conversation. All I remember is going back to class and everything the professor said sounded like mumbo jumbo. A classmate of mine noticed something wasn't right with me. She asked me what was wrong, and I told her. Then, she shared with the professor, and the professor stopped teaching and they all prayed for me. I was so grateful for caring people being around me in that moment. I felt like I was losing it.

That evening, I made the necessary calls to my siblings and family members to share the news. Everyone was distraught, we all knew it was coming, but it had only been three months since we had Thanksgiving and he was still strong then. The calls drained me emotionally, but I still had one more call to my dad.

I finally got myself together enough to call him back. He was very calm, cool, and collected and I was still distraught. Crazy enough, he was the one trying to console me. I was snorting and crying on the phone. Then, he said something that I will never forget. Amid my crying, he said to me, "Rick, you're not going to understand this right now, but I have to die in order for you to become the man you are supposed to be. In order for you to become all God called you to be, I have to die."

He was right, I couldn't understand that. I believed I could be the man I was supposed to be and have him alive. I thought, "Why would he say something like that?" It just didn't make sense. I was just getting him back. We finally had the relationship I always longed for. We were finally at a great place in life. This was what I always wanted. My dad was not just my dad, he was my best friend! And now he's getting ready to die. I felt like this was more than I could bear. But it was evident that he was in another spiritual place than I was.

What has always been astounding to me is the fact that my father was so in tuned with God in his last days that he could see beyond his own fate to see my future. In the end, he was concerned about me fulfilling my purpose in life. In some way, perhaps, my father knew that even though his life would end, what he poured into me and so many others would continue to live.

It wouldn't be until a few years later that I began to understand those powerful words he said to me. I realized I had learned to heavily depend on my dad when it came to spirituality and leadership matters. He was my go-to person when I needed to make big decisions. It wasn't until much later that I had to truly learn to depend on God and the other people he placed in my life. I had to learn to trust what God said and how God was leading me. More importantly, I had to trust and believe that I had what it took to lead and make good decisions. I still had a counsel of people I shared things with; however, I had to learn to give God the final say.

That weekend after my dad was placed on hospice, Racheal and I went to see him. I knew he had gotten weaker, but I was not prepared for how much weight he had lost since we were there three weeks prior. Georgia said he barely had an appetite to eat. He looked like he had lost almost 30 to 40 pounds in just that short amount of time. I was even more sad when I saw him stand up to walk. I knew it wouldn't be long.

Later that weekend, we took my dad to get something to eat and he told us he had already met with the funeral home and had everything arranged. He wanted us to drive to see where the funeral home was. While we were in the car, he told us about his revelation regarding the Lord healing him. He said, "I thought when I heard the Lord tell me he was going to heal me that it meant I would be cured of cancer, and I would continue to live here on earth. Yet, what God meant was this healing was concerning me getting a new body in heaven. A new body that is cancer and pain free. I didn't realize it, but death can be a form of healing. When we die, we will go to heaven to be with God. All the pain, doctors, medications, feeling sick, hospitals, tubes, monitors, and everything else will be gone. I will be free!"

I just listened. I could not wrap my mind around it at first. I needed time to process what this meant and more importantly, what it meant concerning him. I was trying to begin to rationalize what he said. After all, healing is just becoming whole, sound, or healthy again. You are technically whole, sound, and healthy again if you are in heaven.

I think it bothered me because I interpreted what he said as meaning my dad had done all he could do regarding his fight against cancer. I saw it as a sign that my father was quitting. It seemed like he had given up. He had given up on any hope of beating the cancer. This new concept of healing forced me to look at what life and death meant to me and what it meant to quit.

I, first, began to look at, intrinsically, what life represented for me. For me, life represented winning, and death represented losing. Winning, for me, was associated with reward and, ultimately, God being on your side. Therefore, if God healed my dad from cancer, it meant God was rewarding him, or even me on some level because I was praying for him. But, fundamentally, it meant God was on our side.

Losing, for me, was associated with punishment and ultimately was a sign that God was not on your side. Therefore, if my father was admitting he was ready to die, he was admitting defeat and it was a punishment from God, who was not on our side. But if my dad said that death was his healing, it meant that he somehow saw death as a win. I was struggling with the concept of how he could lose and still win.

Or perhaps, was this a new level of spiritual maturity that my selfish desires for my dad to live caused me to develop a blind spot for? Or was it my small in-the-box thinking that would not allow me to see how God had the ability to work through life and death. Whether I was ready to accept it or not, death was coming for my father. My question was, "Can death be another way of healing someone? Especially, someone who is in constant agony and pain?"

But I also had to wrestle with the idea of quitting. I felt like my dad was quitting, and I felt disappointed because, in some way, I felt he was not just quitting on life, but on us. It wasn't until one day while watching a wholistic doctor on a talk show, that I saw quitting in a new light. This doctor explained how the word "quit" had gone through a transformation and even had been perverted and robbed of its original meaning. The word "quit" today has a negative connotation. When we hear the word "quit" we think, to stop, cease, discontinue, and give up. However, the original meaning of "quit" meant to be clear, free, release, let go, and rest. That discovery gave me a new meaning to the word and what my dad's revelations really meant.

I finally understood that what my father was saying was God's healing was coming in the form of rest for my father. He fought the fight of his life and he won! My dad had fought cancer for two and a half long years. He gave it all he had and fought valiantly. He kicked cancer in the butt and gave it a black eye. He never let cancer get the best of him nor take his essence. He remained faithful and kept growing as a person through it all. I concluded that my dad deserved rest after the way he lived his life at the end. It would be a punishment for him not to be able to rest after that kind of constant fighting. It reminds me of what the prophet Nathan said to King David in 2 Samuel 7:12. *"When your days are fulfilled and you rest with your fathers, I will set up your seed after you, who will come from your body, and I will establish his kingdom."* My father's days were fulfilled, and it was now time for him to prepare to rest from all his labor. He was right, my dad wasn't being punished. This form of healing was a sign of God being pleased with him and showing him honor by giving him rest.

I had to realize my reasoning for not accepting his new revelation was because I was being selfish. It was selfish of me to rather have my dad in pain and still be here, than healed and not be here. I had to welcome the idea that my dad and I had done everything we could in our relationship. Our relationship had become more than I think either of us could ever have dreamed or hoped for. I was grateful for what we had accomplished and the hard work that had gone into reconciling and creating something new that would be with each of us for however amount of time we both had left. But also, how the work we did would serve as a model and blueprint for others to follow.

Donnie McClurkin's song, "Stand," gave us a blueprint to follow when we find ourselves having reached the point when we've done all we can...just stand. Meaning hold on, be strong, and confident that you have done your best. Now, wait, knowing God will provide the rest. Keep standing knowing that your rest is on the way.

REFLECTIONS

You will appreciate what you have built in relationships with those you love, when you can say you have done all you could do. When you can say you were vulnerable when you needed to be, forgave when it was called for, and open to reconciling even when it was hard. When you can look back over your relationships, you can be proud, not that you didn't make mistakes, but that you kept trying to get it right. You kept jumping in and risking everything for someone you knew was valuable to you. Even when they did not know, show, or seemed to care that you loved them. You made the sacrifice to love them because you knew how important they were to you, and you to them.

That kind of love won't work if you only give half the effort. You won't see the same results if you only play it safe. This kind of reconciliation that goes beyond your imagination and expectations, requires you to put it all on the line and risk comfort, pride, ego, time, money, and most of all, your heart being broken. It will seem crazy at first and even others may not see it, but trust your gut, trust that small, still voice whispering through your loud ego and hear what it is saying. Hear it saying, "Keep pursuing them, keep forgiving them, and keep looking in the mirror and changing you. Keep seeing the best in them. There is a reason for all of this. This is where your satisfaction will come from. It's not just for them, this is also for you. You need this just as much as they do."

In other words, when you can say you put yourself out there, then you can rest knowing you've given all you could. You can be satisfied knowing you became all you could be in the process, because this forgiveness and reconciliation is as much about you as it is about them.

TWENTY

"My father wasn't the only one who became a better man; I became a better man, too"

IT WAS ALL WORTH IT

How do you know if something you do will be worth it or not? How do you know if what you will receive or gain from something will at least be equivalent to what you gave or sacrificed? None of us want to waste our time, energy, efforts, or money. But truth be told, there are not many things in life that can guarantee that we will always get back at least what we put in it, especially when it comes to people and reconciling relationships.

The other hard thing about giving in a relationship that you're trying to reconcile is, sometimes, you must front most of the cost yourself. In the beginning, you must make most of the sacrifices emotionally, spiritually, and mentally without getting anything in return. Meaning, you and the other person do not split everything 50/50 initially. Sometimes the splits will look like 75/25 or 80/20, or God forbid, 100/0. It's like going into business with someone and investing most, if not all the money, time, and sweat equity. But you trust that your partner won't always be in that position. Eventually, they will be in a better position to contribute to the partnership, and you will begin to receive back what you invested.

But, you still won't know if your sacrifice and what you gave was worth it until that moment comes when you can reflect and weigh it all out. The great poet and activist, Maya Angelou said, "Life is not measured by the number of breaths we take, but the moments that take our breath away." You measure life by the moments you had along the journey, not the destination. You don't measure a relationship's worth by where you end up with that person. You measure the relationship by the journey you took and what you experienced and learned along the way. They become the story, the account of what happen, the evidence of your evolution. Maya Angelou also said, "There is no greater agony than bearing an untold story inside you." Your story is the way you know if that sacrifice was worth it or not. It is the story of how you transformed, changed, grew, developed, and became a better person. That's how you will know, that's when it will all make sense. When the stories and memories you have are more valuable than whatever you had to sacrifice to create them, you will know that relationship was worth it.

The moments I had with my dad became more and more valuable as time went on. Our morning meetings kept getting shorter and farther apart. My dad and I spoke less and less a few weeks after he was put in hospice care. He was getting more and more tired. He couldn't hold conversations for long before he had to get off the phone. His voice had gotten weaker. It used to be that my dad and I both talked a lot on the phone, however, it had just started being me doing most of the talking. I knew we didn't have long before he would die.

As I was experiencing my father's decline, I could feel myself isolating from other people. Although I knew my family, friends, and church family were there for me, I still felt very alone. I felt distant from everyone and everything. I had a hard time concentrating on any and everything. I had already started grieving even before he died. I was grieving the times we talked and how I couldn't share what I was going through with him. I had a limited capacity to do anything that was not necessary. I began to share with our church leaders the plan for when my father passed. I wanted to make sure we had people and processes in place when I needed to be away from the church. I wanted to give myself ample time to grieve before I jumped back into leading the church. I had been preparing leaders for years and I had full confidence in their abilities. It helped that we had some phenomenal leaders.

I also began to prepare my wife and daughters. I let them know I would start spending more time riding the motorcycle, connecting with God, and reminiscing on the times my dad and I would go to motorcycle shops together. I knew riding motorcycles would be a healthy outlet for me. Besides, I had a lot of good friends who rode as well that I could connect with. My wife was very supportive. Unfortunately, two months earlier she had gone through her own loss. Both Robyn's mother and her closest cousin passed away suddenly, and just two weeks apart. She was still grieving, and I was beginning to grieve for my dad. We were doing all we could to try to be there for each other.

My daughters tried their best to be there for me by checking on me and asking me if I was ok. They would ask me to watch movies with them as an attempt to get my mind off my dad. I also prepared some of my friends to check on me. I knew I would need support, even if sometimes I said I did not. I also solicited the prayers of close friends and mentors. I knew I would need people praying for me and my family. I spent more time praying about experiencing and feeling God's presence as I prepared to be without my dad's presence. Like my dad felt like he was not alone in this, I prayed that I would not feel alone.

Racheal called me on a Friday night and said, "I just got this feeling we need to go to Atlanta." I told her I had that same feeling. We both agreed to listen to that feeling and go that weekend. Right after I got off the phone with Racheal, my aunt, Sissy, called and let me know she had just gotten to Atlanta, and my dad had my uncle, Tony, drop him off at the hospice facility. He told my uncle he did not want to die in the house. She explained how he had gotten worse and was barely speaking. We decided to go immediately after church on that Sunday.

We arrived in Atlanta and went directly to the hospice center. What we saw will forever be etched in our minds. My dad was so small and frail. We had just seen him three weeks prior. In that short period, he had dwindled down to almost nothing. He was a shell of his former self.

We stood at the door trying to gather ourselves for a moment, and then we finally went in. He said four words, "Thank y'all for coming." Subsequently, those would be his last audible words. He was still polite and hospitable even on his death bed. If his weight loss and frailty wasn't bad enough, he was also shaking and jerking violently. He was experiencing what is called, myoclonic seizures, which means his muscles were contracting and tightening uncontrollably. His whole body was violently shaking. I was not prepared to see him like that. My dad was always a strong man with a muscular build. It was hard to see a man who I viewed as my first superhero now dying and he could not even control his own muscles.

The nurse checked on him and gave him some more medication. She reassured us that they were doing everything they could to keep him comfortable. The medication they gave him helped with some of the jerking, but it did not completely stop it. I asked her how long they thought he had to live. She said, "I would be surprised if he lived longer than 72 hours. I think you should be prepared for less." She was so sweet and attentive to my dad. We were grateful for her heart, honesty, and service.

But, the news we received from the nurse was devastating to us. The moment almost seemed surreal. My sister and I just cried. We held his hand and just talked with him. Even though he could not answer, we still shared how much we loved him and appreciated all he was and did for us. The same hands that held us as children, that guided us as children, and spanked us when we were wrong, those strong hands we used to admire, were now weak, feeble, and life was quickly draining out of them. By the end of the night, he was no longer consciously aware or alert of our presence. He no longer made eye contact, nor was there any indication that he was conscious. I intellectually knew this time would come, but nothing could prepare me for actually going through it.

I called Ricketa, Rueben, and Ryan. Reuben was still having a hard time with losing his wife just four months prior and could not bring himself to come. He said, he couldn't see Dad like that. He wanted to remember him as strong. Ryan was still dealing with his own issues. Ricketa immediately booked a flight and arrived the next day. I picked her up from the airport and we went straight to the hospice facility. She broke down when she saw him. Racheal and I just held her.

After Ricketa got herself together, we just sat there talking and sharing stories about Dad. One thing was for sure, Dad could make you laugh. He had an infectious smile and laugh. His personality was so big, it always filled whatever room he walked in. It even made strangers feel at home. Ricketa had that same personality. She also was blessed with his infectious smile. Her smile was a reminder that a little piece of Dad would still be in all of us.

We decided to spend the night at the hospice facility. We vowed that Dad would not die alone. We all agreed that the worst thing for anyone, especially Dad, was for him to die and no one would be there holding his hand. The next day, things got worse. We could tell it was coming to an end. His body was still jerking, but his breathing became spaced out with long pauses. The nurse notified us that it would not be long. At this point, we were relieved. We had seen him suffer violent shakes and muscle jerks for three days straight. We just wanted him to be at peace and rest.

Often, when I can't find the right words to say in tough situations, I just sing. I started singing the hymn, "It Is Well With My Soul." The words just began to roll off my tongue:

"When peace like a river, attendeth my way, and sorrows like sea billows roll, whatever my lot, thou has taught me to say, it is well, it is well with my soul. It is well, it is well, with my soul, with my soul, It is well, it is well with my soul."

My sisters began to sing with me. We formed a natural trio. Our voices matched beautifully, better than any choir or group I have ever sung with or directed. We were in perfect sync and harmony. It was as if God anointed our voices with an angelic melody that would welcome my father into those pearly gates in heaven. I have never heard anything so beautiful and sweet. The nurses came to listen outside the doors. A peace fell, not just in our room, but it also fell over the entire facility.

We moved from one song to the next seamlessly. Then, Racheal started singing the end of Vanessa Bell Armstrong's song, "Peace Be Still." The words began to minister to us. It gave us a sense that everything was going to be alright. She started singing, "*Peace, there will be peace, peace be still, whenever the Lord says peace, there'll be peace...*" The song was about when Jesus was on the boat with his disciples during a storm and he calmed the stormy winds by saying, "Peace be still." We sang those words over and over again, and the more we sang it, the more peaceful my father became, and the less his body shook. A few short minutes after that, he had completely stopped shaking. He had this serene look on his face as if he had just been told some good news. We all just held his hands and watched him peacefully pass on.

When he took his last breath, it was as if he was released to rest. I felt, in that moment, this was the healing my father spoke about. His passing was the healing he needed. No more pain, no more suffering, no more cancer. God allowed him to beat cancer because he was now free. Free from the restraints and chains cancer kept his physical body under for more than two years. My dad was now free!

We sang for a few more minutes and then we prayed. We thanked God for answering our prayers to stop the violent physical seizures. We thanked God for my dad and the blessing we experienced by him being our dad. We also thanked God for the journey of reconciliation and God giving us a chance to reconnect with him before it was too late. We praised God for giving my dad and us the peace we desperately sought after. We were grateful for the time we had with our dad. We were particularly grateful that we were there with him in the end. As a result, my dad's fear of dying alone would never come to fruition because we were there with him until the end. Now, he was in more capable hands than ours. He was now in the hands of his heavenly father.

The arrangements were set for his homegoing. Saturday, April 30, 2017. It was about 14 days between my dad's death and the funeral. It seemed like an eternity. Each day seemed to be longer than the day before. I may have seemed like I was calm and in control, but I was just going through the motions. Some days I felt like a zombie. I was having conversations, but I could not hear anyone. Many days I even felt physically numb. I knew something was wrong when I did not want to watch TV. I would just stare at the walls with the TV off. I got very little sleep in those 14 days. I would look at the ceiling most of the night. I was forgetful and could not remember appointments or if I had paid certain bills or not. I was a mess. But I knew I had to, at least, try to keep it together until after the funeral.

A few months before my father passed, he asked me to preach his eulogy. This was a sermon that was already written because of his life. More specifically, his comeback and reconciliation with so many people. I already knew what scripture I wanted to use: 2 Timothy 4:7-8 (NIV)

"7) I have fought the good fight, I have finished the race, I have kept the faith. 8) Now there is in store for me the crown of righteousness, which the Lord, the righteous Judge, will award to me on that day—and not only to me, but also to all who have longed for his appearing."

I knew what stories I wanted to share about him and his journey with cancer. I had been working on this sermon since he asked me. I was taking mental notes of everything. It didn't hurt that I felt like I knew my dad better than anyone else.

The day of the funeral finally arrived. The funeral was happening. It was not all a dream. I wanted to grieve like everyone else, but I could not grieve just yet, because it was time to preach. I could not get emotional because it was time to preach. I could not cry because it was time to preach. I knew my dad; he loved church and he wanted a real homegoing with great singing and preaching. And I was not going to let my dad down.

The stage was set. My family was there. My dad's wife, Georgia, my mom and Irie, my sisters, aunts, uncles, cousins, my dad's siblings, nieces and nephews, family from down south, friends, and church members all came to Atlanta for my dad's homegoing. My Uncle Tommy was there to officiate the service. All I had to do was preach. I knew my uncle would handle the rest.

I was standing in the pulpit, the same place I had stood for so many other people's deceased loved ones. But this time was different. This time it was not someone else's father, it was my own. I decided if I was going to get through this, I had to tuck that emotional, grieving part of me to the side and place it in a box and close the lid. I knew I just needed to finish the sermon. Then, I could let myself grieve and cry when it was all over; Uncle Tommy would do everything else.

While standing over my father's casket, preaching his eulogy, the question my mother asked me years before came to my mind. "Why are you doing this? You know how he is. Why are you going through all of this? Why are you fighting so hard for this?"

The last two and a half years I had with my father washed over me, looking at his casket. I began to reflect on how we became best friends. How he became my confidant and my covering. How he became my prayer partner. How he became my early morning conversation partner after dropping off my daughters to school. How he became the one that I talked to when I was bored and everybody else was at work or busy. How he became the one I looked forward to seeing and talking to about motorcycles. How he was the one that I first went into a motorcycle shop with and fell in love with motorcycles. How I realized I was more like him than I ever wanted to admit. How I learned being like him wasn't a curse, it was blessing! I reflected on how he finally became, not the father I always dreamed of having, but so much more. I finally got my answer.

The Holy Spirit revealed it to me, I was fighting so hard for this because some things are worth fighting for. I didn't know it when I started this journey. And if I am being honest, I asked myself the same question my mother asked. In the beginning, I thought I was wasting my time. I thought it was all in vain. But standing there, knowing the unbreakable bond we formed, I knew in that moment, everything we went through was all worth it. Every heartbreak, tear, disappointment, and set back was a set up for one of the greatest father and son relationships ever. I am grateful that I kept pursuing the relationship even though I did not understand why. I am grateful I kept reaching out even though I could not see what would become of it. I'm so glad I was obedient to God's calling to reconcile with my father because it was all worth it.

Praise be to God, I was able to get through the sermon. I was even able to hold it together as we started walking out of the funeral home in front of the casket leading to the hearse. But as we got to the hearse, I could no longer keep it together. All the emotions I had been holding back seemed to hit me all at once. My legs gave out, and I started to collapse. As I was going down, I thought I was going to hit the ground, but I felt something catch me. It was my best friend, Keith. He caught me and helped me walk to my car. I was finally able to let it all go. I had done what my dad asked of me. Preaching his eulogy was difficult, and at times I wasn't sure if I was going to make it, but even that sacrifice was worth it.

My relationship with my father was worth fighting for. Was it hard? Yes! Was it difficult? Yes! Did I want to sometimes give up? Yes! Did it take everything I had and then some? Yes! But in the end, after the tears, the anger, the embarrassment, the suffering, the surrendering, the hurt, the restoration, rebuilding, and after all the healing, it was all worth it!

But I didn't pursue this relationship with my dad on my own. I leaned on family members, friends, and most of all, something greater than myself, the Holy Spirit. The Holy Spirit's job is to remind, strengthen, counsel, and advocate. I thank God I was obedient. I found out during this process that obedience is God's love language, and he rewards those who speak it well. I believe my reward was gaining a better father and a better friend.

But, my father wasn't the only one who became a better man; I became a better man, too! Forgiveness freed me to love without restrictions or limitations. Forgiveness allowed me to love the man inside my father. As I forgave him, somehow it gave me permission to forgive myself. It is hard to forgive yourself when you cannot forgive others for their mistakes. Because we usually hold ourselves to higher standards than we hold others. If I could forgive the man who hurt me the most, I could forgive others, and most importantly, the man in the mirror.

REFLECTIONS

Perhaps you are in a similar situation. Your anger and unforgiveness have given you a sense of false security or power. True security or power is felt and demonstrated when forgiveness is allowed to lead your heart. You will have to risk being hurt. You will have to trade comfort for a deeper calling. Forgiveness is the deeper calling that can only come from God. That calling will continue to tug at you no matter how angry, hurt, disappointed, or betrayed you may feel. Forgiveness begs us to peer into a future that can be better than what we are experiencing right now. Forgiveness beckons us forward to be the best versions of ourselves, so that others may see and hear the voice within, calling them to be the best versions of themselves.

Maybe you will not have an ending like mine. Perhaps the person you forgive and want to reconcile with will not become a better version of themselves like my father. I cannot guarantee that your relationships will turn around like ours did. However, one thing I do know, if you decide to embark on this journey to forgive and reconcile, you will not be able to help becoming a better man or woman because of it. You might not know why you are fighting so hard right now, but hold on to the fact that some things are worth fighting for. It will be worth it for you, too. Whatever happens, trust God is on your side, and he will give you what you need to get through this.

TWO YEARS LATER

I would continue a journey I started with my dad. I was standing at my graduation for my doctorate and when they called my name, tears started flowing down my face. I knew I was not alone. My father was right there with me. I could hear him saying, "Well done. I'm so proud of you, son. You did it. Now there is a real Dr. Rickey McCray in the family. It was all worth it."

Dr. Rickey McCray

ABOUT THE AUTHOR

Dr. Rickey McCray is a pastor, teacher, preacher, author, entrepreneur, leadership consultant, singer, songwriter, worship leader and musician who has been featured on several nationally recorded albums. His belief is that "The Word of God must be spread through preaching, teaching, song, dance and creative art."

Dr. Rickey Allen McCray Jr. is the Senior Pastor of The Way Church in Indianapolis, Indiana. He and his wife Robyn McCray have four daughters, Brittany, Aaliyah, Melodey and Scyia. He has a bachelor's degree from St. Joseph's College, a Master of Divinity from Christian Theological Seminary, as well as a Doctor of Ministry degree earned from Christian Theological Seminary.

God gave Dr. McCray the awesome privilege of birthing THE WAY CHURCH into existence in 2012; one of the fastest growing churches in the Indianapolis area. Because of his belief that God has destined everyone for greatness, he is passionate about standing for those who are oppressed, silenced, and marginalized.

One of Dr. McCray's other passions is meeting the needs of youth and teens. In 2014, Dr. McCray started We Care Indy; a youth organization that employs and mentors' youth while they perform free lawn care services for senior citizens. This program has served over 200 youth in the Indianapolis community. We Care Indy is committed to teaching entrepreneurship, financial literacy, conflict resolution, career, and college readiness.

In 2019, Dr. McCray released his first children's book entitled, *"What's All the Fuss Over Mr. Wilson?"*. This book is an amazing illustration of the story of a teenage boy that discovers the true meaning of God's love. This publication was birthed and developed from a personal experience Dr. McCray had as a child. His latest book, *"Some Things Are Worth Fighting For"* is about his personal story of forgiveness and reconciliation with his father. Which will be released September 2022. Dr. McCray's vision is to inspire and encourage everyone to discover, embrace, and live out their God given greatness.

ACKNOWLEDGEMENTS

To my daughters Brittany, Aaliyah, Melodey, and Heava-Scyia. You have my heart! I have grown closer to God because of you. I know what real love is because of how you love me unconditionally. Thank you for being my teachers of life. I have learned how to forgive, persevere, laugh, play, and enjoy life by watching you. You four ladies will always have my heart! I love you!! BAMS Forever!!

To my parents, LaTonia and Irie Smith, thank you for encouraging me to believe I can do and be anything. Thank you for being my biggest cheerleaders. Mom, thank you for always being the loudest one calling my name! I am strong, courageous, crazy, and a man of faith because of you. I know how to praise the Lord at all times because I watched you. You have always been my inspiration. Dad, you taught me what it means to be a man who loves and provides for his family. I am the man I am today because of you.

To my dad Dr. Rickey A. McCray Sr. (Rest in peace. With God's help we did it!!) You were my best friend, confidant, advisor, accountability partner, encourager, and motorcycle riding buddy. I will always love you and miss you! Thank you for introducing me to Jesus, ministry, preaching, and motorcycles!

To my grandparents James and Pearl Meyers, thank you for always supporting me. Grandpa thank you for your stories and your example of being a godly man. Grandma thank you for believing in me and praying for me. Rest in peace grandma! I love you and miss you!

To my father-in-law Eugene Akers, thank you for showing me what it means to love your daughter and to help people. The true measure of a man is not how far he goes, but who he helps along the way.

My sister Rachael Martin-Clark, you are my ride-or-die! Thank you for allowing me to cry on your shoulders, to talk crazy, and to share my heart. You are one of my best friends on the planet! I love you!

To my siblings Ricketa, Reuben (thank you for helping write "Meaning of Christmas") and Ryan, thank you for continuing to remind me what is important. I love you all dearly!

The Way Church for being so patient and supportive and allowing me to be creative. Lisa Washington (my fabulous publisher), and Markel Washington

Kevin Clark, Hans & Emilee Meyers, Rev. John Akers, Georgia McCray, Tammy Mitchell, Gloria & Ray Willis-Smith, Rita & Otis Green, Tony McCray, Leon McCray, Noel, Bre'Ann, BraLynn, Sadie, Irvin, Antonio, Candice, Alexa Sublett, Dominique Bryant,

Yvonne Singfield, Kelvin & Katrena Greer, Nicole Perdue, Paula Glover, Anteria Gross, Uncle Dewitt, Chris Daniels, Mike and Tracey Palmer, Pastor Arthur Sample, Pastor Eric Whitaker, Pastor Tommie Harris, Pastor Antwaun Johnson, Pastor Jeffrey Brown, Danielle Brown, Pastor Norell Taylor, Rev. John Ray, Dr. Michael Miller, Pastor Corey Duncan, Dr. Milton Keys, Dr. Terrance Bridges, Dr. Twana Harris, Deacon Anita Walls, Trent Cowles, Shalisa Humphrey, Nicole Perdue, LaRon Avery, Mike Nowlin, Rolando Urbina, Dr. Carmin Frederick-James, Rev. Monique Crain-Spell, Julian Grace, Aaron Thomas, Terrill Krigger, Aundre Hogue, Cindy Neal, Keith Taylor, Lyndal Tipton, James Brown, Michael Carter, Justin Jeter, Jeremy Taylor, Shawn Parker, Mary & Gregory Wise, Zakiya & Joseph Smith, Tina & Rob Hardiman, Pastor Richard Reynolds, Robert & Erica Porter, Dwayne Jarrett, Ralph Hankerson, Dr. Leah Gunning-Francis, Rev. Jason Powell, Ministers of The Way Church, The Way Church Leadership, We Care Indy, Shalonda Johnson, Nathaniel McGuire, Bob Seagar, Rev. Curtis Mundy

www.ingramcontent.com/pod-product-compliance
Lightning Source LLC
Chambersburg PA
CBHW021617120626
46545CB00001B/264